BLOOMSBURY KITCH

C000319053

Rice

Bloomsbury Books
London

This edition published 1994 by Bloomsbury Books,
an imprint of The Godfrey Cave Group,
42 Bloomsbury Street, London, WC1B 3QJ.

ISBN 1 85471 537 2

Printed and bound in Great Britain.

Contents

Toasted Brown Rice Cereal with Orange and Cocoa

Serves 6

Working time: about 15 minutes

Total time: about 30 minutes

Calories 215
Protein 3g
Cholesterol 0mg
Total fat 10g
Saturated fat 0g
Sodium 100mg

175 g	brown rice	**6 oz**
¼ tsp	salt	**¼ tsp**
2 tbsp	unsweetened cocoa powder	**2 tbsp**
90 g	dark brown sugar	**3 oz**
12.5 cl	fresh orange juice	**4 fl oz**
1	orange, peeled and cut into segments	**1**

Toast the brown rice in a heavy frying pan over medium-high heat, shaking the pan occasionally, until the rice begins to crackle and some of the kernels start to burst – 7 to 10 minutes. Transfer the rice to a blender and grind it until it resembles coarse sand.

Put the ground rice and salt into a saucepan; add ¾ litre (1¼ pints) of cold water and bring the mixture to a simmer over medium-high heat. Reduce the heat to medium low, then cover the pan and cook the rice until all but about ¼ litre (8 fl oz) of the water has been absorbed and the rice is tender – approximately 15 minutes. Remove the pan from the heat. Sift the cocoa on to the rice and then stir it in. Add the brown sugar and orange juice; stir the mixture well.

Spoon the cereal into warm bowls, then top each serving with several of the orange segments. Serve the cereal with semi-skimmed milk, if you like.

Chicken Soup with Chilies, Cabbage and Rice

Serves 4

Working
time: about
20 minutes

Total time:
about
1 hour

Calories
285
Protein
20g
Cholesterol
60mg
Total fat
11g
Saturated fat
2g
Sodium
275mg

1 tbsp	safflower oil	**1 tbsp**
750 g	chicken thighs, skinned, fat trimmed	**1½ lb**
1	garlic clove, finely chopped	**1**
3	spring onions, trimmed and sliced into thin rounds	**3**
½ litre	unsalted chicken stock	**16 fl oz**
1 tbsp	fresh thyme, or ¾ tsp dried thyme	**1 tbsp**

	freshly ground black pepper	
¼ tsp	salt	**¼ tsp**
90 g	long-grain rice	**3 oz**
2	large dried mild chili peppers, stemmed, split lengthwise and seeded	**2**
1	large carrot, julienned	**1**
175 g	shredded Chinese cabbage	**6 oz**

Heat the safflower oil in a large, heavy-bottomed saucepan over medium-high heat. Add the chicken thighs and sauté them, turning them frequently, until they are evenly browned – 3 to 4 minutes. Push the chicken to one side of the pan; add the garlic and spring onions and cook them for 1 minute, stirring constantly. Pour in the stock and ¾ litre (1¼ pints) of water. Add the thyme and some pepper, and bring the liquid to the boil. Simmer, partially covered, for 20 minutes. Skim the surface and simmer the liquid for 20 minutes more.

Meanwhile, bring ¼ litre (8 fl oz) of water and ⅛ teaspoon of the salt to the boil in another pan. Add rice and stir once, reduce the heat and

cover the pan. Simmer the rice until water is absorbed – about 20 minutes.

While rice is cooking, pour ¼ litre (8 fl oz) of boiling water over the chilies and soak for 15 minutes. Purée with their liquid.

Remove the chicken thighs. When cool enough to handle, remove the meat from the bones with your fingers and cut it into small pieces. Return the chicken pieces to the pan. Add the carrot, cabbage, rice, and the remaining salt. Simmer the soup until the carrot is tender – 3 to 4 minutes. Strain the chili purée through a fine sieve into the soup. Stir to incorporate the purée and serve the soup at once.

Clam and Rice Soup

Serves 4

Working time: about 35 minutes

Total time: about 50 minutes

Calories 140

Protein 7g

Cholesterol 25mg

Total fat 4g

Saturated fat 1g

Sodium 40mg

24	small hardshell clams, scrubbed	24
1 tbsp	virgin olive oil	1 tbsp
90 g	onion, finely chopped	3 oz
2 tsp	finely chopped garlic	2 tsp
1	small bay leaf	1
45 g	long-grain rice	1½ oz

4 tbsp	dry white wine	4 tbsp
⅛ tsp	crushed saffron threads	⅛ tsp
½ tsp	fresh lemon juice	½ tsp
1	large, ripe tomato, skinned, seeded and finely chopped	1
2 tbsp	finely chopped fresh parsley	2 tbsp

Bring 1 litre (1¾ pints) of water to the boil in a large pan. Add the clams, cover the pan tightly, and cook the clams until they open – about 5 minutes. Transfer the clams to a plate, discarding any that remain closed, and reserve the cooking liquid. When the clams are cool enough to handle, remove them from their shells. Discard the shells and set the clams aside.

Heat the oil in a heavy frying pan over medium heat. Add the onion, garlic and bay leaf, and sauté them, stirring frequently, until the onion is translucent – about 5 minutes.

Strain the clam-cooking liquid through a sieve lined with muslin, then pour the liquid back into the pan. Add the contents of the frying pan along with the rice, wine, saffron and lemon juice, and bring to the boil. Reduce the heat and cover the pan, leaving the lid ajar; simmer for 10 minutes, stirring once or twice. Add the tomato and simmer for 5 minutes more. Stir in the parsley and cook for 2 minutes longer. Return the clams to the pan and heat them through. Serve immediately.

Lamb and Wild Rice Soup

Serves 6

Working time: about 50 minutes

Total time: about 2 hours

Calories 375
Protein 19g
Cholesterol 1mg
Total fat 13g
Saturated fat 6g
Sodium 275mg

1 tbsp	safflower oil	1 tbsp
2	lamb shoulder joints, knuckle end (about 1 kg/2 lb), trimmed of fat	2
750 g	onions, coarsely chopped	1½ lb
½ litre	dry white wine	16 fl oz
400 g	canned tomatoes, drained and chopped	14 oz
¾ litre	unsalted chicken or veal stock	1¼ pints
1	carrot, sliced into 5 mm (¼ inch) thick rounds	1
8	garlic cloves, chopped	8
1	stick celery, chopped	1
	freshly ground black pepper	
½ tsp	salt	½ tsp
1½ tbsp	fresh rosemary, or 1 tsp dried rosemary	1½ tbsp
160 g	wild rice	5½ oz

Heat oil in a frying pan over medium-high. Sauté the lamb joints until dark brown all over – about 15 minutes. Transfer the lamb joints to a pan.

Reduce heat to medium. Add onions, cook, stirring, until lightly browned – 10 to 15 minutes.

Add onions to the pan. Return to the heat and pour in the wine. Scrape up the caramelized pan juices from the bottom, stirring to dissolve them. Add tomatoes and boil until it is reduced by half – about 5 minutes. Pour the reduced liquid into the pan, then add the stock, 2.5 litres (4 pints) of water, carrot, garlic, celery and some pepper.

Place over medium heat and simmer, skim off any foam that rises to the surface. Stir in the salt and rosemary. Reduce heat and simmer until lamb is tender – 1½ to 2 hours.

After meat has cooked for 1 hour, put the rice into a pan with ¼ litre (8 fl oz) of water and bring to a simmer over medium heat. Reduce to low and cook the rice slowly until the water is absorbed – about 15 minutes. Set the rice aside.

Transfer the lamb joints to a clean work surface. When they are cool enough to handle, remove the meat from the bones. Cut the meat into small pieces; discard the bones. Return the meat to the pot. Add the partially cooked rice and simmer the soup until the rice is tender – about 20 minutes. Serve the soup hot.

Curried Swede Soup

Serves 4

Working time: about 20 minutes

Total time: about 1 hour

Calories 185
Protein 4g
Cholesterol 0mg
Total fat 7g
Saturated fat 2g
Sodium 425mg

1 tbsp	safflower oil	1 tbsp	$\frac{1}{2}$ tsp	ground coriander	$\frac{1}{2}$ tsp
1	onion (about 125 g/4 oz), chopped	1	$\frac{1}{4}$ tsp	ground cumin	$\frac{1}{4}$ tsp
350 g	swedes, diced	12 oz	$\frac{1}{8}$ tsp	ground turmeric	$\frac{1}{8}$ tsp
175 g	parsnips, diced	6 oz	$\frac{1}{8}$ tsp	ground ginger	$\frac{1}{8}$ tsp
1	small sweet red pepper, seeded, deribbed and diced	1	1	garlic clove, crushed	1
1	small cooking apple (about 90 g/3 oz), diced	1	$\frac{1}{2}$ tsp	salt	$\frac{1}{2}$ tsp
30 g	brown basmati rice	1 oz	30 cl	tomato juice	$\frac{1}{2}$ pint
$\frac{1}{2}$ tsp	medium-hot curry powder	$\frac{1}{2}$ tsp	90 cl	unsalted vegetable stock	$1\frac{1}{2}$ pints
			15 g	sultanas	$\frac{1}{2}$ oz
			15 g	desiccated coconut, toasted	$\frac{1}{2}$ oz

Heat the oil in a large, heavy-bottomed saucepan or fireproof casserole and sweat the onion, swedes and parsnips over medium heat for 5 minutes. Add the red pepper and cook for a further 2 to 3 minutes, stirring occasionally. Then add the apple, rice, spices and garlic and cook, stirring constantly, for 2 minutes. Finally, mix in the salt, tomato juice, stock and sultanas and bring the mixture to the boil. Reduce the heat to a simmer, cover the pan, and cook the soup for 30 minutes. Just before serving, stir in the coconut.

Suggested accompaniment: sourdough rye bread.

Editor's Note: To toast desiccated coconut, spread the coconut out on a baking sheet and place it in a 180°C (350°F or Mark 4) oven for 10 minutes, stirring it once.

Stuffed Mushroom Caps

Serves 6

Working time: about 35 minutes

Total time: about 1 hour and 10 minutes

Calories
185

Protein
7g

Cholesterol
15mg

Total fat
6g

Saturated fat
3g

Sodium
260mg

6	large field, or open cup, mushrooms, wiped clean, stalks removed and finely chopped	6
½ tsp	salt	½ tsp
	freshly ground black pepper	
1 tbsp	virgin olive oil	1 tbsp
1	onion, finely chopped	1
1	small sweet red pepper, seeded, deribbed and finely chopped	1
125 g	Italian round-grain rice	4 oz
2	garlic cloves, crushed	2
30 g	pine-nuts	1 oz
35 cl	unsalted vegetable stock	12 fl oz
2 tbsp	shredded fresh basil leaves	2 tbsp
125 g	low-fat mozzarella cheese, diced	4 oz
30 g	fresh wholemeal breadcrumbs	1 oz
1 tbsp	chopped parsley	1 tbsp

Preheat the oven to 200°C (400°F or Mark 6).

Place the mushrooms in a shallow ovenproof dish with 2 tablespoons of cold water. Season the mushrooms with a little of the salt and some freshly ground black pepper. Cover the dish with a lid or aluminium foil, and set it aside.

Heat the oil in a large, heavy-bottomed saucepan over medium heat. Add the onion and red pepper and cook gently for 6 to 8 minutes, until soft. Stir in the chopped mushroom stalks, the rice, garlic and pine-nuts, and cook for 5 minutes, stirring occasionally, until the rice is very lightly browned. Add the stock, basil, the remaining salt, and some pepper. Bring to the boil, then reduce the heat to low and cover the pan tightly. Cook gently for 20 to 25 minutes, until the rice is cooked and the stock has been absorbed. Put the mushrooms in the oven to cook for 20 minutes, until they are almost soft.

Remove the rice mixture from the heat and stir in the diced mozzarella cheese, then divide the mixture evenly among the mushrooms, mounding it neatly on top of each one. Sprinkle on the wholemeal breadcrumbs and return the mushrooms to the oven for another 10 minutes, or until the mozzarella cheese begins to melt. Serve the mushrooms sprinkled with the chopped parsley.

Spring Onion and Rice Muffins

Makes 12
muffins

Working
time: about
20 minutes

Total time:
about
45 minutes

Per muffin:

Calories
105

Protein
3g

Cholesterol
25mg

Total fat
3g

Saturated fat
1g

Sodium
130mg

45 g	long-grain rice	1½ oz
225 g	plain flour	7½ oz
2 tsp	baking powder	2 tsp
2 tsp	caster sugar	2 tsp
¼ tsp	salt	¼ tsp
¼ tsp	ground white pepper	¼ tsp

1	egg	1
17.5 cl	semi-skimmed milk	6 fl oz
2 tbsp	safflower oil	2 tbsp
2	spring onions, trimmed and finely chopped	2

Preheat the oven to 220°C (425°F or Mark 7). Lightly oil a muffin or deep bun tin. Bring 15 cl (¼ pint) of water to the boil in a saucepan. Stir in the rice, then reduce the heat to low, and cover tightly. Cook the rice until it is tender and all the liquid has been absorbed – 15 to 20 minutes. Uncover and set aside to cool.

Sift the flour, baking powder, sugar, salt and pepper into a bowl. In another bowl, lightly beat the egg, then whisk in the milk and oil; stir in the cooled rice and the spring onions. Pour the rice mixture into the flour mixture, then stir until the ingredients are just blended.

Spoon the batter into the cups in the tin, filling each no more than two-thirds full. Bake the muffins until lightly browned – 18 to 22 minutes. Remove the muffins from the cups immediately and serve hot.

Sweet Pepper Rice Ring

Serves 6

Working time: about 30 minutes

Total time: about 1 hour

Calories 125

Protein 3g

Cholesterol 0mg

Total fat 3g

Saturated fat 1g

Sodium 135mg

½ tsp	salt	½ tsp	
150 g	long-grain rice	5 oz	
1	small sweet red pepper	1	
1	small sweet green pepper	1	
1	small sweet yellow pepper	1	
1 tbsp	virgin olive oil	1 tbsp	
1 tbsp	white wine vinegar	1 tbsp	
1	garlic clove, crushed	1	
4 tbsp	finely chopped parsley	4 tbsp	
	freshly ground black pepper		
	red, green and yellow pepper rings, for garnish		

Bring a saucepan of water to the boil with ¼ teaspoon of the salt. Add the rice, stir it once, then cover the pan and reduce the heat to low. Simmer the rice for 20 minutes, until it is cooked but still slightly firm. Drain it thoroughly and set it aside to cool.

Meanwhile, skin the peppers, then seed and derib them, retaining their juice. Cut the peppers into small dice.

Put the oil, vinegar, garlic and parsley into a large bowl, and add the remaining salt and some pepper. Mix the ingredients well. Add the diced peppers to the dressing, with 1 tablespoon of their juice, then add the rice and mix everything together thoroughly.

Fill a 1.25 litre (2 pint) ring mould with the rice salad, pressing the mixture down firmly. Cover the mould with plastic film and refrigerate it.

To serve, turn the rice salad out on to a serving plate and arrange the pepper rings in the centre.

Rice and Apricot Ring

Serves 8

Working time: about 1 hour and 10 minutes

Total time: about 3 hours and 30 minutes (includes chilling)

Calories 125

Protein 6g

Cholesterol trace

Total fat 1g

Saturated fat trace

Sodium 60mg

60 cl	skimmed milk	**1 pint**	**½ tsp**	pure almond extract	**½ tsp**
60 g	round-grain rice, washed	**2 oz**	**90 g**	low-fat fromage frais	**3 oz**
5	large ripe apricots, peeled, halved	**5**	**1 tbsp**	powdered gelatine	**1 tbsp**
	and stoned, or 400 g (14 oz)		**2**	egg whites	**2**
	canned apricot halves in fruit		**75 g**	caster sugar	**2½ oz**
	juice, drained		**175 g**	fresh raspberries	**6 oz**

Boil milk in a pan. Reduce heat to low and add rice and almond extract. Simmer, uncovered, until rice has absorbed the milk – about 50 minutes – stirring occasionally.

If using fresh apricots, place, cut side down, in a pan and pour in 17.5 cl (6 fl oz) of boiling water. Simmer gently for 2 to 3 minutes, until just tender. Drain.

Arrange eight apricot halves, skinned surfaces down, in the base of a 20 cm (8 inch) ring mould. Reserve the remaining two.

When rice has absorbed milk, remove from heat, allow to cool slightly, then stir in *fromage frais*. Dissolve gelatine in 2 tablespoons of water and stir into rice. Whisk egg whites until they stand in soft peaks. Whisk in 60 g (2 oz) of sugar in three batches,

ensuring the mixture is stiff and glossy each time before adding further sugar. Stir one spoonful of egg whites into the rice, then fold in remainder of egg whites. Spoon mixture into prepared ring mould, being careful not to disturb the apricot. Level the surface and refrigerate for 2 hours, or until set.

Put the raspberries in a pan and add remaining caster sugar. Heat berries and sugar gently until the juice runs, simmer the berries until they fall apart – 2 to 3 minutes. Allow them to cool. Purée the cooked raspberries with the reserved apricot halves. Press the purée through a fine sieve.

To unmould the dessert, dip the base of the mould in hot water for 2 or 3 seconds, then turn the ring out on to a flat plate. Serve the dessert in slices, with the raspberry-apricot purée.

Spiced Tomato Rice Mould

Serves 6 as a first course	
Working time: about 20 minutes	
Total time: about 2 hours (includes cooling)	

Calories 235	
Protein 5g	
Cholesterol 0mg	
Total fat 6g	
Saturated fat 1g	
Sodium 10mg	

1	large onion, roughy chopped	1
750 g	tomatoes, quartered	1½ lb
1	large sweet red pepper, roughly chopped	1
12.5 cl	dry white wine	4 fl oz
2 tbsp	virgin olive oil	2 tbsp
¼ tsp	cayenne pepper	¼ tsp
1 tbsp	paprika	1 tbsp
	bouquet garni	
250 g	Italian round-grain rice	8 oz
3 tbsp	finely chopped parsley	3 tbsp
	cherry tomatoes, for garnish (optional)	
	sweet yellow or red pepper slices, for garnish (optional)	

Put the onion, tomatoes and chopped sweet pepper in a large bowl with the wine, oil, cayenne pepper, paprika and bouquet garni. Cover the bowl with plastic film, pulling back one corner, and cook in a microwave on high for 12 to 14 minutes, until the vegetables are soft.

Remove the bouquet garni and rub the remaining ingredients through a sieve into a large bowl. Stir the rice into the resulting purée, cover with plastic film, again pulling back one corner, and microwave on high for 10 minutes, stirring twice. Cook on defrost for about 10 minutes more, stirring twice; the rice should have absorbed all the liquid. Add the parsley and blend well.

Lightly oil six 9 cm (3½ inch) diameter brioche moulds. Spoon the spiced rice into the moulds, packing it down with the back of the spoon and smoothing the surface. Leave to cool and set for about 1 hour.

To serve, turn out the rice moulds on to individual plates. Garnish, if you like, with cherry tomatoes and sweet pepper slices.

Basmati and Wild Rice Moulds with Artichokes

Serves 6

Working time: about 1 hour and 30 minutes

Total time: about 2 hours and 30 minutes (includes soaking)

Calories 405
Protein 14g
Cholesterol 25mg
Total fat 12g
Saturated fat 5g
Sodium 245mg

125 g	wild rice	**4 oz**
125 g	basmati rice, rinsed well under cold water, soaked in 60 cl (1 pint) water for 1 hour	**4 oz**
½ tsp	salt	**½ tsp**
6	globe artichokes	**6**
2	lemons, grated rind of one, juice of both	**2**
1 tbsp	virgin olive oil	**1 tbsp**
3 tbsp	chopped mint	**3 tbsp**
2	garlic cloves, finely chopped	**2**
125 g	fresh chestnuts, peeled, or 60 g (2oz) dried chestnuts, soaked in hot water for 8 hours or overnight	**4 oz**
60 g	unsalted butter white pepper	**2 oz**

Boil 1.25 litres (2 pints) of water in a pan. Stir in wild rice, reduce heat and simmer, uncovered, until tender – about 45 minutes. Drain the basmati rice and boil it rapidly, with the salt in 90 cl (1½ pts) water, uncovered, for 5 minutes until rice is cooked. Drain, and set it aside.

Put 3 litres (5 pints) of water in a bowl; add a third of the lemon juice. Cut the stem off an artichoke. Pull off any tough outer leaves and trim away dark green leaf bases on the bottom. Cut off top ⅔ and remove the hairy choke. Halve and cut each half into six wedges and keep in acidulated water until required. Repeat with remaining artichokes.

Heat oil in a frying pan, add mint and garlic; cook for 1 minute. Drain artichokes and stir-fry for 1 minute. Add remaining lemon juice and ¼ litre (8 fl oz) of water, cover, simmer for about 10 minutes. Remove lid and cook for a further 5 to 10 minutes, until artichokes are tender.

Drain the wild rice. Chop chestnuts finely. Melt butter in a pan and fry chestnuts for 2 to 3 minutes. Mix in basmati and wild rice and heat through. Press into six 20 cl (7 fl oz) moulds and turn onto plates. Serve moulds with artichoke. Sprinkle tops with lemon rind and juices from pan.

Rice Congee

Serves 8

Working time: about 30 minutes

Total time: about 1 hour

Calories 165

Protein 10g

Cholesterol 20mg

Total fat 1g

Saturated fat 0g

Sodium 130mg

135 g	long-grain rice	**4½ oz**
1 litre	unsalted brown or chicken stock	**1¾ pints**
1 tbsp	safflower oil	**1 tbsp**
6	garlic cloves, finely chopped	**6**
60 g	fresh ginger root, julienned	**2 oz**
125 g	bean sprouts	**4 oz**
45 g	fresh coriander leaves	**1½ oz**
1	lime, cut into 16 wedges	**1**

2 tbsp	sugar	**2 tbsp**
1 tsp	fish sauce or low-sodium soy sauce	**1 tsp**
1 tsp	salt	**1 tsp**
	freshly ground black pepper	
250 g	beef fillet, trimmed of fat and cut into thin strips	**8 oz**
3	spring onions, trimmed and cut into 1 cm (½ inch) lengths	**3**

Put the rice, stock and 1 litre (1¾ pints) of water into a large saucepan; bring the liquid to the boil. Stir the mixture, then reduce the heat to medium, and simmer the rice, uncovered, until it is very soft and begins to break apart – about 1 hour.

While the rice is cooking, heat the safflower oil in a small frying pan over medium-low heat. Add the garlic and cook it, stirring often, until it is crisp and brown – 4 to 5 minutes. Transfer the garlic to a paper towel and let it drain. Put the garlic, ginger, bean sprouts, coriander and lime wedges into small serving bowls, and set them aside.

About 5 minutes before serving, stir the sugar, fish sauce or soy sauce, salt and some pepper into the hot soup. Add the beef strips and spring onions, and bring the liquid to the boil. Reduce the heat to medium and simmer the soup until the beef is just cooked – about 3 minutes.

Ladle the soup into individual bowls. Pass the garnishes separately inviting the diners to season their own soup with them.

Brown Rice and Mango Salad

Serves 8
as a side
dish

Working
time: about
20 minutes

Total time:
about
1 hour and
30 minutes

Calories
140
Protein
2g
Cholesterol
0mg
Total fat
4g
Saturated fat
0g
Sodium
70mg

185 g	brown rice	6½ oz	1	small shallot, finely chopped	1
4 tbsp	red wine vinegar	4 tbsp	⅛ tsp	ground cardamom	⅛ tsp
¼ tsp	salt	¼ tsp		mace	
2 tbsp	safflower oil	2 tbsp		cayenne pepper	
1	sweet green pepper, seeded and deribbed	1	1	ripe mango, peeled and diced	1

Bring 1.5 litres (2½ pints) of water to the boil in a large saucepan. Stir in the rice, reduce the heat and simmer the rice, uncovered, until it is tender – about 35 minutes. Drain the rice and put it in a serving bowl. Stir in the vinegar and salt, and allow the mixture to cool to room temperature – about 30 minutes.

When the rice is cool, stir in the oil, pepper, shallot, cardamom and a pinch each of mace and cayenne pepper. Add the mango pieces and stir them in gently so that they retain their shape. Cover the salad; to allow the flavours to meld, let the salad stand, unrefrigerated, for about 30 minutes before serving it.

Apricots and Water Chestnuts in Wild Rice

Serves 8
as a side
dish

Working
time: about
30 minutes

Total time:
about
1 hour

Calories
130
Protein
4g
Cholesterol
0mg
Total fat
0g
Saturated fat
0g
Sodium
75mg

160 g	wild rice	**5¼ oz**
125 g	dried apricots, cut into 1 cm (½ inch) pieces	**4 oz**
175 g	fresh water chestnuts, peeled and quartered, or 250 g (8 oz) canned whole peeled water chestnuts, drained, rinsed and quartered	**6 oz**
2 tbsp	chopped parsley	**2 tbsp**

Spicy Lemon Dressing		
2 tbsp	fresh lemon juice	**2 tbsp**
1 tbsp	red wine vinegar	**1 tbsp**
⅛ tsp	ground ginger	**⅛ tsp**
⅛ tsp	cinnamon	**⅛ tsp**
	ground cloves	
¼ tsp	salt	**¼ tsp**
	freshly ground black pepper	

Bring 1.5 litres (2½ pints) of water to the boil in a saucepan. Stir in the wild rice, reduce the heat, and simmer the rice, uncovered, until it is tender but still chewy – approximately 45 minutes.

While the rice cooks, prepare the apricots and dressing: put the apricots into a small bowl and pour in enough hot water to cover them by about 2.5 cm (1 inch). Soak the apricots for 20 minutes to soften them. Drain the apricots, reserving 4 tablespoons of their soaking liquid, and set them aside.

Pour the reserved apricot-soaking liquid into a small bowl. Add the lemon juice, vinegar, ginger, cinnamon, a pinch of cloves, the salt and some pepper; whisk the mixture vigorously until it is thoroughly combined.

When the rice finishes cooking, drain and rinse it, and transfer it to a serving bowl. Pour the dressing over the rice, then add the apricots, water chestnuts and the parsley; toss the ingredients well and serve the salad at room temperature.

Saffron Rice Salad with Peppers and Chick-Peas

Serves 12
as a side
dish

Working
time: about
30 minutes

Total time:
about
2 hours and
45 minutes

Calories
180
Protein
5g
Cholesterol
0mg
Total fat
7g
Saturated fat
1g
Sodium
145mg

135 g	dried chick-peas, picked over	**4½ oz**	
¼ tsp	salt	**¼ tsp**	
275 g	long-grain rice	**9 oz**	
60 cl	unsalted chicken stock or water	**1 pint**	
½ tsp	saffron threads, soaked for 10 minutes in very hot water	**½ tsp**	
1	strip lemon rind	**1**	
500 g	fresh peas, shelled, or 150 g (5 oz) frozen peas, thawed	**1 lb**	

30 g	whole unskinned almonds	**1 oz**
1	sweet red pepper, seeded, deribbed and cut into thin slices	**1**
1	sweet green pepper, seeded, deribbed and cut into thin slices	**1**
2	ripe tomatoes, seeded and chopped	**2**
6	oil-cured black olives, thinly sliced	**6**
6 tbsp	vinaigrette	**6 tbsp**

Rinse chick-peas under cold water. Put in a pan and pour in enough cold water to cover by about 5 cm (2 inches). Discard any that float to surface. Cover , leaving lid ajar, bring to the boil; cook for 2 minutes. Turn off heat, cover, and soak the peas for at least 1 hour.

When peas finish soaking, drain. Return to pan and pour in water to cover by about 5 cm (2 inches). Simmer; until soft – about 45 minutes. Stir in salt, cook until tender – 10 to 15 minutes.

About 20 minutes before peas finish cooking, start the rice: bring the stock to the boil in a pan, add the rice, saffron and its liquid, the lemon rind. Stir rice to distribute the saffron and return

to the boil. Cover, cook the rice over medium-low until tender and has absorbed liquid – about 20 minutes. Discard the lemon rind.

While the rice is cooking, boil the fresh peas until tender – 5 to 7 minutes. Drain the peas and set them aside. Heat the almonds in a small frying pan over medium heat, stirring frequently until they are lightly toasted – about 5 minutes.

Drain the chick-peas well and transfer them to a large bowl. Add the rice, peas, toasted almonds, red and green peppers, tomatoes and olives. Pour the prepared vinaigrette over the salad and toss well. Transfer the salad to a serving dish. Serve at room temperature or barely chilled.

21

Black Bean, Rice and Pepper Salad

<table>
<tr><td>Serves 4
as a main
course</td></tr>
<tr><td>Working
time: about
20 minutes</td></tr>
<tr><td>Total time:
about
11 hours
(includes
soaking and
chilling)</td></tr>
</table>

Calories
635

Protein
21g

Cholesterol
2mg

Total fat
10g

Saturated fat
1g

Sodium
385mg

185 g	black beans, soaked overnight	6½ oz
1	small onion, coarsely chopped	1
1	garlic clove	1
2 tsp	fresh thyme, or ½ tsp dried leaves	2 tsp
1	bay leaf	1
½ tsp	salt	½ tsp
1 litre	unsalted chicken stock	1¾ pints
370 g	long-grain rice	13 oz
1	sweet red and green pepper, seeded, deribbed and sliced into short, thin strips	1
1	fresh hot green chili pepper, seeded and finely chopped	1

2	shallots, finely chopped	2
3	spring onions, thinly sliced	3
2 tbsp	chopped coriander or parsley	2 tbsp
	Chili Dressing	
1 tsp	Dijon mustard	1 tsp
1 tbsp	sherry or white wine vinegar	1 tbsp
1 tbsp	unsalted chicken stock	1 tbsp
2 tbsp	virgin olive oil	2 tbsp
½ tsp	chili powder	½ tsp
4	drops Tabasco sauce	4
1	garlic clove, finely chopped freshly ground black pepper	1

Drain beans and boil in plenty of fresh water for 10 mins. Drain.

Return beans to the pan, add water to cover by 7.5 cm (3 inches) and bring to boil. Add onion, garlic, thyme and bay leaf, cover ,and simmer until they are soft – about 50 minutes. Skim foam from surface. Stir in salt and cook beans until quite tender – 30 minutes to 1 hour.

Drain and remove the garlic clove and bay leaf; rinse beans.

Bring stock to boil in a pan. Add rice and shallots, simmer. Cook rice, covered, until tender and the liquid is absorbed – about 20 minutes.

Mix the mustard, vinegar and the stock in a bowl. Whisk in the oil, then the chili powder, Tabasco sauce, garlic and some pepper.

Transfer the hot rice to a large bowl. Add the peppers, spring onions and beans. Pour the dressing over the salad, toss well, and chill the salad for at least 1 hour. Sprinkle with the fresh coriander or parsley just before serving.

Red Lentils with White Rice and Pearl Onions

Serves 6
as a side
dish

Working
time: about
15 minutes

Total time:
about 30
minutes

Calories
200

Protein
8g

Cholesterol
0mg

Total fat
3g

Saturated fat
0g

Sodium
20mg

190 g	red lentils, picked over	**6¼ oz**
90 g	long-grain rice	**3 oz**
2 tbsp	sugar	**2 tbsp**
4 tbsp	raspberry vinegar	**4 tbsp**
6 tbsp	unsalted chicken stock	**6 tbsp**

175 g	pearl onions, blanched for	**6 oz**
	2 minutes in boiling water	
	and peeled	
1 tsp	Dijon mustard	**1 tsp**
	freshly ground black pepper	
1 tbsp	safflower oil	**1 tbsp**

Bring the lentils and ¾ litre (1¼ pints) of water to the boil in a small saucepan. Reduce the heat and simmer the lentils until they are tender – 15 to 20 minutes. Avoid overcooking or the lentils will lose much of their colour. Drain the lentils and put them into a large bowl.

Start cooking the rice while the lentils are simmering. Bring the rice and ¼ litre (8 fl oz) of water to the boil in a small saucepan over medium-high heat. Reduce the heat, cover the saucepan, and simmer the rice until the liquid has been absorbed and the rice is tender – about 20 minutes. Add the rice to the lentils.

While the rice is cooking, sprinkle the sugar into a sauté pan and set it over medium heat.

Cook the sugar until it liquefies and starts to caramelize. Pour in 3 tablespoons of the vinegar and 4 tablespoons of the chicken stock. As the liquid comes to a simmer, stir it to incorporate the caramelized sugar, then add the pearl onions. Cook the onions, stirring from time to time, until they are glazed and nearly all the liquid in the pan has evaporated. Add the glazed onions to the lentils and rice in the bowl.

To prepare the dressing, combine the remaining raspberry vinegar and chicken stock, the mustard and some pepper in a small bowl. Whisk in the oil, then pour the vinaigrette over the lentil and rice mixture, and toss well. This salad is best served cold.

Mussel Salad

Serves 4
as a first
course

Working
time: about
30 minutes

Total time:
about
1 hour

Calories
175

Protein
7g

Cholesterol
25mg

Total fat
5g

Saturated fat
1g

Sodium
125mg

90 g	rice	**3 oz**
1 tbsp	fennel seeds	**1 tbsp**
2 tbsp	finely chopped sweet green pepper	**2 tbsp**
4 tbsp	finely chopped red onion	**4 tbsp**
1	small ripe tomato, skinned, seeded and chopped	**1**
1	small garlic clove, finely chopped	**1**
1 tbsp	grated horseradish, drained	**1 tbsp**
3 tbsp	white wine vinegar	**3 tbsp**
24	mussels, scrubbed and debearded	**24**
1 tbsp	virgin olive oil	**1 tbsp**
	parsley sprigs for garnish	

Put the rice, the fennel seeds and ¼ litre (8 fl oz) of water into a small saucepan over medium-high heat. Bring the water to the boil, then reduce the heat, cover the pan, and simmer the rice until it is tender – 20 to 25 minutes. Set the rice aside.

While the rice is simmering, prepare the marinade. In a bowl, mix together the green pepper, onion, tomato, garlic, horseradish and vinegar.

Bring ¼ litre (8 fl oz) of water to the boil in a large pan. Add the mussels and cover the pan. Steam the mussels until they open – 2 to 3 minutes. Discard any mussels that remain closed. Strain the cooking liquid through a sieve lined with doubled muslin, taking care not to pour any

of the sand into the sieve. Reserve the liquid.

Using a slotted spoon, transfer the mussels to a large bowl. When the mussels are cool enough to handle, remove them from their shells, reserving one half of each shell. Dip each mussel into the reserved liquid to rinse away any residual sand. Pat the mussels dry, then add them to the marinade, and let them stand at room temperature for 30 minutes.

Stir the rice and oil into the marinated mussels. Fill each reserved mussel shell with one mussel and about 2 teaspoons of the rice-and-vegetable mixture. Arrange the stuffed shells on a platter; garnish the platter with the parsley just before serving.

Green and White Rice Salad

Serves 12 as a side dish

Working time: about 25 minutes

Total time: about 45 minutes

Calories 105
Protein 2g
Cholesterol 0mg
Total fat 5g
Saturated fat 1g
Sodium 123mg

45 cl	unsalted vegetable stock	¾ pint
175 g	long-grain rice	6 oz
400 g	fresh peas, shelled, or 125 g (4 oz) frozen peas, thawed	14 oz
½	cucumber, cut into 5 mm (¼ inch) dice	½
125 g	courgettes, trimmed and julienned	4 oz
6	spring onions, trimmed and thinly sliced diagonally	6
1 tbsp	finely cut chives	1 tbsp
3 tbsp	chopped parsley	3 tbsp
1	crisp round lettuce, leaves washed and dried	1
	Tarragon Vinaigrette	
½ tsp	French mustard	½ tsp
⅛ tsp	salt	⅛ tsp
⅛ tsp	freshly ground black pepper	⅛ tsp
2 tbsp	tarragon vinegar	2 tbsp
4 tbsp	walnut or virgin olive oil	4 tbsp

Bring stock to the boil in a small pan and add the rice. Reduce heat to a simmer and cook the rice, covered, until it is just tender and all the stock is absorbed – 15 to 20 minutes. Set aside to cool.

Blanch the fresh peas in a saucepan of boiling water for about 30 seconds; if you are using frozen peas, add them to boiling water and just bring the water back to the boil. Drain the peas, refresh them under cold running water and drain them again.

Transfer the cooled rice to a large bowl, add the blanched peas, the cucumber and courgettes, and mix the ingredients together well. Stir in the spring onion slices, the chives and the parsley.

To make the dressing, whisk the mustard, salt, black pepper, vinegar and oil together in a small bowl. Pour the dressing over the salad, and toss it thoroughly.

Line a large serving bowl with the lettuce and pile the salad in the centre.

Avocado, Flageolets, Almonds and Brown Rice

Serves 6

Working time: about 25 minutes

Total time: about 3 hour (includes soaking)

Calories 300

Protein 10g

Cholesterol 0mg

Total fat 11g

Saturated fat 2g

Sodium 80mg

125 g	dried flageolet beans, picked over	**4 oz**
250 g	brown rice	**8 oz**
¼ tsp	salt	**¼ tsp**
1	small ripe avocado	**1**
1	lemon, juice only, strained	**1**
60 g	blanched and skinned almonds, toasted	**2 oz**
6 tbsp	chopped parsley	**6 tbsp**
2 tbsp	chopped fresh wild fennel	**2 tbsp**
4 tbsp	plain low-fat yogurt	**4 tbsp**
1 tbsp	virgin olive oil	**1 tbsp**
1 tsp	Dijon mustard	**1 tsp**
1	garlic clove, crushed	**1**
	Large lettuce leaves, for garnish	

Rinse beans under cold water, put into a pan, and pour in cold water to cover by about 7.5 cm (3 inches). Discard beans that float to surface. Cover, leaving lid ajar, and slowly bring to the boil. Boil for 2 minutes, turn off the heat, and soak the beans, covered, for at least 1 hour.

Rinse beans, place in a clean pan, pour in enough water to cover by about 7.5 cm (3 inches). Bring to the boil. Boil for 10 minutes, drain and rinse again. Wash the pan, replace beans and pour in enough water to cover again by about 7.5 cm (3 inches). Bring to the boil, reduce heat to maintain a strong simmer and cook, covered, until tender – about 1 hour. Drain beans in a colander, rinse, and set them

aside to cool for about 30 minutes.

Bring 2 litres (3½ pints) of water to the boil in a pan. Stir in rice and salt, reduce heat, simmer, uncovered, until rice is tender – about 40 minutes. Drain the rice in a strainer, rinse under cold water and leave to drain and cool thoroughly.

Halve, stone, peel and chop the avocado and coat the pieces in half of the lemon juice to prevent them from discolouring. In a bowl, mix the avocado, almonds, parsley and fennel with the beans and the rice. In a bowl, beat together the yogurt, olive oil, mustard, garlic and remaining lemon juice. Fold dressing into the rice salad.

To serve, line a large bowl with the lettuce leaves and spoon the rice salad into the middle.

Caribbean Spiced Rice

Serves 4

Working (and total) time: about 50 minutes

Calories 540

Protein 9g

Cholesterol 0mg

Total fat 6g

Saturated fat 2g

Sodium 250mg

350 g	basmati rice, rinsed	**12 oz**
1 tsp	ground allspice	**1 tsp**
½ tsp	salt	**½ tsp**
2	garlic cloves, sliced	**2**
	freshly ground black pepper	
90 cl	unsalted vegetable stock	**1½ pints**
2	green bananas	**2**
1 tbsp	white wine vinegar	**1 tbsp**
1	small carrot, finely chopped	**1**
¼	sweet red pepper, finely chopped	**¼**
1	stick celery, finely chopped	**1**
125 g	okra, finely sliced	**4 oz**
2	small ripe mangoes	**2**
12	spring onions, finely sliced	**12**

6 tbsp	chopped parsley	**6 tbsp**
½	lime, cut into slices, for garnish	**½**
	Coriander Sauce	
20 g	fresh coriander leaves	**¾ oz**
4	spring onions, roughly chopped	**4**
1	garlic clove, roughly chopped	**1**
½	onion, roughly chopped	**½**
1 cm	piece fresh ginger root, peeled and roughly chopped	**½ inch**
½	green chili pepper, seeded, chopped	**½**
	freshly ground black pepper	
4 tsp	wine vinegar	**4 tsp**
½	fresh lime, juice only	**½**
2 tbsp	virgin olive oil	**2 tbsp**

For the sauce: blend all ingredients with 2 tbsp water until smooth. Leave, covered, in a bowl.

Cover and simmer rice with allspice, salt, garlic, some black pepper, and the stock until water is absorbed – about 20 minutes.

Cut bananas in half lengthwise without peeling. Score the skin through to the flesh in a few places. Boil, in vinegar and enough water to cover; simmer for 20 minutes. Drain and peel. Cut each half lengthwise into three or four thin slices. Keep warm.

While rice and bananas are cooking, steam the vegetables. Put carrot in steamer and steam for 3 minutes; add the sweet red pepper, celery and the okra. Steam until cooked but crisp.

Peel and dice half the mangoes; slice the other half. Stir diced mangoes, spring onions, steamed vegetables and parsley into rice. Serve with coriander sauce, garnished with fruit.

Gateau of Crêpes with Wild Rice and Mushrooms

Serves 6

Working time: about 1 hour

Total time: about 2 hours

Calories 215
Protein 8g
Cholesterol 40mg
Total fat 7g
Saturated fat 2g
Sodium 185mg

125 g	plain flour	**4 oz**	**1½ tbsp**	dry Madeira	**1½ tbsp**
1 tsp	freshly grated nutmeg	**1 tsp**	**1½ tbsp**	safflower oil	**1½ tbsp**
1	small egg	**1**	**250 g**	button mushrooms, wiped	**8 oz**
1	egg white	**1**		clean, thinly sliced	
30 cl	skimmed milk	**½ pint**	**½ tsp**	salt	**½ tsp**
60 g	wild rice	**2 oz**	**60 g**	low-fat fromage frais	**2 oz**
30 g	dried ceps or other wild mushrooms	**1 oz**		freshly ground black pepper	

Sift flour and nutmeg into a bowl. Add egg, egg white and a little milk. Mix. Gradually mix in rest of milk to make smooth batter. Set aside.

Bring 30 cl (½ pint) of water to boil in a pan. Stir in wild rice; simmer, uncovered, until rice is tender – approx 45 mins. Drain.

Put the ceps in a bowl, add 1 tablespoon of the Madeira and 60 cl (1 pint) of tepid water to cover them. Soak for 20 to 30 mins.

Heat ¼ tsp oil in a crêpe pan over medium heat. Spread over entire surface. Heat until very hot. Put 3 tablespoons of the batter into the pan and swirl to coat the bottom with a thin, even layer. Cook until bottom is browned – about 1 min. Lift edge and turn over. Cook second side – 15 to 30 seconds. Repeat to make six crêpes. Set aside.

Preheat the oven to 180°C (350°F or Mark 4).

Drain and rinse the ceps and strain their soaking liquid; reserve the liquid. Sauté button mushrooms with remaining oil for 3 to 5 minutes, until lightly cooked. Add ceps, the reserved soaking liquid, the salt and the remaining 2 tablespoon of Madeira. Boil fast for 30 seconds. Reduce heat, stir in wild rice and cook for about 2 mins, to heat through. Drain, reserve liquid. Season mixture with pepper and keep warm in pan.

Reduce liquid to 3 tbsp by boiling over high heat. Remove from heat. Stir in *fromage frais* – do not boil, but warm through.

Sandwich crêpes with alternating layers of rice and mushroom mix. Warm in oven for a few mins and serve with sauce.

Atlantic Kedgeree

Serves 6

Working time: about 45 minutes

Total time: about 2 hours and 30 minutes (includes cooling)

Calories 280
Protein 23g
Cholesterol 90mg
Total fat 2g
Saturated fat trace
Sodium 170mg

500 g	mussels, scrubbed and debearded	**1 lb**		$\frac{1}{2}$	sweet yellow pepper, seeded, deribbed and thinly sliced	$\frac{1}{2}$
300 g	long-grain rice	**10 oz**		**175 g**	peeled cooked prawns	**6 oz**
3	sticks celery, sliced	**3**			freshly ground black pepper	
90 cl	unsalted vegetable stock	**1½ pints**		**2 tbsp**	fresh lemon juice (optional)	**2 tbsp**
150 g	French beans, trimmed, cut into 2.5 cm (1 inch) lengths	**5 oz**		**1 tbsp**	finely cut chives	**1 tbsp**
350 g	cod fillets	**12 oz**			samphire, for garnish (optional)	
$\frac{1}{2}$	sweet orange pepper, seeded, deribbed and thinly sliced	$\frac{1}{2}$				

Place mussels in a bowl. Sharply tap any that are open; if they remain open, discard them. Cover with plastic film, pulled back at one edge, and cook on high for 5 to 6 mins, stirring the mussels after 3 mins. Cool, discard any that remained closed during cooking. Remove from their shells. Strain any cooking liquid through a muslin-lined sieve into a bowl, and set it aside.

Place the rice and celery in a bowl. Bring stock to the boil, then add it to the reserved mussel-cooking liquid. Cover with plastic film as before, and cook the rice on high for 10 mins. Quickly stir in the French beans. Set rice aside to cool; any stock that was left at the end of the

cooking time will be absorbed as the rice cools.

Put cod on a plate, thinner pieces towards the centre, cover with film pulled back at one edge. Cook on high for 3 to 4 mins, until flesh flakes easily. Discard skin and bones. Set aside to cool.

Place the orange and yellow pepper strips in a bowl. Cover the bowl as before, and cook the strips on high for 1½ minutes, until tender. Pour away any juices, and leave the peppers to cool.

Toss together the French beans and rice, the flaked fish, peppers, mussels and prawns. Season the mixture, and add the lemon juice, if using.

Arrange the kedgeree on a platter, sprinkle on the chives and garnish the dish with the samphire.

Pumpkin and Pecorino Risotto

Serves 4

Working (and total) time: about 1 hour and 15 minutes

Calories
305

Protein
6g

Cholesterol
5mg

Total fat
6g

Saturated fat
2g

Sodium
280mg

1 tbsp	virgin olive oil	1 tbsp
2	shallots, finely chopped	2
250 g	Italian round-grain rice	8 oz
500 g	pumpkin, peeled, seeded and finely grated	1 lb
¼ tsp	powdered saffron	¼ tsp
8 cl	dry white wine	3 fl oz
90 cl	unsalted vegetable stock	1½ pints

1 tbsp	finely chopped fresh oregano or 1 tsp dried oregano	1 tbsp
½ tsp	salt	½ tsp
	freshly ground black pepper	
30 g	pecorino cheese, finely grated	1 oz
2 tbsp	finely chopped flat-leaf parsley, for garnish (optional)	2 tbsp

Heat oil in a 2 to 3 litre (3½ to 5 pint) casserole. Add shallots, cook over medium heat for about 5 minutes, stirring from time to time, until soft but not brown. Reduce heat to low, add rice, stir to ensure each grain is coated with a little oil. Add pumpkin, stir over medium heat for about 3 minutes, until heated through. Stir saffron into white wine. Increase heat and pour wine into casserole. Stir, until all liquid has been absorbed – about 3 minutes. Heat stock in a separate pan.

Reduce heat under rice and ladle about 15 cl (¼ pint) of hot stock into casserole. Stir, then place lid on casserole to almost cover the top. Simmer, until all stock has been absorbed – about 5 minutes. Stir in another ladleful of stock

and cover as before. This time, stir contents of casserole once or twice while stock is being absorbed, replacing lid after stirring. Mix in oregano, continue to add stock by the ladleful, stirring, until rice is soft but still a little resilient to the bite, and pumpkin has almost melted into a sauce – about 30 minutes. Once this stage has been reached, stir in remaining stock and replace lid on casserole. Turn off heat, leave to stand for 5 minutes, during which time remaining stock will be absorbed. Warm four serving bowls.

Season the risotto with the salt, some pepper and the pecorino cheese, stirring well until melted. Serve immediately; if you like, sprinkle ½ tablespoon of parsley over each portion.

Pea and Mushroom Risotto

Serves 6

Working
time: about
45 minutes

Total time:
about
1 hour and
15 minutes

Calories
410

Protein
12g

Cholesterol
20mg

Total fat
10g

Saturated fat
5g

Sodium
430mg

350 g	peas, shelled, or 125 g (4 oz) frozen peas, thawed	**12 oz**		**250 g**	tomatoes, skinned, seeded and chopped	**8 oz**
30 g	unsalted butter	**1 oz**		**½ tsp**	salt	**½ tsp**
125 g	shallots, chopped	**4 oz**		**250 g**	chestnut mushrooms, wiped clean and coarsely grated	**8 oz**
500 g	brown round-grain rice	**1 lb**		**60 g**	Parmesan cheese, grated	**2 oz**
20 cl	dry white wine or dry vermouth	**7 fl oz**			freshly ground black pepper	
45 cl	tomato juice	**¾ pint**			chopped parsley, for garnish	
45 cl	unsalted vegetable stock	**¾ pint**				

If you are using fresh peas, boil until barely tender – 3 to 4 minutes. Drain, then refresh them under cold running water. Drain again and set aside. (Frozen peas do not need precooking.)

In a large, heavy-bottomed saucepan, melt the butter and sauté the shallots over medium heat until they are transparent, stirring occasionally – 3 to 5 minutes. Stir the rice into the shallots and cook for 2 to 3 minutes, stirring constantly to ensure that the grains are well coated with the butter.

Pour the wine into the rice and simmer, stirring frequently, until it has been absorbed by the rice. Pour in the tomato juice and 30 cl (½ pint) of the stock, bring the liquid to the boil, then reduce the

heat to a simmer. Cover the saucepan and cook the rice, stirring occasionally, for about 20 minutes. Stir the tomatoes and the salt into the rice, cover and simmer for a further 10 minutes, adding more stock, a ladleful at a time, if the rice dries out.

Add the mushrooms, peas and any remaining stock to the pan, increase the heat to high and cook rapidly, stirring constantly, until the stock is absorbed but the rice is still very moist. Stir the Parmesan cheese into the risotto and season it generously with freshly ground pepper. Turn the risotto into a warmed serving dish and sprinkle it with chopped parsley.

Rice Cakes with Onion Relish

Serves 4

Working
time: about
35 minutes

Total time:
about
1 hour and
45 minutes
(includes
soaking)

Calories
255
Protein
8g
Cholesterol
15mg
Total fat
6g
Saturated fat
3g
Sodium
300mg

175 g	basmati rice, rinsed and soaked	**6 oz**	**60 g**	Cheddar cheese, grated	**2 oz**
½ tsp	safflower oil	**½ tsp**	**¼ tsp**	salt	**¼ tsp**
1	onion, finely chopped	**1**			
125 g	carrots, grated	**4 oz**		**Onion relish**	
2	green chili peppers, finely chopped	**2**	**1**	onion, cut into paper-thin rings	**1**
2	garlic cloves, crushed	**2**	**½**	sweet red pepper, finely chopped	**½**
½ tsp	cardamom seeds, crushed	**½ tsp**	**1**	lime, finely grated rind and juice	**1**
1 tbsp	chopped fresh coriander	**1 tbsp**	**¼ tsp**	salt	**¼ tsp**
½ tsp	ground cumin	**½ tsp**	**½ tsp**	paprika	**½ tsp**
¼ tsp	ground turmeric	**¼ tsp**	**½ tsp**	brown sugar	**½ tsp**

First make the onion relish. Place the onion in a bowl with the red pepper, and add lime rind, lime juice, salt, paprika and sugar. Toss the ingredients together until well combined, transfer to a serving bowl and set aside for the flavours to develop while you prepare the rice cakes.

After soaking for 1 hour drain the rice and bring to the boil in 1.5 litres (2½ pints) of water. Boil rapidly, uncovered, until thoroughly tender – about 10 minutes. The rice needs to be well cooked so that the rice cakes will hold together when grilled. Drain.

Heat oil in a frying pan over medium heat and fry onion for 3 to 4 minutes, until softened and beginning to brown. Stir in carrots, chili peppers, garlic, and spices, and cook, stirring, until the carrots have softened – about 2 minutes. Remove from the heat, stir in rice, cheese and salt, and mash with a potato masher, until the rice is broken up and sticky.

Preheat grill to medium. Lightly flour your hands and shape the mixture into 20 small balls. Thread five balls on to each of four skewers. Place skewers on a foil-covered rack and grill for about 15 minutes, turning once, until they are pale golden. Serve hot, with the onion relish.

Gingered Black Beans with Saffron Rice

Serves 6

Working time: about 35 minutes

Total time: about 2 hours and 45 minutes (includes soaking)

Calories 390

Protein 12g

Cholesterol 0mg

Total fat 14g

Saturated fat 2g

Sodium 150mg

175 g	dried black kidney beans	**6 oz**
2 tbsp	virgin olive oil	**2 tbsp**
7.5 cm	piece fresh ginger root, peeled, 5 cm (2 inches) thinly sliced, the remainder grated	**3 inch**
1 tbsp	chopped fresh oregano, or 1 tsp dried oregano	**1 tbsp**
1 tsp	chopped fresh sage, or ¼ tsp dried sage	**1 tsp**
1 tsp	saffron threads	**1 tsp**
½ tsp	salt	**½ tsp**

250 g	long-grain white rice	**8 oz**
90 g	shelled walnuts, roughly chopped	**3 oz**
3	garlic cloves, crushed	**3**
60 g	dried cloud-ear mushrooms, soaked for 20 minutes in hot water and drained	**2 oz**
125 g	button mushrooms, wiped and sliced	**4 oz**
2	limes, grated rind and juice freshly ground black pepper	**2**
¼ tsp	paprika, for garnish	**¼ tsp**

Soak beans overnight. Rinse the beans, place in a clean pan, and pour in enough cold water to cover again by about 7.5 cm (3 inches). Bring to the boil. Boil for 10 minutes, then drain and rinse again.

In a clean pan, heat 1 tablespoon of oil over medium heat; add sliced ginger root, oregano and sage, sauté for 1 minute. Add beans and cold water to cover by about 7.5 cm (3 inches). Bring to the boil and boil steadily until tender – about 1 hour. Drain, return to pan with all the flavourings and keep warm.

Boil saffron, salt and rice in 60 cl (1 pint) water, stir once. Cover and simmer for about 15 minutes, or until rice is just cooked and water absorbed. Remove from heat and stir in walnuts. Leave while walnuts warm.

Heat remaining oil in a wok over medium heat, add the garlic, cloud-ear and button mushrooms and grated ginger. Stir fry them rapidly for 5–6 minutes. Add them to beans, with lime juice, rind and some pepper. Serve on a large platter surrounded by rice garnished with paprika.

Phyllo Pastry Fruits

<table>
<tr><td>Makes 12
pastry fruits

Working
time: about
30 minutes

Total time:
about
1 hour and
20 minutes</td><td></td><td>Per fruit:
Calories
50
Protein
1g
Cholesterol
10mg
Total fat
2g
Saturated fat
1g
Sodium
15mg</td></tr>
</table>

4	apricots, halved and stoned	4
4	plums, halved and stoned	4
4	figs, peeled and halved	4
4	sheets phyllo pastry, each about 45 by 30 cm (18 by 12 inches)	4
30 g	unsalted butter, melted	1 oz
1 tsp	flaked almonds	1 tsp

	icing sugar, to decorate	
	Rose Rice Filling	
15 cl	skimmed milk	¼ pint
30 g	ground rice	1 oz
1 tsp	caster sugar	1 tsp
3 tsp	rose-water	3 tsp

Put milk into a pan and bring to the boil over medium heat. Sprinkle in ground rice and stir until it comes back to the boil. Simmer for 2 minutes, stir in caster sugar and rose-water, set aside to cool.

Meanwhile, cut phyllo into 24 15 cm (6 inch) squares. Stack the squares in a pile and cover with a damp cloth, removing them as required.

Fill the cavities in the apricots and plums with the filling, then sandwich the fruit halves back together with more filling to form whole fruits.

Preheat the oven to 200°C (400°F or Mark 6). To wrap the apricots, place each fruit on its side at the centre of one edge of one phyllo square and roll up. Twist both ends, brush with melted

butter; repeat with a second square of phyllo. For the plums, place each fruit, stem end up, in the centre of a phyllo square. Gather the pastry up round the fruit and twist it at the top. Brush with melted butter, then wrap the fruit in a second square. Smooth the top edges of pastry down over the fruit. Wrap figs in the same way as plums, but tease open the layers of pastry at the top of the fruit rather than smoothing them flat.

Place the wrapped fruits, spaced well apart, on a lightly buttered baking sheet. Brush a little more butter on to each fruit and sprinkle almonds over the apricots. Bake the fruits for about 10 minutes, until lightly browned. When they are cool, dust with a little icing sugar.

Avocado Sushi with Olives and Peppers

Makes 24 sushi

Working time: about 50 minutes

Total time: about 1 hour and 30 minutes

Per sushi:

Calories
40

Protein
1g

Cholesterol
0mg

Total fat
2g

Saturated fat
trace

Sodium
35mg

150 g	sushi rice	**5 oz**		**½**	small sweet red papper, skinned, seeded and deribbed	**½**
½ tsp	salt	**½ tsp**		**20**	black olives, stoned	**20**
1½ tsp	sugar	**1½ tsp**		**⅛ tsp**	wasabi powder	**⅛ tsp**
1	lemon, juice strained, rind of one quarter pared	**1**		**1 tsp**	rice vinegar	**1 tsp**
2	spring onions	**2**		**4**	sheets nori	**4**
½	small firm avocado	**½**				

Stir rice gently in a bowl with about five times its volume of water, then carefully pour off the water. Repeat twice, drain the rice and leave in a sieve for about 45 minutes to absorb any residual water.

Boil rice in ¼ litre (8 fl oz) of water, partially covered, over high heat. Cover, and simmer gently for 10 minutes. Turn off heat and leave for 10 to 15 minutes. Dissolve salt and sugar in 2 tablespoons of the lemon juice, and mix into the rice.

Blanch lemon rind for 5 seconds, drain and dry. Cut lemon rind and spring onions into five slivers. Peel avocado and cut into 5 mm (¼ inch) wide strips. Toss avocado strips with 1 teaspoon of remaining lemon juice to prevent discolouring. Cut pepper into narrow strips. Trim olives, then cut in half lengthwise. Mix wasabi powder and a little water to a paste.

Mix vinegar with 3 tablespoons of water. Trim off a third of each nori sheet with scissors along a long edge, and discard. Divide rice into four. Toast one piece of nori by waving it above a high flame for a few seconds until it turns papery, then lay it on a bamboo rolling mat with a long edge towards you. Moisten your fingers in the vinegar and water. Starting at the edge nearest you, spread one portion of the rice over about three quarters of a toasted nori sheet, firming the rice with your fingertips.

For each nori: smear a line of wasabi; along middle of rice and place a quarter of olives end on line. Add a quarter of pepper, spring onion and lemon rind. Roll up. Cut each roll into 6 slices with a wet knife. Serve.

Yellow Squash Quiche with a Rice Crust

Serves 4
as a main
dish

Working
time: about
30 minutes

Total time:
about
1 hour and
15 minutes

Calories
320

Protein
17g

Cholesterol
160mg

Total fat
11g

Saturated fat
5g

Sodium
290mg

3	yellow squashes, halved lengthwise, seeded, flesh grated	3
250 g	cooked rice	8 oz
4	eggs, whites only of 2	4
90 g	Emmenthal cheese, grated	3 oz
2 tsp	safflower oil	2 tsp
6	shallots, finely chopped	6
12.5 cl	vermouth	4 fl oz
¼ tsp	salt	¼ tsp

	freshly ground black pepper	
½ tsp	chopped fresh marjoram, or ¼ tsp dried marjoram	½ tsp
½ tsp	fresh thyme, or ¼ tsp dried thyme	½ tsp
¼ litre	skimmed milk	8 fl oz
⅛ tsp	grated nutmeg	⅛ tsp
12	thin strips of sweet red and green peppers, blanched	12

Preheat the oven to 190°C (375°F or Mark 5). To prepare the rice crust, combine the cooked rice, one of the egg whites and half of the cheese. Press the mixture into a 23 cm (9 inch) quiche or flan tin. Prebake the crust until the cheese is just melted – 3 to 4 minutes. Remove the crust from the oven and set aside.

Heat the oil in a heavy frying pan over medium heat. Cook the shallots until soft – about 2 to 3 minutes – stirring occasionally. Pour the vermouth into the pan, and cook until the vermouth has nearly evaporated – about 3 minutes. Add the squash and cook, stirring occasionally, until the squash is tender – about

3 minutes. Season the mixture with the salt, pepper, marjoram and thyme, and remove from the heat.

In a large mixing bowl, lightly beat the two whole eggs, the remaining egg white, the skimmed milk and nutmeg. Stir in the remaining cheese and the squash mixture. Pour this mixture into the crust and bake until the filling begins to set – about 20 minutes. Remove the quiche from the oven and arrange the pepper strips on top. Return the quiche to the oven and bake until the filling is set in the centre – 5 to 7 minutes more. Cut the quiche into wedges and serve.

Saffron Pork with Quail and Prawns

Serves 4

Working
(and total)
time: about
1 hour

Calories
380

Protein
22g

Cholesterol
75mg

Total fat
9g

Saturated fat
3g

Sodium
100mg

250 g	pork fillet, trimmed of fat and cut into eight pieces	8 oz
2	quail	2
1 tbsp	virgin olive oil	1 tbsp
1	red onion, finely chopped	1
250 g	Italian round-grain rice	8 oz
¼ tsp	saffron powder	¼ tsp
2	pinches saffron threads	2
½ tsp	salt	½ tsp

	freshly ground black pepper	
1–1.25 litres	unsalted chicken stock or water	1½–2 pints
1	green chili pepper, seeded and finely sliced	1
1	red chili pepper, seeded and finely sliced	1
4	large cooked prawns	4

Divide each quail in two by cutting down the back and up along the breastbone. Remove any innards that remain, wash the quail pieces and pat them dry with paper towels. Rub the quail with a little of the olive oil, then set aside.

Heat the remaining oil in a heavy paella pan or frying pan, and sweat the onion in it for 1 minute. Add the rice and sauté for about 1 minute, then add the pork and sauté the whole mixture for a further 2 minutes, until the pork is sealed. Add the saffron powder and saffron threads, season with the salt and some pepper, and pour on enough chicken stock or water to cover.

Bring slowly to the boil, then simmer the mixture gently for 35 to 40 minutes, adding the remaining stock or water as necessary and stirring occasionally. After 30 minutes, test the rice for doneness. When it is still a little hard but nearly cooked, add the chili peppers and prawns to heat through.

While the rice mixture is cooking, grill the quail under a hot grill until they are well browned – about 10 minutes. Transfer the rice and pork mixture to a large dish or individual plates and serve immediately with the prawns and quail to one side.

Kale Gratin with Ricotta and Parmesan Cheese

Serves 10

Working time: about 40 minutes

Total time: about 1 hour and 15 minutes

Calories 130

Protein 7g

Cholesterol 5mg

Total fat 4g

Saturated fat 1g

Sodium 165mg

1.5 kg	kale, washed, stems removed	**3 lb**
¼ litre	unsalted chicken or vegetable stock	**8 fl oz**
1	onion, chopped	**1**
90 g	long-grain rice	**3 oz**
1 tbsp	chopped fresh thyme, or 1 tsp dried thyme	**1 tbsp**

125 g	low-fat ricotta	**4 oz**
5 tbsp	freshly grated Parmesan cheese	**5 tbsp**
¼ tsp	grated nutmeg	**¼ tsp**
¼ tsp	salt	**¼ tsp**
	freshly ground black pepper	
15 g	fresh white breadcrumbs	**½ oz**
1 tbsp	virgin olive oil	**1 tbsp**

Pour the stock into a small saucepan, add the onion and bring the liquid to the boil over high heat. Add the rice and thyme. Reduce the heat to medium-low, cover the pan, and simmer the rice until it is tender – about 15 minutes.

Preheat the oven to 200°C (400°F or Mark 6).

Meanwhile, put the kale in a large saucepan, cover the pan tightly and cook the kale over medium-high heat until it wilts – 3 to 4 minutes. (The water clinging to the leaves provides enough moisture.) Drain the kale and coarsely chop it. Combine the kale with the rice, ricotta,

4 tablespoons of the Parmesan cheese, the nutmeg, salt and pepper.

Put the mixture into a lightly oiled 1½ litre (2½ pint) gratin dish. Sprinkle on the breadcrumbs and the remaining Parmesan cheese. Dribble the olive oil over the top and bake in the upper third of the oven until the juices begin bubbling – about 30 minutes. Remove the gratin from the oven and turn on the grill. Place the gratin under the grill to brown – about 5 minutes. Serve immediately.

Artichoke Bottoms with Tomato and Rice

Serves 8

Working time: about 25 minutes

Total time: about 45 minutes

Calories 205

Protein 6g

Cholesterol 15mg

Total fat 9g

Saturated fat 4g

Sodium 190mg

4	artichoke bottoms	4
$\frac{1}{2}$	lemon	$\frac{1}{2}$
40 g	unsalted butter	$1\frac{1}{4}$ oz
2 tbsp	virgin olive oil	2 tbsp
125 g	mushrooms, wiped and sliced	4 oz
1	small onion, finely chopped	1
1	garlic clove, finely chopped	1
2 tsp	chopped fresh basil, or $\frac{3}{4}$ tsp dried basil	2 tsp

2	tomatoes, skinned, seeded and chopped	2
$\frac{1}{2}$ litre	unsalted chicken or vegetable stock	16 fl oz
175 g	rice	6 oz
$\frac{1}{4}$ tsp	salt	$\frac{1}{4}$ tsp
	freshly ground black pepper	
60 g	Parmesan cheese, freshly grated	2 oz
10 g	parsley, chopped	$\frac{1}{3}$ oz

In a large saucepan, bring 1 litre (1¾ pints) of water to the boil. Squeeze the juice of the lemon into the water and add the lemon itself. Cook the artichoke bottoms in the boiling water for 10 minutes. Drain, and cut each into six wedges.

In a small, heavy-bottomed saucepan, heat 15 g (½ oz) of the butter with the olive oil over medium heat. Add the mushrooms and salt, and sauté until the liquid from the mushrooms has evaporated. Stir in the onion and continue cooking for 2 minutes, stirring frequently. Add the chopped garlic, basil and tomatoes, and 12.5 cl (4 fl oz) of the stock. Bring the mixture to the boil, then reduce the heat and simmer for 10

minutes. Remove the saucepan from the heat.

In a heavy, 4 litre (7 pint) saucepan or a fireproof casserole with a lid, melt the remaining butter over medium-low heat. Add the rice and cook, stirring constantly, until the rice is opaque – 3 to 4 minutes. Stir in the vegetable mixture, ¼ litre (8 fl oz) of the stock and the pepper, and bring to the boil. Reduce the heat and simmer, covered, for 10 minutes.

Gently stir in the artichoke, the remaining stock and the Parmesan cheese, and continue to cook the dish, covered, until the rice is tender and the liquid is absorbed – 10 to 15 minutes.

Garnish with the parsley; serve immediately.

Sweet Peppers with Herbed Rice

Serves 8

Working time: about 30 minutes

Total time: about 1 hour and 15 minutes

Calories 235

Protein 4g

Cholesterol 0mg

Total fat 5g

Saturated fat 1g

Sodium 15mg

6	red, yellow or green peppers, grilled and peeled	6
175 g	long-grain brown rice	6 oz
2 tbsp	virgin olive oil	2 tbsp
1	onion, chopped	1
90 g	raisins, soaked in 12.5 cl (4 fl oz) dry white wine	3 oz
1	5 cm (2 inch) strip of lemon peel	1
6 cl	unsalted chicken or vegetable stock	2 fl oz
1	lemon, juice only	1
3 tbsp	chopped parsley	3 tbsp
1 tsp	fresh thyme, or ¼ tsp dried thyme	1 tsp
⅛ tsp	ground coriander	⅛ tsp

Bring 1 litre (1¾ pints) of water to the boil in a saucepan. Add the rice and the lemon peel. Simmer for 25 minutes over medium heat.

Remove the stems, ribs and seeds from the peeled peppers. Cut the peppers in half lengthwise. Set eight of the pepper halves aside as a garnish. Coarsely chop the remaining pepper halves and set them aside too. Preheat the oven to 200°C (400°F or Mark 6).

Heat 1 tablespoon of the oil in a large, heavy frying pan. Add the onion, and cook until it is translucent – about 5 minutes. Add the raisins and wine, stock, and lemon juice. Bring to the boil and add the rice. Stir in the parsley, thyme, coriander and the chopped peppers. Transfer the rice mixture to a 1.5 litre (2½ pint) gratin dish. Mound up the rice slightly and arrange the pepper halves on top. Bake the dish for 20 minutes. Brush the peppers with the remaining oil before serving.

Rolled Vine Leaves

Serves 8

Working time: about 45 minutes

Total time: about 2 hours and 30 minutes

Calories 110

Protein 4g

Cholesterol 20mg

Total fat 5g

Saturated fat 2g

Sodium 65mg

125 g	lean minced lamb	4 oz
1	onion, chopped	1
2	garlic cloves, chopped	2
90 g	brown rice	3 oz
2 tbsp	chopped fresh mint	2 tbsp
2 tbsp	chopped parsley	2 tbsp
2	tomatoes, skinned, seeded and chopped	2
1 tbsp	tomato paste	1 tbsp
	freshly ground black pepper	
125 g	fresh vine leaves, blanched for 1 minute in boiling water, rinsed and drained well	4 oz
1 tbsp	virgin olive oil	1 tbsp
1	lemon, juice only	1
	lemon wedges, for garnish	

In a non-stick or cast-iron frying pan, cook the lamb over low heat until the meat begins to release its juices. Increase heat to medium and continue to fry until it has browned. Place a colander over a bowl and transfer lamb and juices to colander to drain. Return 1 tablespoon of the juices to the pan and sauté onion and garlic over low heat, until soft – about 10 minutes. Discard the remaining meat juices.

Return lamb to the frying pan and stir in the rice, mint, parsley, tomato paste, tomatoes and some pepper. Add 20 cl (7 fl oz) of water, and bring to the boil. Cover and cook the stuffing for 10 minutes; set it aside for a few minutes to cool. Preheat the oven to 180°C (350°F or Mark 4).

Lay vine leaves out flat on the work surface. Place a spoonful of stuffing on the centre of each leaf. Fold stem end up over the stuffing, fold both sides towards the middle, roll into a small parcel. Take care not to wrap the parcels too tightly: rice needs room to expand as it cooks.

Lay any spare or damaged vine leaves in the base of a heavy casserole. Set the stuffed parcels in the casserole, packing them in tightly to keep them from unrolling. Pour the oil, lemon juice and 45 cl (¾ pint) of water over the rolls.

Cover casserole and cook vine leaves in oven for about 1¼ hours, adding extra water if the liquid in the casserole evaporates. Leave parcels to cool. Serve cold, garnished with lemon.

Mushroom Risotto

Serves 8

Working
(and total)
time: about
1 hour and
20 minutes

Calories
285

Protein
7g

Cholesterol
20mg

Total fat
8g

Saturated fat
4g

Sodium
100mg

60 g	dried mushrooms	**2 oz**
45 g	unsalted butter	**1½ oz**
1	onion, finely chopped	**1**
1 litre	unsalted chicken stock	**1¾ pints**
400 g	round-grain brown rice	**14 oz**

4 tbsp	white wine	**4 tbsp**
45 g	freshly grated Parmesan cheese	**1½ oz**
2 tbsp	chopped parsley	**2 tbsp**
	freshly ground black pepper	

Soak the dried mushrooms in warm water for 5 minutes to remove grit. Drain them in a colander and soak them again in 60 cl (1 pint) of warm water until they are soft – 10 to 15 minutes. Strain off and reserve their second soaking liquid.

In a large, heavy-bottomed saucepan, heat 30 g (1 oz) of the butter and sauté the onion until it is transparent – 3 to 5 minutes. Meanwhile, bring the chicken stock to the boil in a second pan, add the soaking water from the mushrooms, and simmer the liquid over low heat.

Chop the mushrooms roughly and add them to the onions in the pan. Stir the rice into the onion and mushroom mixture and cook it over a gentle heat for about 5 minutes, stirring constantly, to ensure that the grains are well coated with the butter.

Pour the wine into the rice, then begin adding the hot stock, 2 or 3 ladlefuls at a time, stirring frequently. When one batch of liquid has almost been absorbed by the rice, add another few ladlefuls and continue to stir. Cook the rice until it is moist but not swimming in stock, and the grains are no longer brittle but still retain a chewy core – 25 to 30 minutes.

Remove the rice from the heat and stir in the remaining butter, the Parmesan cheese, 1 tablespoon of the parsley and some pepper. Cover the pan and leave the risotto to rest for 5 minutes before serving it in soup plates, sprinkled with the remaining parsley.

Risotto with Carrots and Coriander

Serves 6		Calories	
		300	
Working		Protein	
(and total)		5g	
time: about		Cholesterol	
1 hour		30mg	
		Total fat	
		11g	
		Saturated fat	
		6g	
		Sodium	
		155mg	

45 g	unsalted butter	**1½ oz**
1	onion, finely chopped	**1**
1 litre	unsalted chicken stock	**1¾ pints**
2 tsp	ground coriander	**2 tsp**
300 g	carrots, peeled and finely diced	**10 oz**

350 g	Italian round-grain rice	**12 oz**
	freshly ground black pepper	
45 g	Parmesan cheese, freshly grated	**1½ oz**
1	small bunch fresh coriander leaves, finely chopped	**1**

In a large, heavy-bottomed pan, heat 30 g (1 oz) of the butter, and sauté the onion until it is transparent – 3 to 5 minutes. Meanwhile, bring the stock to the boil in a saucepan, stir in the ground coriander, reduce the heat and keep the liquid simmering gently.

Add the diced carrots to the onion, and sauté them for about 5 minutes. Add the rice, and stir well to ensure that the grains are coated with butter.

Ladle a few spoonfuls of the hot chicken stock into the rice, stir well, and let the mixture cook, stirring occasionally, until most of the liquid has been absorbed by the rice. Continue adding hot stock, a little at a time, stirring the mixture constantly and replenishing the liquid as the rice absorbs it. Cook the rice until it is moist but not swimming in the stock, and the grains have lost their brittleness but still retain a chewy core – about 20 minutes.

Remove the rice from the heat and add the remaining butter, the Parmesan cheese and some pepper. Stir the mixture well, cover the pan, and let the risotto stand for 5 minutes. Stir the rice once more, and sprinkle it with coriander before serving.

Kedgeree

Serves 8

Working
time: about
30 minutes

Total time:
about
1 hour and
30 minutes

Calories
30
Protein
18g
Cholesterol
90mg
Total fat
3g
Saturated fat
1g
Sodium
250mg

500 g	fresh haddock fillet	1 lb	$\frac{1}{2}$ tsp	ground cumin	$\frac{1}{2}$ tsp
125 g	smoked haddock fillet	4 oz	$\frac{1}{4}$ tsp	mixed spice	$\frac{1}{4}$ tsp
1 tbsp	safflower oil	1 tbsp	$\frac{1}{2}$ tsp	salt	$\frac{1}{2}$ tsp
1	onion, thinly sliced	1		freshly ground black pepper	
2 tsp	mild chili powder	2 tsp	500 g	long-grain rice	1 lb
1 tsp	turmeric	1 tsp	2	hard-boiled eggs, quartered	2
1 tsp	ground ginger	1 tsp		chopped fresh chives or parsley,	
$\frac{1}{2}$ tsp	ground coriander	$\frac{1}{2}$ tsp		for garnish	

Put the fresh haddock into a large saucepan and add water to cover. Bring the water to a simmer and poach the fish for 5 minutes. Add the smoked haddock and continue poaching for 5 to 10 minutes or until both fish are cooked and flake easily when tested with a fork.

Drain the fish, reserving the cooking liquid. When the fish are cool enough to handle, flake them, discarding all skin and bones. Set the flaked fish aside and keep it warm.

Strain the cooking liquid and measure it; you will need 1.25 litres (2 pints); if necessary, add a little water.

Heat the oil in a large casserole or saucepan. Add the onion and cook gently, covered, for

about 7 minutes or until softened. If necessary, add a few spoonfuls of the reserved cooking liquid to prevent the onion sticking and burning.

Stir in all the spices, the salt, some pepper and 2 to 3 more spoonfuls of the cooking liquid. Add the rice and stir until it is coated with the spice mixture. Add the remaining liquid and bring to the boil. Stir once, then cover and cook over very low heat for about 20 minutes or until the rice is cooked and tender and all the liquid has been absorbed.

Fluff the rice up with a fork. Gently fold in the flaked fish. Turn mixture into a warmed serving dish. Garnish with the egg quarters and sprinkle with chopped chives or parsley. Serve hot.

Rice-Coated Fish Balls with Mange-Tout

Serves 4

Working
(and total)
time: about
35 minutes

Calories
105

Protein
14g

Cholesterol
50mg

Total fat
1g

Saturated fat
0g

Sodium
60mg

45 g	long-grain rice	1½ oz
300 g	white fish fillet (such as cod, haddock or plaice), skinned	10 oz
4	spring onions, finely sliced	4
1	garlic clove, crushed	1

2.5 cm	piece fresh ginger root, grated	1 inch
1 tsp	fresh lemon juice	1 tsp
	freshly ground black pepper	
90 g	mange-tout, topped and tailed	3 oz
4	lemon slices, for garnish	4

Cook the rice in boiling water for 5 minutes. Drain it in a colander and set it aside.

In a food processor, process the fish for about 10 seconds until it begins to break down. Place it in a mixing bowl with the spring onion, garlic, ginger, lemon juice and some black pepper, and mix well.

Divide the fish mixture into eight equal portions. Moisten your hands with a little water and shape each portion into a ball. Roll each ball in the parboiled rice so that the rice forms a coating.

Arrange the fish balls in one layer in a steamer and place them over boiling water. Cover the pan and steam the fish balls for 7 minutes.

Just before serving, bring some water to the boil and blanch the mange-tout for 1 minute. Drain them thoroughly in a colander.

Remove the cooked fish balls from the steamer with a slotted spoon. Arrange them on individual serving plates with the mange-tout, garnish with the lemon slices, and serve hot.

Salad of Monkfish and Wild Rice

Serves 8

Working time: about 25 minutes

Total time: about 2 hours

Calories 310

Protein 18g

Cholesterol 30mg

Total fat 8g

Saturated fat 1g

Sodium 300mg

500 g	monkfish fillets	1 lb
¼ litre	fish stock or court-bouillon	8 fl oz
4 tbsp	chopped shallots	4 tbsp
2	garlic cloves, finely chopped	2
1½ tbsp	chopped fresh sage, or 1½ tsp dried sage	1½ tbsp
½ tsp	salt	½ tsp
	freshly ground black pepper	
250 g	wild rice	8 oz

¼ litre	dry white wine	8 fl oz
1	lemon, juice only	1
175 g	shelled young broad beans, thawed if frozen	6 oz
4 tbsp	thinly sliced sun-dried tomatoes	4 tbsp
250 g	mange-tout, strings removed, pods cut diagonally in half	8 oz
3 tbsp	virgin olive oil	3 tbsp

Pour the stock and 45 cl (¾ pint) of water into a pan. Add 2 tablespoons of shallots, half of garlic and half of sage, ¼ teaspoon of salt and some pepper; bring to the boil. Stir in rice, reduce heat to low and partially cover pan. Simmer rice with the lid slightly ajar until the rice has absorbed the liquid and is tender – 40 to 50 minutes.

In a sauté pan over medium heat, combine the wine, 12.5 cl (4 fl oz) of water, lemon juice, remaining shallots, garlic and sage, and remaining salt. Grind in a generous amount of pepper.

Rinse fillets and cut into bite-sized pieces. When poaching liquid is hot, reduce heat and place fish in the liquid. Poach fish for 5 minutes until flesh just flakes.

Cool fish slightly on a plate, then refrigerate it. Do not discard the liquid.

When rice is done, refrigerate it. Increase heat to high and boil poaching liquid for 5 minutes to reduce it slightly. Add beans and tomatoes; cook for 3 minutes. Stir in the mange-tout and cook for 1 minute, stirring; there should be just 2 or 3 tablespoons of liquid remaining.

Transfer the vegetables to the bowl with rice. Whisk the olive oil into the reduced liquid in the pan and pour over rice and vegetables. Toss well. Add fish to the bowl and gently toss the salad once more. Serve chilled.

Grilled Eel in Ginger-Sherry Sauce on Rice Fingers

Serves 4
as a first
course

Working
time: about
30 minutes

Total time:
about
40 minutes

Calories
420

Protein
20g

Cholesterol
95mg

Total fat
14g

Saturated fat
3g

Sodium
370mg

500 g	eel, filleted	**1 lb**	
1 tsp	rice vinegar	**1 tsp**	
200 g	glutinous rice, preferably sushi rice	**7 oz**	
1 tsp	wasabi (Japanese horseradish powder) mixed with enough water to form a paste	**1 tsp**	

	Ginger-Sherry Sauce	
4 tbsp	dry sherry	**4 tbsp**
2 tbsp	low-sodium soy sauce or shoyu	**2 tbsp**
1 tbsp	finely chopped fresh ginger root	**1 tbsp**
1 tbsp	sugar	**1 tbsp**
1 tbsp	honey	**1 tbsp**
⅛ tsp	cayenne pepper	**⅛ tsp**

Bring ½ litre (16 fl oz) of water and the vinegar to the boil. Add rice, cover and reduce heat to medium low. Cook rice, stirring occasionally, until all the liquid has been absorbed – about 20 minutes. Set the rice aside to cool.

Rinse eel fillets under water and cut each in half diagonally. Pour enough water into a pan to fill it 1cm (½ inch) deep. Put a bamboo steamer basket in the water. (Alternatively, put a heatproof cup in the centre of the pan and lay a heatproof plate on top of it.) Place the fillets in the basket or on the plate, and bring water to the boil. Reduce heat to low, cover and steam the fillets for 7 minutes.

While eel is steaming, make the sauce. Mix sherry, soy sauce, ginger, sugar, honey and cayenne pepper in a pan. Bring to the boil, then reduce heat to low. Simmer until it thickens – 7 to 10 minutes. Preheat the grill.

Brush some sauce on both sides of the fillets and leave to stand for 5 minutes. Brush more sauce on and grill until crisp – 2 to 4 minutes. Turn fillets over, brush on more sauce and grill on the second side until crisp – 2 to 3 minutes.

While the eel is cooking, form the cooled rice into cakes; each should be about 5 cm (2 inches) long, 2 cm (¾ inch) wide and 2 cm (¾ inch) thick. Arrange the rice cakes or fingers on a serving platter.

Cut the fillets diagonally into 16 pieces. Set a piece of eel on top of each rice cake; brush the pieces with the remaining sauce and serve them with the wasabi.

47

Clams and Rice Yucatan-Style

Serves 4

Working time: about 30 minutes

Total time: about 1 hour

Calories 470

Protein 16g

Cholesterol 35mg

Total fat 8g

Saturated fat 1g

Sodium 200mg

36	clams, scrubbed	36
3	ripe tomatoes, skinned, seeded and coarsely chopped	3
1	large onion, coarsely chopped	1
3	garlic cloves, coarsely chopped	3
3	fresh hot green chili peppers, seeded and coarsely chopped	3
55 cl	fish stock or water	18 fl oz

2 tbsp	safflower oil	2 tbsp
275 g	long-grain rice	9 oz
¼ tsp	salt	¼ tsp
	freshly ground black pepper	
75 g	shelled peas, blanched for 1 minute if fresh	2½ oz
1	lime, juice only	1
	several fresh coriander sprigs	

Purée the tomatoes, onion, garlic, chilies and 12.5 cl (4 fl oz) of the fish stock or water in a food processor or blender. Preheat the oven to 200°C (400°F or Mark 6).

Heat the oil in a large shallow fireproof casserole over medium heat. Add the rice and sauté it in the oil, stirring constantly, until it is lightly browned – 3 to 4 minutes. Stir in the puréed tomato, the remaining stock or water, the salt and black pepper. Bring the mixture to a simmer, reduce the heat to medium low and cook the rice, covered, until most of the liquid

has been absorbed – about 15 minutes. Stir in the peas.

Tap the clams and discard any that do not close. Arrange them on top of the rice, cover with foil and bake them until they open – about 10 minutes. Dribble the lime juice over the clams and garnish the dish with the coriander sprigs. Serve immediately.

Suggested accompaniments: warm tortillas; chicory and orange salad or chopped avocado salad.

Mussel Risotto

Serves 6

Working (and total) time: about 45 minutes

Calories 310

Protein 20g

Cholesterol 90mg

Total fat 9g

Saturated fat 3g

Sodium 450mg

1.5 kg	mussels, scrubbed and debearded	**3 lb**
1 tbsp	safflower oil	**1 tbsp**
1	onion, finely chopped	**1**
185 g	risotto rice	**6½ oz**
4 tbsp	dry white wine	**4 tbsp**
8 to 10	saffron threads, crushed (⅛ tsp)	**8 to 10**
90 g	small broccoli florets	**3 oz**
15 g	unsalted butter	**½ oz**
60 g	Parmesan cheese, freshly grated	**2 oz**
¼ tsp	white pepper	**¼ tsp**

Put mussels in a large pan with 4 tablespoons of water. Bring to the boil, cover. Steam mussels until they open – 5 to 6 minutes. Transfer the opened mussels to a bowl; discard any that remain closed. Strain mussel-cooking liquid into a jug and set it aside.

Heat oil in a casserole over medium heat. Add onion and cook, stirring occasionally, until it is translucent – 2 to 3 minutes. Add rice and stir to coat it with the oil. Cook for 1 minute more. Pour in wine and cook, stirring, until it has evaporated.

Strain into the jug any liquid that has accumulated from mussels. Add water to yield 35 cl (12 fl oz). Pour liquid into the casserole and stir in saffron. Bring to the boil, reduce the heat to maintain a simmer. Cook rice, stirring, until it has absorbed most of the liquid – 10 minutes.

Stir in ¼ litre (8 fl oz) of hot water and continue to cook rice, stirring, until water is absorbed. Pour in another ¼ litre (8 fl oz) of hot water; if necessary to maintain a very moist consistency, pour in an additional 12.5 cl (4 fl oz) of water. The rice is done when it is tender to the bite – 25 to 30 minutes.

While rice is cooking, remove mussels from their shells and set aside; discard the shells. Bring 1 litre (1¾ pints) of water to the boil in a pan. Add the broccoli and blanch until barely tender. – about 2 minutes. Drain the broccoli and refresh it under cold running water.

Melt the butter in a frying pan over medium-high heat. Add reserved mussels and broccoli, sauté until heated through – 1 to 2 minutes. Stir the cheese and pepper into the cooked rice, then stir in the mussels and broccoli; serve at once.

Roulades of Plaice with Seaweed, Spinach and Rice

<table>
<tr><td>Serves 4</td></tr>
<tr><td>Working
time: about
20 minutes</td></tr>
<tr><td>Total time:
about
45 minutes</td></tr>
</table>

Calories
245

Protein
25g

Cholesterol
55mg

Total fat
2g

Saturated fat
1g

Sodium
665mg

500 g	plaice or sole fillets, cut lengthwise into 8 equal pieces	**1 lb**
90 g	rice	**3 oz**
30 cl	unsalted tomato juice	**½ pint**
½ tsp	fennel seeds	**½ tsp**
¼ tsp	salt	**¼ tsp**
250 g	fresh spinach	**8 oz**
	white pepper	

2	sheets nori (dried roasted seaweed)	**2**
1 tbsp	cornflour	**1 tbsp**
¼ litre	fish stock	**8 fl oz**
2 tbsp	mirin or cream sherry	**2 tbsp**
2 tbsp	low-sodium soy sauce or shoyu	**2 tbsp**
2 tsp	rice vinegar	**2 tsp**
4 or 5	drops Tabasco sauce	**4 or 5**
2 tbsp	chopped parsley	**2 tbsp**

To prepare filling, combine rice, tomato juice, fennel and salt in a 1 litre (2 pint) measuring jug and cover it. Microwave the filling on high for 12 minutes, then set it aside, still covered.

Wash and stem the spinach. Put the spinach with just the water that clings to it into a 2 litre (3½ pint) baking dish. Cover the dish with plastic film and microwave it on high for 3 minutes. Remove spinach from the oven and let it cool.

Rinse fillets under cold water and pat dry with paper towels. Lay fillets side by side, with their darker sides up, on a work surface; season with white pepper. Spread a thin layer of the rice filling on each fillet. Cut a strip of *nori* to fit each fillet. Lay the strips in place on the rice, then cover each strip of *nori* with some spinach. Roll each fillet into a roulade, rolling end to end as you would do to form a swiss roll.

Mix the cornflour with 2 tablespoons of the stock; then, in the same dish you used to cook the spinach, stir together the remaining stock, the cornflour mixture, the mirin, soy sauce, vinegar and Tabasco sauce. Microwave the mixture on high for 3 minutes; stir the resulting sauce until it is smooth. Lay the roulades in the sauce, their seam sides down; they should be close but not touching. Cover the dish and microwave on high for 6 minutes. Let dish stand for 3 minutes. Before serving roulades, spoon some sauce over and garnish them with parsley.

Sushi of Prawn and Seaweed Wrapped in Radicchio

Makes 24
sushi

Working
time: about
30 minutes

Total time:
about
1 hour and
20 minutes

Per sushi:

Calories
40

Protein
1g

Cholesterol
5mg

Total fat
trace

Saturated fat
trace

Sodium
75mg

200 g	sushi rice	7 oz	2 tbsp	rice vinegar, plus 1 tsp	2 tbsp
1 tsp	salt	1 tsp	90 g	shelled cooked prawns	3 oz
2 tsp	sugar	2 tsp	$\frac{1}{8}$ tsp	wasabi powder	$\frac{1}{8}$ tsp
24	chives, or two spring onions	24	$1\frac{1}{2}$ tsp	dried wakame	$1\frac{1}{2}$ tsp
	cut into very fine ribbons		12	large radicchio leaves	12

Put rice in a bowl and add about five times its volume of water. Stir gently, then carefully pour off the water. Repeat the rinsing twice, drain the rice and leave it in a sieve for about 45 minutes to allow the grains to absorb any residual water.

Put the rice in a saucepan with $\frac{1}{4}$ litre (8 fl oz) of water and bring to the boil, partially covered, over high heat. Reduce the heat to very low, cover the pan and simmer for 10 minutes. Leave the pan on the stove, with the heat turned off, for 10 to 15 minutes. Dissolve the salt and sugar in 2 tablespoons of the vinegar, and mix into the rice with a wet wooden spoon.

While the rice is being prepared, blanch the chives or spring onions by pouring boiling water over them in a deep bowl. Refresh them immediately in cold water, drain, then lay out on paper towels to dry. Devein and dice the

prawns. Mix the wasabi powder with a little water to make a paste. Soak the wakame in water for 5 to 10 minutes (it will quadruple in size), then squeeze it dry in a towel.

Cut each radicchio leaf in half lengthwise and trim away the thick, white centre ribs. Mix the remaining teaspoon of vinegar with 3 tablespoons of water in a small bowl; dip your fingers in the bowl and spread the rice over three quarters of the length of each leaf with your fingers, pressing it down. Spread a thin layer of wasabi paste over the rice, followed by the wakame, and then the prawns.

Roll up each leaf to enclose rice and filling, wrapping the empty quarter of the leaf neatly round the roll. Tie a ribbon of chive or spring onion round each to secure it, trim sides with a sharp knife to neaten. Arrange on serving plates.

Lemon Sole Roulades

Makes 24
roulades

Working
time: about
35 minutes

Total time:
about
50 minutes

Per roulade:

Calories
40

Protein
6g

Cholesterol
20mg

Total fat
1g

Saturated fat
trace

Sodium
45mg

12	large Chinese cabbage leaves	12
2	lemon soles (about 350 g/12 oz each), cut into eight fillets and skinned	2
	lemon slices, for garnish	
	Spicy Rice Filling	
60 g	long-grain brown rice	2 oz

¼ tsp	salt	¼ tsp
60 g	button mushrooms, chopped	2 oz
2	tomatoes, skinned, seeded and chopped	2
30 g	creamed coconut	1 oz
½ tsp	curry powder	½ tsp
1 tsp	grated fresh ginger root	1 tsp

To prepare the filling, add the rice and salt to 17.5 cl (6 fl oz) of water. Bring to the boil in a tightly covered saucepan, then reduce the heat and simmer until the rice is tender and all of the water is absorbed – about 20 minutes. Stir in the mushrooms, tomatoes, coconut, curry powder and ginger. Mix well and set aside.

Preheat the oven to 200°C (400°F or Mark 6). Soak 24 cocktail sticks in water for about 10 minutes to prevent them from scorching in the oven. Line a baking sheet with non-stick parchment paper.

Blanch the Chinese cabbage in boiling water for 15 seconds. Drain and refresh under cold running water, then drain again thoroughly. Cut each leaf lengthwise into two, removing and discarding the stem. Fold each cabbage piece to form a strip about 15 cm (6 inches) long by 2 cm (¾ inches) wide. Divide the rice filling into 24 portions and cover each leaf strip evenly with one portion of the filling.

Using a sharp knife, cut each sole fillet into three strips about 2 cm (¾ inches) wide. Place a strip of sole on each rice-topped leaf. Roll up the leaf neatly and secure with a cocktail stick.

Place the rolls on the prepared baking sheet and bake until the fish is tender and the leaves are still bright green – 5 to 6 minutes.

Serve warm, garnished with the lemon slices.

Chicken with Dried Fruits and Caramelized Onions

Serves 4

Working
time: about
30 minutes

Total time:
about
1 hour and
45 minutes

Calories
585
Protein
34g
Cholesterol
110mg
Total fat
20g
Saturated fat
6g
Sodium
470mg

8	chicken thighs, skinned	8
1 tbsp	safflower oil	1 tbsp
15 g	unsalted butter, plus ½ tsp	½ oz
½ tsp	salt	½ tsp
	freshly ground black pepper	
175 g	long-grain brown rice	6 oz
1	small onion, chopped	1
60 cl	unsalted chicken stock	1 pint
1	bouquet garni	1
45 g	dried apricots, cut in half	1½ oz
45 g	sultanas	1½ oz
45 g	currants	1½ oz
1 tbsp	grainy mustard	1 tbsp
¼ tsp	grated orange rind (optional)	¼ tsp
125 g	pearl or pickling onions, blanched for 30 seconds and peeled	4 oz
⅛ tsp	sugar	⅛ tsp

In a casserole, heat oil and the 15 g (½ oz) butter. Cook four of the thighs on one side until lightly browned – about 4 minutes. Turn the thighs and sprinkle with ⅛ teaspoon of the salt and some pepper. Sauté on second side for 3 minutes. Repeat the process with the remaining thighs and set them aside.

Reduce heat to medium. Add rice and onion to the casserole and cook until the grains of rice are translucent – about 5 minutes. Add 35cl (12 fl oz) of the stock, remaining salt and bouquet garni. Bring to the boil. Cover the casserole, and simmer for 20 minutes. Preheat the oven to 180°C (350°F or Mark 4).

Stir the apricots, sultanas, currants, mustard and orange rind, into the casserole. Return the chicken pieces to the casserole, pressing them down into the rice. Pour remaining stock over. Cover and bake for 35 minutes.

Put onions in a pan with sugar and the ½ teaspoon of butter. Pour in water to cover the onions. Boil until no water remains – 10 to 15 minutes. Watching onions carefully lest they burn, shake the pan until evenly browned.

Add the onions to the casserole and bake until the rice is tender – about 15 minutes. Remove the bouquet garni and serve.

Chicken-Stuffed Peppers

Serves 6

Working time: about 45 minutes

Total time: about 7 hours (includes chilling)

Calories 140

Protein 9g

Cholesterol 20mg

Total fat 4g

Saturated fat 1g

Sodium 75mg

3	small sweet red peppers, tops cut off and reserved, seeds and ribs removed	3
3	small sweet yellow peppers, tops cut off and reserved, seeds and ribs removed	3
15 cl	unsalted chicken stock	¼ pint
1 tbsp	virgin olive oil	1 tbsp
	Spiced Chicken Stuffing	
½ tbsp	virgin olive oil	½ tbsp
1	onion, finely chopped	1
125 g	long-grain rice	4 oz
2	garlic cloves, crushed	2
½ tsp	ground cardamom	½ tsp
½ tsp	ground cumin	½ tsp
250 g	boned chicken breast, skinned and cut into tiny cubes	8 oz
30 cl	unsalted chicken stock	½ pint
¼ tsp	salt	¼ tsp
	freshly ground black pepper	

Fry the onion in oil until softened but not browned – 5 to 6 minutes. Stir in rice, garlic, cardamom and cumin. Cook for 1 to 2 minutes, stir in the chicken, stock, salt and some pepper. Bring to the boil, reduce heat, cover pan and cook gently until rice is tender and the stock has been absorbed – 25 to 30 minutes.

Preheat the oven to 180°C (350°F or Mark 4).

Cook the peppers and their lids in boiling water until they soften slightly – 4 to 5 minutes. Place in a large colander, rinse and drain them.

Fill the peppers with the rice and chicken mixture and cover them with their lids. Stand the peppers in a deep ovenproof dish, add the chicken stock and cover the dish with a lid or with foil. Bake the peppers in the oven until they are very tender – about 1½ hours.

Carefully transfer the cooked peppers to a serving dish. Pour the juices left in the baking dish into a pan, bring to the boil and boil rapidly until they are reduced by half, then whisk in the olive oil. Pour this liquid over the peppers, and set aside to cool. When cooled, cover with plastic film and chill in the refrigerator. Serve.

Vine Leaves with a Rice and Date Stuffing

Serves 4		Calories
		170
Working time: about 35 minutes		Protein 5g
		Cholesterol 0mg
Total time: about 1 hour		Total fat 2g
		Saturated fat 0g
		Sodium 90mg

90 g	round-grain brown rice	**3 oz**
125 g	fresh dates, stoned and chopped	**4 oz**
1 tbsp	pine-nuts, tossed in a frying pan over medium heat until golden, coarsely chopped	**1 tbsp**
1	lemon, grated rind and juice of one half, the remainder halved vertically and thinly sliced	**1**
1 tbsp	chopped parsley freshly ground black pepper	**1 tbsp**
8	large fresh vine leaves, blanched for a few seconds, patted dry	**8**

	Tomato sauce	
1	small onion, chopped	**1**
250 g	ripe tomatoes, skinned, seeded and chopped	**8 oz**
15 cl	tomato juice	**$\frac{1}{4}$ pint**
6 tbsp	unsalted chicken stock or water	**6 tbsp**
$\frac{1}{8}$ tsp	sugar	**$\frac{1}{8}$ tsp**
1	bay leaf	**1**
1	fresh thyme sprig freshly ground black pepper	**1**

Boil the rice in 2 litre (16 fl oz) of water until it is tender – 25 to 30 minutes. Drain it thoroughly in a colander.

Meanwhile, place all the sauce ingredients in a small saucepan. Bring the mixture to the boil, cover the pan and simmer over low heat for 15 minutes. Remove the herbs and purée the sauce until it achieves a smooth consistency. Preheat the oven to 190°C (375°F or Mark 5).

Put the rice in a bowl and stir in the dates, pine-nuts, lemon rind and juice, parsley and some pepper. Place a spoonful of the rice mixture in the centre of each vine leaf. Fold the stem end up over the filling, fold both sides towards the middle, then roll into a small, tight parcel. Lay the parcels on a sheet of foil and wrap them tightly. Bake until heated – about 15 minutes.

Before serving, reheat the sauce over gentle heat. Serve the parcels with a pool of the sauce and one or two lemon slices.

Spanish-Style Chicken and Saffron Rice

Serves 4

Working time: about 30 minutes

Total time: about 1 hour and 30 minutes

Calories 570

Protein 41g

Cholesterol 105mg

Total fat 20g

Saturated fat 4g

Sodium 410mg

1.25 kg	chicken, skinned, cut into serving pieces	**2½ lb**
	freshly ground black pepper	
½ tsp	salt	**½ tsp**
3 tbsp	virgin olive oil	**3 tbsp**
2	medium onions, thinly sliced	**2**
175 g	long-grain brown rice	**6 oz**
12.5 cl	dry white wine	**4 fl oz**
⅛ tsp	crushed saffron threads	**⅛ tsp**
35 cl	unsalted chicken stock	**12 fl oz**
2 tbsp	mildly hot chilies	**2 tbsp**
⅛ tsp	crushed cumin seeds	**⅛ tsp**
2	garlic cloves, finely chopped	**2**
2	large ripe tomatoes, skinned, seeded and chopped	**2**
1 each	red and yellow sweet pepper, grilled, skinned, seeded and cut into 2.5 cm (1 inch) strips	**1 each**
	fresh coriander for garnish (optional)	

Sprinkle the chicken pieces with pepper and ¼ teaspoon of salt. In a lidded fireproof 4 litre (7 pint) casserole, heat 2 tablespoons of the olive oil over medium-high heat. Sauté the chicken until golden-brown – about 4 minutes on each side – and remove to a plate.

Add the remaining tablespoon of oil to the casserole and cook the onions over medium heat until translucent – about 10 minutes. Add the brown rice and cook for 2 minutes, stirring constantly to coat the grains thoroughly; pour in the white wine, bring to the boil, then reduce the heat, cover, and simmer until all the liquid has been absorbed – about 8 minutes. Add the saffron to the stock and pour over the rice. Stir in the chilies, cumin seeds, the remaining salt and the garlic. Simmer 15 minutes more and add the tomatoes and chicken, pushing them down into the rice. Cook until the juices run clear when a thigh is pierced with the tip of a sharp knife – about 15 minutes more. Garnish with the pepper strips and coriander.

Greek-Style Chicken and Rice Casserole

Serves 8
as a
main dish

Working
time: about
30 minutes

Total time:
about
1 hour

Calories
275

Protein
17g

Cholesterol
50mg

Total fat
11g

Saturated fat
3g

Sodium
245mg

2 tbsp	safflower oil	2 tbsp
8	chicken thighs, skinned	8
175 g	long-grain rice	6 oz
1	onion, chopped	1
4	garlic cloves, finely chopped	4
¼ litre	unsalted chicken stock	8 fl oz
800 g	canned whole tomatoes	1¾ lb
3 tbsp	chopped fresh oregano, or	3 tbsp
	2 tsp dried oregano	
1 tbsp	fresh thyme, or 1 tsp dried thyme	1 tbsp
12	oil-cured olives, stoned and quartered, or 12 stoned black olives, coarsely chopped	12
30 g	feta cheese, rinsed and crumbled	1 oz

Heat the oil in a large, heavy fireproof casserole over medium-high heat. Add four of the thighs and cook them until they are lightly browned – about 4 minutes on each side. Remove the first four thighs and brown the other four. Set all the thighs aside.

Reduce the heat to medium and add the rice, onion, garlic and 4 tablespoons of the stock. Cook the mixture, stirring constantly, until the onion is translucent – about 4 minutes. Add the remaining stock, the tomatoes, the oregano and the thyme. Push the thighs down into the rice mixture. Bring the liquid to the boil, reduce the heat, and simmer the chicken, tightly covered, until the rice is tender – 20 to 30 minutes.

Stir the olives into the chicken and rice, and serve the casserole with the feta cheese on top.

Prunes Stuffed with Wild Rice and Turkey

Makes 14
stuffed
prunes

Working
time: about
30 minutes

Total time:
about
1 hour and
30 minutes

Per stuffed
prune:

Calories
25

Protein
2g

Cholesterol
5mg

Total fat
trace

Saturated fat
trace

Sodium
30mg

30 g	wild rice	**1 oz**
¼ litre	unsalted chicken, beef or veal stock or water	**8 fl oz**
14	large ready-to-eat prunes	**14**
60 g	smoked turkey or chicken, finely chopped	**2 oz**

	freshly grated nutmeg	
¼ tsp	salt	**¼ tsp**
	freshly ground black pepper	
1 tbsp	finely cut chives	**1 tbsp**

Put the rice and stock or water into a heavy-bottomed saucepan, bring to the boil, then simmer, covered, until the husks of the rice have split – 50 to 60 minutes. Drain off any remaining cooking liquid and set the rice aside to cool.

Using a sharp knife, slit open one side of each prune from end to end. Mix the turkey with the rice, season with some nutmeg, the salt and a little pepper, and stuff the prunes with this mixture. Sprinkle the chives over the stuffed prunes and serve.

Editor's Note: The prunes used in this recipe are sold for eating straight from the packet, and do not require either pre-soaking or stoning. If you use ordinary dried prunes, soak them for 10 minutes in boiling water with a dash of Madeira, and then stone them.

Duck and Wild Rice Salad with Raspberry Vinaigrette

Serves 6
as a main
course at
lunch

Working
time: about
30 minutes

Total time:
about
3 hours and
10 minutes
(includes
chilling)

Calories
310

Protein
25g

Cholesterol
75mg

Total fat
12g

Saturated fat
4g

Sodium
110mg

2 kg	duck, rinsed and patted dry	4 lb
5 tbsp	raspberry vinegar	5 tbsp
160 g	wild rice	5½ oz
1	garlic clove, finely chopped	1
100 g	carrot, julienned	3½ oz
120 g	celery, julienned	4 oz
1	large ripe tomato, skinned, seeded and coarsely chopped	1

1 tsp	Dijon mustard	1 tsp
1 tbsp	finely chopped shallot	1 tbsp
	freshly ground black pepper	
3 tbsp	unsalted chicken stock or water	3 tbsp
2 tsp	safflower oil	2 tsp
1	small red-leaf lettuce	1
1	small Batavian endive	1

Trim any excess fat from around the neck of the duck. Remove any fat from the cavity. Lightly prick the duck, taking care not to pierce the flesh below the layer of fat. Sprinkle the inside of the cavity with 1 tablespoon of the vinegar. Place the duck breast side down in a microwave-safe roasting pan and cover it with greaseproof paper. Microwave on medium high (70 per cent power) for 15 minutes. Drain off and discard fat in roasting pan. Turn duck breast side up and cover with fresh paper. Continue cooking on medium high until juices run clear when a thigh is pierced with tip of a knife – about 20 minutes. Drain and discard fat; cool.

Pour the 60 cl (1 pint) boiling water into a bowl and add the wild rice and garlic. Cover and microwave on medium low (30 per cent power) until tender – about 30 minutes. Drain rice; refrigerate in a bowl.

Put the carrot and celery into a bowl with 2 tablespoons of hot water. Cover and microwave the vegetables on high until tender – 2 to 3 minutes. Drain and mix with the rice; leave in refrigerator.

When duck is cool, pull off its skin. Remove meat and slice it into thin strips. Toss with the rice-and-vegetable mixture. Stir in the tomato and 2 tbsp of vinegar.

Combine mustard, shallot, pepper, remaining vinegar and stock, whisking in oil until well combined. Pour over duck mixture and toss. Chill, and serve as illustration.

Shoulder Stuffed with Wild Rice and Spinach

Serves 12

Working time: about 1 hour

Total time: about 4 hours

Calories 225
Protein 22g
Cholesterol 75mg
Total fat 13g
Saturated fat 5g
Sodium 140mg

1.5 kg	shoulder of lamb, boned and trimmed of fat	**3 lb**
60 g	wild rice	**2 oz**
2 tsp	virgin olive oil	**2 tsp**
4	shallots, coarsely chopped	**4**
175 g	fresh spinach, washed, stems removed	**6 oz**

175 g	celeriac, grated	**6 oz**
½ tsp	finely grated nutmeg	**½ tsp**
¾ tsp	salt	**¾ tsp**
	freshly ground black pepper	
30 cl	unsalted chicken stock	**½ pint**
1 tsp	cornflour	**1 tsp**

Wash the wild rice and put it into a saucepan in twice its volume of water. Bring to the boil, cover and simmer until the husks have split and rice is soft – 50 minutes to 1 hour. Drain rice and allow to cool. Fry shallots and cook over very low heat until soft but not brown. Add celeriac and continue cooking until it looks transparent – about 3 minutes – add the spinach and cook for 1 minute, until it wilts. Blend this mixture briefly to make a rough-textured purée; do not over process. Mix the purée with the wild rice, and season with the nutmeg, ½ teaspoon of the salt and some black pepper.

Preheat the oven to 230°C (450°F or Mark 8). Stuff and tie the shoulder into a melon shape. Put the lamb in a roasting pan and season with

the remaining salt and some pepper. Roast lamb in oven until well browned – 10 to 15 minutes – reduce the oven temperature to 200°C (400°F or Mark 6) and cook for a further 1¼ to 1½ hours for medium-rare to medium. Transfer the lamb to a carving board and allow it to rest in a warm place for 15 minutes.

While meat is resting, make the gravy. Skim off any fat from surface of the roasting juices and transfer the pan to the stove top. Add stock and boil over high heat, stirring to loosen any sediment from bottom of pan. Mix the cornflour with 1 tablespoon of water and add to the pan, stirring until gravy thickens. Season with black pepper. Cut off the string and carve the lamb into wedges. Serve the gravy separately.

Lamb and Orange Pilaff

Serves 4

Working
time: about
30minutes

Total time:
about
1 hour and
25 minutes

Calories
385
Protein
16g
Cholesterol
55mg
Total fat
8g
Saturated fat
3g
Sodium
205mg

350 g	lean lamb (from the leg or loin), trimmed of fat and finely diced	**12 oz**
1 tsp	safflower oil	**1 tsp**
1	onion, chopped	**1**
1	large leek, trimmed, washed and sliced	**1**
200 g	long-grain brown rice	**7 oz**
1 tsp	chopped fresh rosemary, or ½ tsp dried rosemary	**1 tsp**

45 cl	unsalted brown or chicken stock	**¾ pint**
¼ tsp	salt	**¼ tsp**
	freshly ground black pepper	
1	orange, rind grated and flesh cut into segments	**1**
2	carrots, peeled	**2**
125 g	courgettes, trimmed	**4 oz**
30 g	raisins	**1 oz**

Preheat the oven to 180°C (350°F or Mark 4).

Heat the oil in a fireproof casserole over high heat. Add the lamb and sear it quickly on all sides. Stir in the onion, leek and rice and cook them for 1 minute. Add the stock, rosemary, salt, pepper and orange rind. Bring the mixture to the boil, then cover the casserole, transfer it to the oven and bake the pilaff until the rice is almost tender and the liquid virtually absorbed – about 40 minutes.

Using a potato peeler, shred the carrots and courgettes into long strips. Reserve a few carrot strips for garnish and stir the remainder into the lamb mixture along with the courgette strips and the raisins. Return the casserole to the oven and cook, covered, until the rice and carrots are tender – about 20 minutes. Stir in the orange segments and garnish with the reserved carrot ribbons just before serving.

Vinegar Pork with Garlic

Serves 6

Working time: about 20 minutes

Total time: about 1 hour and 40 minutes (includes marinating)

Calories 300

Protein 33g

Cholesterol 80mg

Total fat 13g

Saturated fat 5g

Sodium 130mg

1 Kg	boned leg of pork, trimmed of fat and cut into 4 cm (1½ inch) cubes	2 lb
350 g	long-grain rice	12 oz
3 tbsp	low-sodium soy sauce or shoyu	3 tbsp
5 tbsp	distilled malt, rice or other clear vinegar	5 tbsp

2 tbsp	safflower oil	2 tbsp
1	head of garlic (about 12 cloves), cloves peeled and quartered	1
1 tsp	black peppercorns, coarsely crushed	1 tsp
350 g	waxy potatoes, quartered	12 oz

Sprinkle the meat with the soy sauce and vinegar, and leave to marinate for at least 30 minutes.

Heat the oil in a large fireproof casserole over high heat. Add the garlic and stir for a few seconds, then reduce the heat and spoon in the meat, reserving the marinade. Turn the meat for 2 to 3 minutes, until it has lost its raw look – do not let it brown. Add the peppercorns, marinade,

potatoes and enough water to cover. Bring to the boil, cover and simmer for 30 minutes. Boil; then simmer rice for 30 minutes or until cooked, drain. Serve with pork.

Remove the lid and increase the heat. Continue cooking for 20 to 30 minutes, stirring often, until the meat is tender and coated with a thick, syrupy sauce.

Picnic Slice

Serves 10

Working time: about 35 minutes

Total time: about 3 hours (includes chilling)

Calories 290
Protein 13g
Cholesterol 70mg
Total fat 15g
Saturated fat 6g
Sodium 275mg

350 g	leg or neck end of pork, minced	12 oz
125 g	brown rice	4 oz
1	bunch spring onions, chopped	1
2	eggs, hard-boiled, roughly chopped	2
2 tbsp	chopped fresh tarragon	2 tbsp
2 tbsp	capers, rinsed and drained	2 tbsp
8	green olives, stoned and chopped	8
50 g	anchovy fillets, rinsed, chopped	1¾ oz
	Flaky Pastry	
200 g	plain flour	7 oz
½ tsp	salt	½ tsp
60 g	unsalted butter, slightly softened	2 oz
60 g	hard white vegetable fat	2 oz

Sift flour and salt into a bowl. Mix together butter and vegetable fat. Rub a quarter of the fat into flour until it resembles breadcrumbs. Add iced water and work: into a dough. Shape into a ball, wrap in plastic film and refrigerate for 30 minutes.

On a floured board, roll dough into a rectangle. Dot top two thirds of rectangle with another quarter of fat, fold bottom third of rectangle over centre and top third over that, chill for 30 minutes. Roll out, dot with fat, fold and chill in same way twice more, then roll out dough to make final folds cohere. Wrap dough in film and refrigerate until ready to use.

Boil, then simmer rice for 30 minutes or until cooked, drain and rinse. Leave rice in a sieve to cool.

Brown pork in a frying pan. Stir in spring onions and. cook for another 2 minutes.

Preheat the oven to 220°C (425°F or Mark 7). Divide dough into two pieces. Roll each into a thin sheet about 30 by 25 cm (12 by 10 inches) and place these on non-stick baking sheets. Spread rice down the centre of each sheet of pastry, leaving about 7.5 cm (3 inches) of bare pastry on each side. On top of rice lay the meat mixture and the eggs, tarragon, capers, olives and anchovies; make sure that each ingredient is evenly spread over the rice.

Paint edges with water and seal. Turn roll over so seam is underneath. Cut slits on top and bake for 15 mins then finish cooking (another 20 mins) at 180°C (350°F or Mark 4.)

Pilaff with Pig's Heart

Serves 6

Working time: about 20 minutes

Total time: about 45 minutes

Calories 565

Protein 15g

Cholesterol 60mg

Total fat 15g

Saturated fat 3g

Sodium 175mg

1	pig's heart (about 250 g/8 oz), trimmed of fat and finely diced	1
2 tbsp	virgin olive oil	2 tbsp
1	onion, finely chopped	1
2 tbsp	pine-nuts	2 tbsp
350 g	long-grain rice	12 oz
2 tbsp	currants	2 tbsp

¼ tsp	sugar	¼ tsp
¼ tsp	ground allspice	¼ tsp
¼ tsp	ground cinnamon	¼ tsp
½ tsp	salt	½ tsp
	freshly ground black pepper	
3 tbsp	finely chopped parsley	3 tbsp

Heat the olive oil in a heavy-bottomed saucepan over medium heat and sauté the diced heart for about 5 minutes. Add the onion and pine-nuts, and cook until both are beginning to colour. Add the rice and stir to coat well with oil, then stir in ¾ litre (1¼ pints) of water and all the remaining ingredients except the parsley. Bring to the boil, reduce the heat, cover and simmer for 10 minutes.

Stir in the parsley, re-cover the pan and leave the pilaff to stand, off the heat, for 15 minutes more. Mix well and serve hot or warm.

Suggested accompaniments: steamed or grilled baby courgettes; grilled and skinned sweet pepper strips.

Pork Risotto

Serves 4

Working time: about 25 minutes

Total time: about 40 minutes

Calories 460
Protein 24g
Cholesterol 55mg
Total fat 12g
Saturated fat 4g
Sodium 100mg

350 g	pork fillet, trimmed of fat and cut into small cubes	12 oz
1 tbsp	virgin olive oil	1 tbsp
1	onion, finely chopped	1
1	garlic clove, crushed	1
125 g	button mushrooms, roughly chopped	4 oz
½ tsp	chopped fresh sage	½ tsp
250 g	Italian round-grain rice	8 oz
½ tsp	salt	½ tsp
	freshly ground black pepper	
30 cl	dry white wine	½ pint
125 g	shelled peas, blanched in boiling water, or frozen peas	4 oz
1 tbsp	freshly grated Parmesan cheese	1 tbsp
3 tbsp	flat-leaf parsley, torn into small pieces	3 tbsp

Heat the olive oil in a heavy-bottomed saucepan over medium heat and brown the cubes of meat. Stir in the onion and continue cooking until the onion begins to turn golden at the edges. Add the garlic, mushrooms and sage. When the mushrooms are wilting, increase the heat, add the rice, salt and some pepper, and stir for a couple of minutes.

Mix the white wine with an equal amount of water and pour half of the liquid into the saucepan. Reduce the heat and stir while bringing the liquid to a gently simmer. Stir the mixture frequently as the liquid is absorbed – 5 to 10 minutes.

Pour in the rest of the liquid and the peas, bring back to a simmer and stir. Cover the pan and leave to cook very slowly, stirring from time to time until the mixture is creamy but not mushy – 10 to 15 minutes. Just before serving, stir in the cheese and parsley.

Suggested accompaniment: tomato salad.

Nasi Goreng

Serves 6

Working
time: about
25 minutes

Total time:
about
1 hour and
15 minutes

Calories
350
Protein
25g
Cholesterol
120mg
Total fat
12g
Saturated fat
3g
Sodium
125mg

350 g	pork fillet, trimmed of fat and cut into 1 cm ($\frac{1}{2}$ inch) cubes	**12 oz**
250 g	long-grain brown rice	**8 oz**
2 tbsp	safflower oil	**2 tbsp**
1	large onion, quartered, thinly sliced	**1**
1	garlic clove, chopped	**1**
1	green chili pepper, seeded and chopped, plus a few thin rings for garnish	**1**
125 g	boneless chicken breast, skinned and cut into 1 cm ($\frac{1}{2}$ inch) cubes	**4 oz**

$\frac{1}{2}$ tsp	ground turmeric	**$\frac{1}{2}$ tsp**
$\frac{1}{2}$ tsp	paprika	**$\frac{1}{2}$ tsp**
$\frac{1}{4}$ tsp	cayenne pepper	**$\frac{1}{4}$ tsp**
2 tbsp	low-sodium soy sauce or shoyu	**2 tbsp**
1	large tomato, skinned, seeded and cut into thin slivers	**1**
175 g	peeled prawns, deveined	**6 oz**
	Rolled Omelette	
1	egg	**1**
1 tsp	low-sodium soy sauce or shoyu	**1 tsp**
1 tsp	safflower oil	**1 tsp**

Cook brown rice in covered saucepan of boiling water until tender – about 40 minutes. Drain, rinse under cold water, drain, and set aside.

Heat oil in a frying pan. Add sliced onion, garlic and chopped chili, cook gently for 4 minutes, stirring frequently. Stir in pork and chicken, and cook gently for 4 minutes, stirring. Add turmeric, paprika and cayenne pepper and mix, stir in drained rice and continue cooking for 4 minutes, stirring. Add soy sauce, tomato and half of the prawns, heat through for 2 to 3 minutes. Turn on to a warmed serving platter

and keep warm while you make the omelette.

In a bowl, beat egg with soy sauce. Heat oil in a 15 to 17.5 cm (6 to 7 inch) diameter frying pan. Add egg mixture and tilt pan to cover base evenly. Cook over gentle heat until omelette is set – 45 seconds to 1 minute. Loosen omelette from the pan and turn it out on to a board, then roll up the omelette and cut it into thin slices.

Arrange the omelette slices either round the base of the rice mixture or over the top. Garnish with the reserved rings of chili pepper and the remaining prawns, and serve immediately.

Prune and Pecan Patties

Serves 4

Working time: about 20 minutes

Total time: about 1 hour and 30 minutes

Calories 280

Protein 16g

Cholesterol 45mg

Total fat 12g

Saturated fat 4g

Sodium 150mg

250 g	pork fillet, minced	**8 oz**
30 cl	unsalted chicken stock or water	**½ pint**
90 g	wild rice	**3 oz**
8	prunes, stoned and soaked in 1 tbsp of dry Madeira for 1 hour	**8**
50 g	pecan nuts	**1¾ oz**

1½ tsp	grated nutmeg	**1½ tsp**
1 tbsp	arachide or sunflower oil	**1 tbsp**
3 tbsp	balsamic vinegar	**3 tbsp**
¼ tsp	salt	**¼ tsp**
	freshly ground black pepper	

In a saucepan, bring the stock or water to the boil and add the wild rice. Cook the rice, covered, for about 1 hour, checking it periodically and adding more stock or water if necessary. Meanwhile, chop the prunes and pecan nuts finely and combine them with the minced pork and ½ teaspoon of the nutmeg. Shape the mixture into eight patties with your hands.

When the rice is cooked – the grain should be split open and soft, but still have some bite – drain it and reserve the cooking liquid. Cover the rice with wet greaseproof paper and keep it warm.

Heat the oil in a heavy frying pan over low heat and cook the patties, turning them and gradually increasing the heat so that they become crisp and brown all over. This should take about 7 minutes. Remove the patties from the pan and keep them warm.

Over high heat, deglaze the pan with the balsamic vinegar. When it has all but disappeared, add 4 tablespoons of the reserved cooking liquid and reduce until it becomes syrupy. Add the remaining nutmeg and season lightly with the salt and some pepper.

Serve the patties on warmed plates with the sauce poured round them and the wild rice to one side.

Editor's Note: To make a richer and more glossy sauce, add reduced chicken stock instead of the rice-cooking liquid to the deglazed frying pan.

Fillet with Rice and Vegetables

Serves 4

Working time: about 30 minutes

Total time: about 1 hour and 20 minutes

Calories 565
Protein 34g
Cholesterol 70mg
Total fat 15g
Saturated fat 4g
Sodium 330mg

500 g	pork fillet, trimmed of fat and cubed	**1 lb**
2 tbsp	safflower oil	**2 tbsp**
1	onion, chopped	**1**
1	large garlic clove, finely chopped	**1**
500 g	ripe tomatoes, skinned and chopped	**1 lb**
45 cl	puréed tomatoes	**¾ pint**
1 tsp	mild chili powder	**1 tsp**
1 tbsp	Worcester sauce	**1 tbsp**

	cayenne pepper	
½ tsp	salt	**½ tsp**
	freshly ground black pepper	
	Tabasco sauce	
1	sweet green pepper, seeded, deribbed and diced	**1**
2	sticks celery, diced	**2**
1	aubergine (about 250 g/8 oz), cubed	**1**
250 g	courgettes, cubed	**8 oz**
250 g	long-grain rice	**8 oz**

Heat 1 tablespoon of the oil in a large fireproof casserole over high heat. Add the pork cubes and cook until the meat is sealed – about 2 minutes – stirring all the time. Stir in the onion and garlic, and cook for a further minute.

Add the chopped tomatoes, puréed tomatoes, chili powder, Worcester sauce, a pinch of cayenne, the salt, some black pepper and a few drops of Tabasco sauce, and stir. Cover, cook gently for 20 minutes, stirring from time to time.

Meanwhile, heat the remaining oil in a frying pan over moderate heat. Add the green pepper,

celery and aubergine, and cook gently for 5 minutes, then stir in the courgettes and cook for a further 5 minutes.

Add the rice and vegetables to the meat in the casserole. Cover again and continue cooking for 10 to 15 minutes, or until rice is tender and all the excess liquid has been absorbed. Depending on how much liquid the vegetables exude, you may need to add a little water from time to time. Fluff up rice with a fork and serve hot.

Suggested accompaniment: tossed green salad.

Roast Loin and Sweetcorn-Watercress Pilaff

Serves 8

Working time: about 1 hour

Total time: about 2 hours and 15 minutes

Calories 275
Protein 30g
Cholesterol 110mg
Total fat 14g
Saturated fat 5g
Sodium 220mg

1 kg	boned loin of veal	2 lb
2 tsp	safflower oil	2 tsp
1	onion, finely chopped	1
1	stick celery, finely chopped	1
2 tbsp	semi-skimmed milk	2 tbsp
300 g	sweetcorn kernels (about 4 ears),	10 oz
	or 300 g (10 oz) frozen, thawed	
125 g	cooked brown rice	4 oz
60 g	watercress leaves, chopped	2 oz
½ tsp	salt	½ tsp
	freshly ground black pepper	
4 tbsp	medium sherry	4 tbsp

Trim excess fat from loin of veal, careful not to cut through the membranes that hold the joint together. Open out the joint on a work surface.

Preheat the oven to 180°C (350°F or Mark 4). Gently fry onion and celery in oil until soft – 5 minutes. Tip vegetables into a bowl.

Blend the milk and 30 g (1 oz) of rice to a smooth paste, then turn the paste into a bowl.

Add the kernels to the onion and celery together with watercress, salt and some pepper, and mix. Add a quarter of this mixture to the rice paste and mix. Spread sweetcorn and rice paste over surface of loin of veal, roll up carefully and tie in a neat shape with string. Put joint into a roasting bag and place in a roasting pan.

Add remaining rice to rest of sweetcorn mixture and spoon into roasting bag round the joint.

Close the end of the bag with a plastic tie, and cut several slits in the bag. Roast for 1¼ to 1½ hours; test if the veal is cooked by piercing it with a skewer through one of the slits in the bag. The juices that run out of the meat should be only faintly pink, or clear.

Cut open the top of the roasting bag and lift the joint on to a carving dish. Transfer the sweetcorn-watercress pilaff to the dish, draining it well and arranging it around the joint. Cover the meat and pilaff and set aside to rest in a warm place for 10 minutes.

Strain cooking juices left in the roasting bag into a pan. Add sherry, and boil for 1 minute.

Carve the veal into thick slices on the bed of pilaff, and serve with the sherried juices.

Rice Pudding with Raspberry Sauce

Serves 8

Working time: about 50 minutes

Total time: about 3 hours

Calories 225

Protein 7g

Cholesterol 45mg

Total fat 3g

Saturated fat 2g

Sodium 140mg

1 litre	semi-skimmed milk	1¾ pints	
90 g	long-grain rice	3 oz	
125 g	sugar	4 oz	
¼ tsp	salt	¼ tsp	
1	egg yolk	1	
3 tbsp	plain flour	3 tbsp	
½ tsp	grated nutmeg	½ tsp	

1 tsp	pure vanilla extract	1 tsp
¼ tsp	almond extract	¼ tsp
45 g	sultanas	1½ oz
250 g	fresh or frozen whole raspberries, thawed	8 oz
	fresh mint leaves (optional)	

Bring ¾ litre (1¼ pints) of the milk to the boil in a heavy-bottomed saucepan over medium heat. Reduce the heat to low and add the rice, 50 g (1½ oz) of the sugar and the salt. Cook the mixture, stirring frequently, for 50 minutes.

To prepare the pastry cream, whisk together the egg yolk and 4 tablespoons of the remaining milk. Whisk in the flour and 50 g (1½ oz) of the remaining sugar; then blend in the remaining milk. Bring the mixture to the boil over medium heat, stirring constantly, then cook it, still stirring vigorously, for 2 minutes more. Remove the pan from the heat and stir in the nutmeg, and vanilla and almond extracts.

When the rice has finished cooking, stir in the sultanas, then fold in the pastry cream. Transfer the pudding to a clean bowl. To prevent a skin from forming on its surface, press a plastic film directly on to the pudding. Refrigerate the pudding until it is cold – about 2 hours.

To prepare the sauce, purée the raspberries and the remaining 25 g (1 oz) sugar in a blender or food processor. Rub the purée through a fine sieve with a plastic spatula or the back of a wooden spoon; discard the seeds.

To serve, divide the sauce among eight serving dishes. Top the sauce with individual scoops of pudding; if you like, sprinkle the scoops with some additional nutmeg and garnish each with a sprig of mint.

Vinegar Cake

Serves 20

Working time: about 20 minutes

Total time: about 3 hours and 30 minutes

Calories 220

Protein 2g

Cholesterol 0mg

Total fat 8g

Saturated fat 2g

Sodium 130mg

350 g	plain flour	**12 oz**
125 g	ground rice	**4 oz**
½ tsp	allspice	**½ tsp**
175 g	polyunsaturated margarine	**6 oz**
125 g	raisins	**4 oz**
125 g	sultanas	**4 oz**
125 g	mixed candied peel	**4 oz**
17.5 cl	milk	**6 fl oz**
3 tbsp	cider vinegar	**3 tbsp**
1 tsp	bicarbonate of soda	**1 tsp**
90 g	icing sugar	**3 oz**
1½ tbsp	fresh lemon juice	**1½ tbsp**

Preheat the oven to 170°C (325°F or Mark 3). Grease a deep 25 by 11 cm (10 by 4½ inch) oblong tin. Line it with greaseproof paper and grease the paper.

Put the flour, ground rice and allspice into a mixing bowl. Add the margarine and rub it in until the mixture resembles breadcrumbs. Stir in the raisins, sultanas and candied peel.

Heat the milk in a saucepan until it is tepid. Stir in the vinegar and bicarbonate of soda, which will froth up. Immediately add the frothy liquid to the fruit mixture in the bowl, so as not to lose too much of the gas. Stir with a wooden spoon to blend the ingredients, then beat them to achieve a smooth, soft consistency. Spoon the

mixture into the prepared tin. Level the top with a small palette knife.

Bake the cake in the centre of the oven until well risen, golden-brown and springy when touched in the centre – about 1 hour and 10 minutes. Loosen the edges with a small palette knife, turn the cake out of the tin on to a wire rack and remove the lining paper. Leave the cake until it has cooled completely.

With a wooden spoon, beat the icing sugar with the lemon juice in a small bowl until smooth. Spoon the icing into a greaseproof paper piping bag and pipe a lattice design over the top of the cake. Leave the cake until the icing has set.

Useful weights and measures

Weight Equivalents

Avoirdupois		Metric
1 ounce	=	28.35 grams
1 pound	=	254.6 grams
2.3 pounds	=	1 kilogram

Liquid Measurements

$^1/_4$ pint	=	$1^1/_2$ decilitres
$^1/_2$ pint	=	$^1/_4$ litre
scant 1 pint	=	$^1/_2$ litre
$1^3/_4$ pints	=	1 litre
1 gallon	=	4.5 litres

Liquid Measures

1 pint	=	20 fl oz	=	32 tablespoons
$^1/_2$ pint	=	10 fl oz	=	16 tablespoons
$^1/_4$ pint	=	5 fl oz	=	8 tablespoons
$^1/_8$ pint	=	$2^1/_2$ fl oz	=	4 tablespoons
$^1/_{16}$ pint	=	$1^1/_4$ fl oz	=	2 tablespoons

Solid Measures

1 oz almonds, ground = $3^3/_4$ level tablespoons
1 oz breadcrumbs fresh = 7 level tablespoons
1 oz butter, lard = 2 level tablespoons
1 oz cheese, grated = $3^1/_2$ level tablespoons
1 oz cocoa = $2^3/_4$ level tablespoons
1 oz desiccated coconut = $4^1/_2$ tablespoons
1 oz cornflour = $2^1/_2$ tablespoons
1 oz custard powder = $2^1/_2$ tablespoons
1 oz curry powder and spices = 5 tablespoons
1 oz flour = 2 level tablespoons
1 oz rice, uncooked = $1^1/_2$ tablespoons
1 oz sugar, caster and granulated = 2 tablespoons
1 oz icing sugar = $2^1/_2$ tablespoons
1 oz yeast, granulated = 1 level tablespoon

American Measures

16 fl oz	=1 American pint
8 fl oz	=1 American standard cup
0.50 fl oz	=1 American tablespoon

(slightly smaller than British Standards Institute tablespoon)

0.16 fl oz	=1 American teaspoon

Australian Cup Measures
(Using the 8-liquid-ounce cup measure)

1 cup flour	4 oz
1 cup sugar (crystal or caster)	8 oz
1 cup icing sugar (free from lumps)	5 oz
1 cup shortening (butter, margarine)	8 oz
1 cup brown sugar (lightly packed)	4 oz
1 cup soft breadcrumbs	2 oz
1 cup dry breadcrumbs	3 oz
1 cup rice (uncooked)	6 oz
1 cup rice (cooked)	5 oz
1 cup mixed fruit	4 oz
1 cup grated cheese	4 oz
1 cup nuts (chopped)	4 oz
1 cup coconut	$2^1/_2$ oz

Australian Spoon Measures

	level tablespoon
1 oz flour	2
1 oz sugar	$1^1/_2$
1 oz icing sugar	2
1 oz shortening	1
1 oz honey	1
1 oz gelatine	2
1 oz cocoa	3
1 oz cornflour	$2^1/_2$
1 oz custard powder	$2^1/_2$

Australian Liquid Measures
(Using 8-liquid-ounce cup)

1 cup liquid	8 oz
$2^1/_2$ cups liquid	20 oz (1 pint)
2 tablespoons liquid	1 oz
1 gill liquid	5 oz ($^1/_4$ pint)

CYCLING *without* TRAFFIC:

THE NORTH

Colin & Lydia Speakman

DIAL
HOUSE

Published by Dial House

an imprint of Ian Allan Ltd,
Terminal House, Station Approach,
Shepperton, Surrey TW17 8AS.
Printed by Ian Allan Printing Ltd,
Coombelands House, Coombelands Lane,
Addlestone, Surrey KT15 1HY.

CONTENTS

The Auckland Walk. *John Price*   **Maps by RS Illustrations, Liss, Hants**

ABOUT THIS BOOK

Cycling is one of the very best ways to enjoy the countryside. The gentler pace of a cycle compared with motorised forms of transport gives the cyclist time to see and enjoy the countryside, to hear natural sounds such as birdsong and to smell the fresh scents of nature. Cycling creates minimal noise to disturb wildlife or local inhabitants, it's virtually pollution-free, and it causes little or no congestion to other users of the countryside.

It's also good for your health, being one of the finest forms of exercise available to most people. Medical experts are unanimous in agreeing that one of the biggest problems now facing our society is car-dependency, which in turn means people are no longer taking enough exercise to meet their body's needs, resulting in obesity, heart disease and degenerative conditions, already observable in many even quite young people who spend too much time in their polluting cars, and not enough time walking or cycling.

So why are there not thousands more people out on their bikes?

Ironically it's because of other people's cars — and lorries.

There are about 20 million bikes in the UK, but only 15% of them are in regular use. The main deterrent for bike owners is not the English weather or laziness, but the fear of traffic on our increasingly congested and dangerous roads. This is especially true of family cyclists who understandably fear for their children's safety.

However, there is light at the end of the tunnel in the form of a whole new network of traffic-free cycleways in town and countryside which are being developed and opened by local authorities, by British Waterways, by Forest Enterprise, and above all by that remarkable visionary cycle path-building charity Sustrans, which, in partnership with local authorities, has pioneered the conversion of many hundreds of miles of former railway lines, canal towpaths and areas of derelict riverside into superb, safe routes where cyclists can travel free of the ever present risk of serious injury or even violent death resulting from the irresponsible actions of drivers.

The problem facing the cyclist at the moment is that information about these routes is virtually impossible to obtain. With a few exceptions, such information as exists is only available locally. In some cases it is totally non-existent. Nor are many railway path routes even marked on maps, and where they are, the print is often too small and the

information too sparse to be of much value.

This book, like its companion volumes for the Midlands and the South East, sets out to remedy the situation, and details 30 traffic-free routes throughout the North of England which enable cyclists to enjoy a day's cycling away from pollution, noise and danger, along attractive green corridors through some of the region's most beautiful countryside.

The routes selected cater for a mix of abilities and experience, ranging from a pleasant short afternoon's ride to a full day's excursion. Some of the routes interlink, and so it is also possible to use this book as a guide to help plan part of a longer cycling tour using traffic-free routes to explore part of the region. Remember, approximate distances indicated in the text are one way only. If you are returning (say) to a parked car you need to double the length to be cycled along the trail — and the time required to do it. The exceptions, perhaps, are one or two trails in Greater Manchester, West Yorkshire and Merseyside where convenient local cycle-carrying train services can avoid the need to cover the route twice.

It must also be pointed out that even as we were undertaking our research, in the summer and autumn of 1995, the situation on the ground was changing rapidly — almost invariably for the better — with new routes being developed and existing routes being extended in a quite remarkable way. This reflects changes in national and local government policies about transport, most notably as a result of the Royal Commission on Environmental Pollution's recent report Transport and the Environment which suggests that cycle provision must now receive high priority in future plans for transport. New routes are opening almost weekly, and such major projects as the Trans-Pennine Trail, the Sea to Sea Cycleway and above all the National Cycle Network, all dealt with elsewhere in this book, will revolutionise opportunities for cycling without traffic in the North of England in the years ahead. We look forward to working on new editions of this guide!

What is also clear from any book about the North of England, is its diversity of landscape which offers an intriguing mix of the deeply rural, with no less than five National Parks (more than half England's total) and areas of extensive agriculture, and some of Europe's most concentrated urban and industrial conurbations. It offers a mixture of topography from the high, open moorland of the Pennine hills to the wide flood plains around York and Merseyside, from the craggy Lakeland peaks to the flat coastlines of East Yorkshire; landscapes which each offer a very different experience, reflected in their scenery, wildlife and local communities.

If nothing else, we hope that these 30 routes will inspire both those cyclists who live in the region and those who are visiting it, to get their bikes out of the garage and discover a different and more peaceful Northern countryside away from traffic noise and congestion and the extensive car parks which deface so much of the countryside. They reveal a world of quiet green tracks and paths, meandering through the valleys, by rivers, canals, along embankments and through deep cuttings, past old industrial landscapes now covered by birch and willow, into richly beautiful, forgotten countryside waiting to be discovered from the saddle.

The River Wear crossing on the Consett-Sunderland Railway Path. *Author*

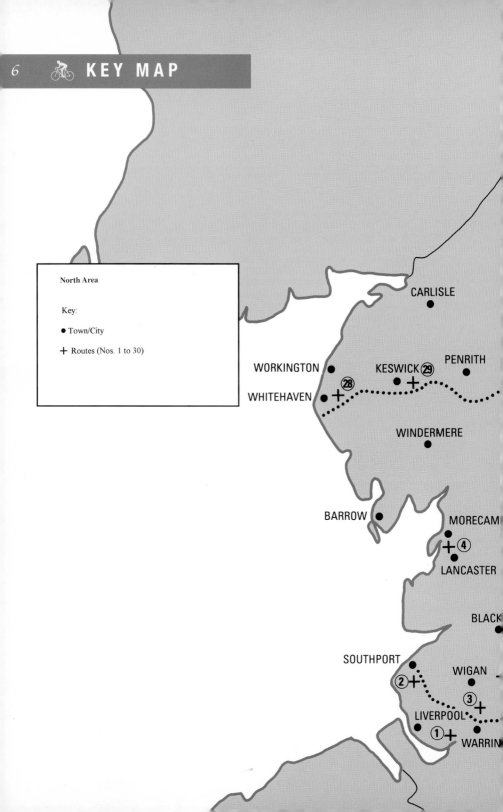

North Area

Key:

● Town/City

✛ Routes (Nos. 1 to 30)

CARLISLE ●

WORKINGTON ●   KESWICK ㉙   PENRITH ●

WHITEHAVEN ● ㉘ ✛ ········· ● ✛ ···········

WINDERMERE ●

BARROW ●

MORECAM ●

✛ ④

LANCASTER

BLACK

SOUTHPORT ●

WIGAN ●

② ✛ ·····

③ ✛

LIVERPOOL ● ····

① ✛   WARRIN

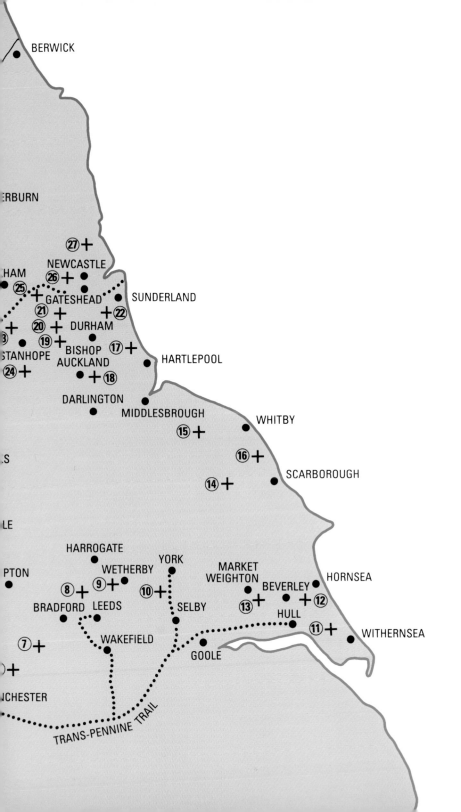

All the routes featured in this book are traffic-free cycle paths which have been created to provide cyclists and walkers with safe and attractive routes to enjoy the countryside.

In the North of England, the development of traffic-free cycle routes is closely linked to the region's industrial heritage. In Tyneside and Durham, the local authorities have used the dense network of waggonways and disused railways that once served the Northumberland and Durham coalfield – to create a network of cycleways, through a now largely rural landscape, where once coal-mining devastated the environment, but where birch and willow now flourish. In other parts of the region where canals were an important part of the industrial development of the area, canal towpaths are being widened and strengthened to enable them to be used for cycling, including the Leeds-Liverpool Canal, St Helens Canal in Merseyside and Manchester's Ashton Canal featured in this book.

Completely new purpose-built cycle paths are also being constructed through former areas of industry and urban dereliction as part of the economic regeneration of the North of England. This has been particularly the case in parts of Tyneside, Merseyside and Greater Manchester, where cycle paths are being built as new 'green ways', perhaps linking new country parks or nature reserves as part of major environmental improvement projects.

Elsewhere in the region cycle paths are being developed around reservoirs such as at Kielder Water, and within the large tracts of Forestry Commission land, providing high quality routes across a variety of terrain, often rich in wildlife interest.

There are basically five broad categories of off-road cycling path featured in this book:

1. Disused railways

Only when you look at the vast network of disused railways within Northern England is it possible to understand the contribution of the railways in the 19th century to industrial development. This network shaped not only the development of industries, but also the towns that grew around them. By the beginning of the 20th century, Britain had over 20,000 route miles of railway, with most towns and villages within England being no more than two or three miles from their nearest railway station.

But ever increasing road competition, both by bus and car (especially after World War 2), and lack of investment, reduced the competitiveness of railways. Lines were being closed before the 1960s, but Dr Beeching's now infamous Report of 1963 saw these closures escalate on a massive scale. By the early 1970s Britain's rail network consisted of just 11,500 miles. Whilst it can be argued that Britain's railways required some rationalisation, many lines if they had survived today could have provided badly needed alternative transport routes. Thanks to the vision of many local authorities and to Sustrans, many remaining sections of trackbed – at least where they have not been sold off piecemeal, shortsightedly, to developers – have been transformed into environmentally friendly cycle paths and walkways, incidentally retaining the infrastructure and right of passage in case at some point in the future they are ever required as railway lines or even tramway lines.

This process has been greatly helped by the work of Sustrans which has not only helped and advised local authorities, but by working in partnership with them and other agencies, has set standards of good practice in terms of quality of surface, the retaining of road bridges and safe crossings, and use of public art to animate the routes. Several Sustrans-built (or inspired) routes are featured in this book including the Liverpool Loop Line, Selby to York, Whitehaven to Ennerdale, and the Consett–Sunderland railway paths, as well as the Trans-Pennine Trail and Coast to Coast Cycleway.

These disused railways make ideal cycle paths, providing a relatively level surface for cyclists, except in cases where bridges have been removed from embankments (requiring steps or steep inclines to cross roads) or, on occasions, a section of rope-hauled incline. The ballast base on which the tracks once rested forms an ideal surface for top dressing. Some of the old railway paths featured in this book are in better condition than others. A few are rather overgrown and have very stony uneven surfaces, little more than the basic railway crushed limestone or ash ballast; others are provided with excellent fine gravel or tarmac paths. Dismantled railways are also popular with walkers, joggers and, in some instances, wheelchair users. So please always be considerate when using these railway paths and always give way to other users on foot, and carry (and use) a bell to give people advance warning of your presence. Nothing irritates non-cyclists more on a path shared by cyclists and walkers than to be almost mown down by a fast-moving rider who approaches without warning.

An indication of the importance of disused railways as a potential cycling resource is that over 20 of the 30 cycle rides featured in this book use dismantled railway lines for all or part of their route, and many of the planned and proposed routes will also use old railway lines.

2. Forest Trails

The Forestry Commission has in recent years been keen to encourage greater recreational use of its forests for walkers and cyclists. Many of the region's forests now contain way-marked trails, and leaflets are available to tell cyclists where they can cycle. As a general rule, cycling is permitted on most hard surfaced forestry tracks, subject to diversions when timber is being extracted. It is best to contact the Forestry Commission, whose address is provided for each of its regional offices at the back of this book. The main Forestry Commission areas in this region are:

- North Riding Forest (North Yorks and South Durham)
- The Border Forest Park, including Kielder Forest
- Grizedale Forest Park

Three cycle routes from the North Riding Forest Park are featured in this book and one from the Border Forest Park. It is likely that the development of Community Forests around some of Britain's largest cities will lead to the establishment of many new off-road cycling opportunities.

3. Canal Towpaths

Like old railways, canal towpaths provide green lungs through urban centres linking to the open countryside. The area around Greater Manchester and West Yorkshire has a particularly rich canal heritage with three Trans-Pennine canals — the Leeds–Liverpool, the Huddersfield Narrow Canal and the Rochdale Canal — linking the two great navigable river estuaries: the Mersey and, via the Aire Calder Navigation, the Humber. Canals and riverside paths are rich in wildlife interest and industrial heritage and, like old railways, provide level easy cycling.

However, cyclists cannot use all of the canal towpath network. A recent survey by British Waterways found that nationally only 10% of its towpaths met the requirements for cycling and the towpaths were categorised: (A) open to cycling with care, (B) open to cyclists with extreme care, and (C) where cycling is not permitted on safety grounds. Cycling is likely to be allowed on towpaths with A and B categories, but there is usually no right of way for cyclists on British Waterways' land. In addition, cyclists sometimes require a permit, available for a small fee, to use a towpath. For further details contact your local British Waterways office, listed at the back of this book.

Cyclists should also be aware that towpaths are narrow and often slippery, and they should not attempt to cycle two abreast. Please, again, always be considerate to other canal users, including walkers and anglers, whose equipment may lie across the path, and be prepared to dismount and push your cycle if the path narrows, passes under a low bridge or alongside a lock, or if a group of anglers are on the path.

The following canal routes, where cyclists are permitted as long as they consider the needs of other users, are featured in this book:

- Ashton Canal
- Leeds–Liverpool canal, between Shipley and Leeds
- St Helens (or Sankey) Canal, Merseyside

4. Country Parks

Some country parks are served by a cycle path, or have cycle routes running through them, providing an attractive way to enjoy the country park. Several of the cycle routes featured in this book are linear country parks or nature parks where cycling is permitted on the marked paths. These include:

- The Derwent Walk
- The North Tyne Cycle Way
- The Rising Sun Country Park
- Sankey Valley Country Park
- Spike Island Country Park
- The Halewood Triangle Country Park
- The Loop Line Nature Park
- The Tame Valley Trail

5. Bridleways and Byways

Cycling is also permitted on public bridleways, byways open to all traffic (BOATs) and roads used as public paths (RUPPS), but is not permitted on public footpaths. Bridleways, RUPPs and some byways are clearly marked on Landranger or Pathfinder Ordnance Survey maps, though it is only when you come to cycle them that you discover their condition. Many are muddy and overgrown and are only suitable for the more dedicated mountain-biker. Some of the routes featured in this book use bridleways for part of the route or as link paths. Many of the cycle paths along disused railways have been given legal bridleway status to enable the route to be used for cyclists and horseriders. Others are technically only 'Permissive' routes which means walkers or cyclists can use them subject to the agreement of the owner — usually in the case of cycle paths, the local authority or in the case of canal towpaths, British Waterways.

There are currently proposals to develop a Pennine Bridleway running parallel to the Pennine Way for 432 kilometres (270 miles) along the Pennine hills from Wirksworth in Derbyshire to Kirkby Stephen in Cumbria. For further details contact: Countryside

Commission, NW Region, 7th Floor, Bridgewater House, Manchester M1 6LT. Tel: 0161 237 1061.

Cycling on the public highway

Gradually cycle lanes and cyclist-friendly junctions along roads are being developed in some of Britain's cities, and cycle lanes created in traffic-calmed streets, but provision remains sparse and all too often the various measures are not interlinked to provide a safe means of crossing the city centre.

At the same time, whilst many cycle owners are understandably nervous at cycling on busy main roads, there are many opportunities for cycling on some of Britain's quieter country lanes. This book is about traffic-free cycling, and the vast majority of our recommended routes involve little or no on-road cycling. However, for those who do wish to explore the countryside beyond the off-road cycle paths, many local authorities are providing 'cycle routes' or cycling guides to their county or district featuring a number of rides using quiet lanes. These are listed at the back of this book. It is also perfectly possible to plan your own trip, perhaps using a mixture of the featured routes and linking bridlepaths or quiet back lanes, including either 'C' roads marked yellow on Ordnance Survey maps (though these are not always quiet roads, especially near towns) or unclassified roads (yellow or white), to develop a circular ride from home or to or from the nearest railway station.

Above: The Auckland Walk. *Author*

In October 1995 Sustrans received confirmation from the Millennium Commission of the success of £42.5 million bid to create a National Cycle Network throughout Britain. When completed, the National Cycle Network will create a high quality network of safe and attractive routes on a combination of completely traffic-free paths, protected sections of cycle track on minor roads, and quiet back roads and byways.

Sustrans, in partnership with over 400 local authorities and other agencies from all over Britain, is seeking to create an environment in which cycling can flourish, to encourage many more people to leave their cars at home and use their bikes to commute to work and school, to go shopping or simply for leisure. The Network will pass through the centre of most cities and towns in England and has been designed to pass within two miles (a 10min cycle ride) of over 20 million people — or more than a third of the population of Britain. Sustrans estimate that when the entire Network is completed, in the year 2005, it will carry over 100 million journeys each year, of which the majority will be local people making local trips.

The Network will consists of 1,800 miles of traffic-free routes, mainly using canal towpaths and disused railways; 3,000 miles of traffic-calmed and signposted quiet roads; and 200 miles of protected sections of road where cyclists will be provided with cycle lanes and special measures at junctions and road crossings.

In addition to creating a network of safe cycling routes, the scheme will also be an important catalyst in improving and landscaping derelict areas, restoring canal towpaths and preserving some of Britain's railway heritage. It will help create wildlife corridors and new recreational opportunities, including for those with disabilities. The routes will include elements of sculpture and public art, and where they pass through urban areas will be designed as demonstration projects to put the needs of people before cars.

In the North of England, the National Cycle Network will use many existing traffic-free routes, many of which are featured in this book. New routes will also be created and existing ones extended. Nationally 2,500 miles of route will be open by Easter 2000 and the rest by the year 2005.

In the North of England the proposed National Cycle Network will include the following routes:

Guisborough–Durham 44.7 miles (incorporating the Haswell–Hart route)

Durham–Sunderland 14.1 miles

Sunderland–Newcastle 10.5 miles

York–Guisborough 67.7 miles

Sunderland–Little Blencow 75.1 miles (incorporating the C2C route)

Durham–Consett 13.8 miles (incorporating the Lanchester Valley Walk)

Consett–Newcastle 24.3 miles (incorporating the Derwent Walk and North Tyne Cycle Way)

Little Blencow–Carlisle 16.4 miles

Carlisle–Glasgow 184.8 miles

Little Blencow–Keswick 20.5 miles (incorporating the C2C route)

Keswick–Whitehaven 30.6 miles (incorporating the C2C and the Ennerdale–Whitehaven rail path

Keswick–Workington 18.2 (incorporating the C2C route)

Hull–Guisborough 108.8 miles (incorporating the Whitby–Scarborough Trailway)

Newcastle–Edinburgh 171.3 miles

Manchester–Preston 34.1 miles

Preston–Keswick 110.8 miles

Leeds–Harrogate and York 42.6 miles (incorporating the Harland Way)

Newcastle–Carlisle 77.8 miles (incorporating the North Tyne Cycle Way)

Newcastle–Berwick (67 miles)

For further information on the National Cycle Network, and up-to-date information on the progress of newly opened routes, contact Sustrans, 35 King Street, Bristol BS1 4DZ. Tel: 0117 926 8893, or at Rockwood House, Barnhill, Stanley, Co Durham DH9 8AN. Tel: 01207 281259.

THE TRANS-PENNINE TRAIL

The Trans-Pennine Trail is an initiative by 30 local authorities in the North of England and the Countryside Commission to create a 180-mile off-road route for walkers and cyclists stretching across the Pennines between Liverpool and Hull. The route is designed to include links into all the main towns and cities which surround the trail, including Manchester, Leeds, York, Sheffield, Chesterfield and the seaside resorts of Southport and Hornsea.

The Trans-Pennine Trail, once complete, will be easily accessible to over 13 million people living within 20 miles. Part of the trail's attraction is that the route cuts right across the heart of northern England and in doing so offers a unique opportunity to experience the many different kinds of landscape which make up this part of Britain. It begins and ends alongside the region's two major river estuaries, the Mersey and the Humber, dominated by a variety of harbours and ports, and in between crosses the Pennines, including the gritstone moors of the Dark Peak in the Peak National Park, and through old industrial areas dominated by coal, steel, engineering, cotton and chemical industries. The Trail, with its mixture of deeply rural countryside and quiet canal and riverside paths, and the newly renatured and landscaped routes through areas once disfigured by slag tips and spoil heaps, will not only provide cyclists with a range of high quality leisure experiences, but many other people with convenient and safe traffic-free routes to work, shopping and school.

The Trans-Pennine Trail will mostly follow disused railways, canal towpaths, riverside paths and existing rights of way, though several new sections of cycleway are being specially created where required. Throughout, the Trail will provide a high quality surface, with gates and other access controls to prevent misuse by motorised vehicles. Wherever possible the route will also be available to those with disabilities and to horseriders. The Trans-Pennine Trail is currently completely accessible to walkers and has recently been designated as forming part of the E8 Euro-route, a long-distance European footpath route with links from Hull to Rotterdam through Holland and Germany to Turkey.

Several substantial sections of the Trail are already available to cyclists, whilst other sections are in the process of construction and planning, and are likely to be ready as or soon after this book is published. Each local authority is responsible for building its own section of the route, and these are being co-ordinated by the Trans-Pennine Trail Project Officer who is based with Barnsley Borough Council in the centre of the trail. A recent successful application to the Millennium Commission has provided £5.33 million towards the construction of two new bridges, the acquisition of several disused railway lines and various structural improvements which will ensure that the Trans-Pennine Trail should be completed as a walking and cycling route before the year 2000. A publication featuring six rides along the Trail is currently in preparation, whilst the official comprehensive cycling guide to the trail should be available in 1999.

The following sections of the trail are currently (1996) already open to cyclists. Those with an asterisk are featured.

* Cheshire Line

(Ainsdale–Magull) **10km, 6.5 miles**
Following the old Cheshire Lines railway across the West Lancashire Moss

* Liverpool Loop Line

(Halewood–Aintree) **16km, 10 miles**
A former railway, the Liverpool Loop Line once connected North at South Docks. It has now been attractively landscaped to create a traffic-free route for cyclists and pedestrians along wooded embankments and sandstone cuttings through the Liverpool suburbs.

* St Helens Canal

(Sankey Bridge–Spike Island) **8km, 5 miles**
The trail follows the St Helens Canal (Sankey Canal) from Sankey Bridge to Spike Island, formerly a centre of the Widnes chemical industry. It is now a small country park and home of the Catalyst Museum.

Warrington–Heatley **11km, 7 miles**

Along the former London and North Western (Altrincham)-Railway and part of the Manchester Ship Canal from Warrington to Heatley, near Lymm. The Trail is almost complete in Warrington.

The River Mersey–North Banks
(Sale Water Park–East Didsbury)
10km, 6 miles.
Following the banks of the River Mersey, through Sale Water Park amidst a landscape of flood plains and disused gravel pits, now a haven for wildlife.

Reddish Vale Railway Path
(Stockport–Brinnington) Several sections of this path are now complete through Reddish Vale and the Tame Valley, between Tiviot Dale to Reddish Visitor Centre .

Hulmes Wood and Haughton Dale
6km, 4 miles
Runs from Stockport Road, Denton to Gibraltar Bridge (Apethorne) following the River Tame through woods.

The Longdendale Trail
(Hadfield–Woodhead) **10.5km, 6 miles**
Follows the course of the old railway between Manchester and Sheffield, past five reservoirs, through fine Pennine scenery into the Peak National Park.

The Dove Valley Trail
(Silkstone–Wombwell) **12km, 7.5 miles**
Once the line of the former Worsbrough Bank railway, the trail follows the Dove Valley, an attractive tree-lined route on the outskirts of Barnsley, passing alongside Worsbrough Country Park.

The Aire and Calder Navigation Towpath
(Leeds Bridge to Woodlesford)
11km, 7 miles
Attractive section along this important commercial waterway from the centre of Leeds, waymarked past Thwaite's Mill (industrial museum) to Woodlesford MetroTrain station (cycles carried); soon to be extended to Wakefield.

* York and Selby Cycle Path
(York–Selby) **24km, 15 miles**
Follows the line of the former main line railway between York and Selby, across the River Ouse flood plain. The cycle path was built by Sustrans and throughout its route there are a series of environmental sculptures reflecting the industrial heritage of the area.

Trail in Humberside
(Barmby on the Marsh–King George Dock, Hull) **60km, 37.5 miles**

The trail follows a mixture of bridleways and minor roads alongside the Humber Estuary. There are plans to waymark the route through Humberside.

* Hornsea Rail Trail
(Hull–Hornsea) **19km, 11 miles**
An attractive route following the line of the old railway to the resort of Hornsea.

Beighton–Staveley Trail 9km, 5.5 miles
This follows the line of the former Great Central Railway. There are plans to extend the path through Rother Valley Country Park and along the River Rother to Rotherham.

Chesterfield Canal
3km, 1.9 miles
Currently only a short section of the Chesterfield towpath around Tapton Lock is accessible to cyclists, but eventually cyclists will be able to use the towpath between Chesterfield and Staveley.

For details of the route taken by the Trans-Pennine Trail and up-to-date information on its progress (see *Useful Addresses)*

THE SEA TO SEA CYCLE ROUTE (C2C)
The Sea to Sea (C2C) is a 140-mile cycle route which has been devised by Sustrans in conjunction with local authorities in the North of England, to link the Irish and the North Seas, from Whitehaven and Workington in Cumbria to Sunderland and Newcastle in Tyne & Wear.

The route mostly follows minor roads and traffic-free cycle paths, and can be cycled in short sections or as part of a longer cycling tour. A C2C Sculpture Trail of mileposts, seats and signs is currently being erected as part of the North of England's celebration of Visual Arts Year 1996.

Some of the route goes through remote and bleak countryside, so cyclists should carry suitable clothing and be prepared to avoid certain sections in severe weather conditions. It is also recommended that the route is ridden west to east taking advantage of the prevailing westerly winds. An all-terrain bike is recommended for the off-road sections.

Five routes are featured in this book, and a detailed map of the entire 140-mile route is available at £3.00 from Sustrans. (See *Useful Addresses)*

Your bike

Most routes in this book are perfectly manageable by what are generally called touring bikes; that is bikes which are reasonably sturdy, with tyres stout enough to cope with gravel and cinder tracks. Mountain bikes — now the most popular style of cycle to be sold in Britain — with a sturdy frame, a wide range of gears and strong tyres with plenty of grip are, however, preferable for many of the routes, including those on forest tracks and canal towpaths and some railway paths where surfaces may be rough or overgrown. In some places steps and narrow anti-motorbike gates require a machine to be lifted or carried, so a light, strong machine, whether for an adult or a child, will make off-tarmac cycling more enjoyable.

Before setting out on any cycling trip, it is essential to check your bike, not only to ensure it is safe, but also to make sure you don't arrive at your chosen starting point to discover a puncture or malfunctioning brakes. Before you leave home, check the following:

■ Brakes

Check front and back brakes are working. Also check that the cables and brake blocks are not worn, otherwise they will require replacement.

■ Tyres

Check tyres are properly pumped up hard. Also check the tread is not worn or the valves damaged, otherwise the tyre or inner tube may need replacing.

■ Chain

Check it is well oiled and not slack.

■ Saddle

Check it is the right height, so that you can touch the ground with your toes when sitting in the saddle, but high enough to have your legs almost straight when pedalling. This is particularly important for children's bikes.

■ Gears

Check these are working, other than minor adjustments. If not, they will usually require the attention of a bike shop if there are problems.

■ Wheels

Check for broken spokes or buckled wheels. If damaged, the bike will need to go to a shop for repair.

■ Lights

Check they are working (back and front) and not in need of a new battery or bulb

■ Bell

Have one fitted — and use it. Be considerate to other users on cycle paths, and use your bell to warn walkers of your approach.

For those unsure of how to maintain the bike, pick up a copy of a book like Richard's New Bike Book, which provides helpful foolproof diagrams to assist even the most non-mechanically-minded cyclist. For those who are not confident of their abilities, or for whom bike repairs go beyond simple adjustments, do not hesitate to take your bike to the nearest cycle repair shop. It is a lot easier to get your bike fixed at your local shop, than be forced to find one miles away from home.

Make sure you know how to fix a puncture — off-road routes are more punishing on tyres than normal roads. Most puncture repair kits have clear instructions on the back of the box to help — but you might practise removing and replacing a tyre and inner tube before you have to do it in the pouring rain on a remote hillside. In addition to the puncture kit, it is also advisable to carry the following items in a basic cycle tool kit:

pump, inner tube, allen keys, adjustable spanner, screwdriver, tyre levers (at least two) and chain link remover.

It is also worth considering joining the Environmental Transport Association (ETA) which like National Breakdown (Green Flag) and AA, offers a comprehensive breakdown service for motorists, but unlike other national breakdown organisations, also offers a recovery service for cyclists. The ETA is also a campaigning organisation supporting sustainable transport policies in both town and countryside, including the creation of better and safer conditions for cyclists and improved public transport with better cycle-carrying provision. Its address and telephone number are listed at the back of this book.

Hiring a bike

Wherever available, the nearest bike hire centre to the route is mentioned in the text. Such centres are ideal for those without their own bike, or for those who do not want the hassle of transporting their own bike to a particular location, especially if travelling by public transport. It is a good idea to ring beforehand and book a bike, especially during the summer holidays and at weekends, to avoid disappointment.

Make sure when you collect your hire bike that the hirer checks you with the bike frame size to ensure that you have the correct size for a comfortable ride. The hirer should also adjust the saddle for you and explain how the gears and brakes work, as the bike may differ from other bikes you have ridden. He should also provide you with a small tool kit, just in case you have an unexpected puncture or minor repair.

Lock Up!

Bicycle thefts are forever on the increase even in rural areas, so even if you are only intending to stop for a short time, it is advisable to lock your bike up, if only to avoid being stranded in a remote location! Always try and lock your bike to something, preferably a solid object such as a lamp post or fence. The best type of locks to use are the reinforced black steel U-locks which require special equipment to cut them open without a key. Other types of lock are easily removed using bolt cutters by enterprising thieves. It is also advisable to have a record of your frame identity number, so that in the event of your bike being stolen, you have some chance of recovering it.

Clothing and footwear

The main thing to consider before setting out on a cycle trip is to ensure that what you are wearing is both comfortable and visible. Even though the routes featured in this book are traffic-free, some do involve road crossings or short stretches on quiet lanes, and it is advisable to wear brightly coloured clothing to ensure you are seen.

For women, whilst it is perfectly possible to cycle in a skirt, do make sure that the skirt isn't too wide or too long to get caught in the wheels. A better option for those who don't wish to wear trousers or shorts, is to wear a divided skirt. Leggings or tracksters which are tight at the leg are ideal for cycling. Avoid baggy tracksuits which can easily be caught in the chain and thick non-stretch material like denim which on a longer ride can get very uncomfortable as the seams can rub the inside of your leg. The best solution, for those intending to do a lot of cycling, is a pair of padded cycling shorts, which do provide excellent protection against saddle-sore behinds.

The best combination of clothing for the upper part of the body is a series of thin layers, rather than one thick sweater. This enables layers to be removed to ensure that as you heat up you can adjust your clothing to find a comfortable temperature. A lightweight fleecy zipped jacket can often prove a very flexible garment for cycling, which can be worn with just a T-shirt in summer and several layers in winter. Make sure that the clothing you are wearing is not tight across your back when you stretch out your arms. In winter, gloves are essential because even if the rest of your body is nice and warm from exercise, your hands remain exceedingly exposed on the handlebars. Specialist cycling gloves, whilst cheap, are not really necessary, unless you cycle regularly. They do, however, provide additional padding around the palms of the hands which can be very welcome on a long ride. For those who don't wish to wear a helmet, a woolly hat can also be advantageous in winter.

You can wear any shoe with a flat sole for cycling; trainers or old tennis shoes are ideal. Do take care to make sure the laces are properly tied to prevent them getting caught in the pedals.

The British weather is at best erratic, and it is always sensible to pack waterproofs. It is amazing how quickly a cyclist can get soaked to the skin in even a relatively light shower compared to a rambler. A lightweight cagoule is usually adequate in summer, especially if you are wearing shorts, but at other times of the year it may be advisable to carry waterproof trousers or a long cycling cape, particularly for longer rides. Once you are soaked, it is often difficult to get dry, and with a cold wind, the ride home can be very uncomfortable.

Helmets

There has been much debate about whether to wear a helmet or not. What is not debatable is that the majority of serious injuries to cyclists are head injuries. Indeed head injuries have been found to be the primary or contributory cause of death in about two thirds of fatalities. Advocates of cycle helmets argue that the majority of serious cycle accidents are not caused by a collision with a motor vehicle, but by cyclists falling off after losing control or encountering a road hazard. Whilst an increasing number of children are now wearing helmets, many adults feel that they are uncomfortable to wear, awkward to carry around off the bike and a hindrance to enjoying the fresh air as they pedal along. Until the wearing of helmets is made compulsory, however, it is a matter of individual choice. The authors of this book can only advise that you do wear one — at all times.

Children
All the routes in this book are suitable for children who are able to cycle. The shorter routes are better for beginners, and it is better to keep trips enjoyable by having frequent stops and returning to a parked car or transport before youngsters are overtired. Take care wherever road crossings do occur to ensure that children await adult supervision before crossing. Minor, seemingly empty, country roads often attract extremely fast cars. Like adults, children require a well-maintained bike, should wear suitable clothing and the wearing of safety helmets should be encouraged at all times — preferably with parents setting a good example.

Refreshments
Even if you intend to stop at a café or a pub for lunch or a snack, always carry a drink with you, as cycling can often be thirsty work, especially in hot weather. Most bikes have a holder to take a plastic container for water or fruit squash. Some fruit, chocolate or a packet of nuts and raisins is also useful to have as emergency rations.

Other essentials
There are a number of other items that it is also sensible to carry on any cycling trip.

Check List
- Cycle repair kit (including a spare inner tube)
- Pump
- Waterproofs
- Water bottle
- Suntan cream (essential on a sunny day, it is amazing how quickly legs, arms and necks can burn)
- Insect repellent (useful if cycling through a forest in summer, where midges and mosquitoes can be rampant!)
- Food, either a snack or packed lunch
- Lock
- Money
- Hand wipes (great for getting oil off your hands after an unexpected repair)
- Lights/reflective belt (essential if there is the remotest chance you will be out after dusk)
- Map/guide book
- Hat/gloves

Having assembled all the items for your cycle trip, you will now need something to carry them in. There are a number of options. Some shopper bikes have a basket on their handles which can be used to carry a selection of items. Other bikes have a metal carrier on their rear wheel to enable a bag such as a rucksack to be strapped on using rubber bungees. The more regular cyclist may wish to use a pannier or set of panniers which fit on to a metal carrier on the rear of the bike. Whenever possible avoid carrying things on your back — a rucksack can not only be a strain on the back but can throw the cyclist off balance, perhaps with disastrous effect. Even a small bag can be in the way and make your back feel rather sweaty. However you chose to carry your possessions, do make sure that you do not leave any loose straps that can get caught in a wheel.

TRANSPORTING YOUR BIKE
The great joy of cycling is that it is a sustainable, green form of transport, powered by human energy and causing no unpleasant emissions. In an ideal world, therefore, cyclists should be able to cycle from home to the start of traffic-free routes to enjoy a day out in the countryside. The reality is that unless cyclists live close to a particular cycle path, they usually need to transport themselves and their bike to the start of the route, either because of the distance involved or because there is no safe route from home. There are two ways of getting to the start of the routes featured in this book: by car or by public transport.

Using your car
In recent years, the growth of leisure cycling has led to the increasing availability of various forms of bike carriers which fix on to a car. A popular method is to use a back carrier which is fitted to the car using a combination of straps, clips and adjustable angles. This type of rack usually carries two bikes. Care is needed to ensure the car numberplate is not obscured, and that you do not scratch the car's or the bikes' paintwork — which is easily done. It is also possible to buy, though more expensive, a system which fits on a car tow bar, in which the bikes fit into individual grooves. This system usually holds between two and four bikes.

Another method of carrying bikes on the outside of the car is to use a roof rack, designed to carry bikes. Some are designed to carry the bikes upside down and others the right way up. The advantage of this system is that it does not restrict the driver's rear view, but it can affect the car's wind resistance and you need to be pretty strong to lift your bike on to the roof especially if it's a heavy mountain bike.

Another option, used by some motorists, is to carry their bikes in the back of an estate car or larger hatchback. Quick release wheels mean that most bikes will fit into the back of a car, though it may restrict the number of passengers you can carry. If carrying more than one bike, use an old blanket to stop the bikes damaging each other. This will also protect the inside of the car when you return to the car park with a wet, muddy bike.

Whichever way you choose to transport your bike by car, make sure that it is secure and the straps are all properly tied. Rubber bungees can be used for additional security. Remember also to remove any accessories such as pumps, panniers and water bottles before fixing the bike to the car, and if carrying several bikes do be careful to ensure that they do not damage one another, such as by getting brake levers caught in gear mechanisms. If you are leaving the bikes on your car unattended for any time, lock the bikes to each other and the rack. Always lock the bike rack in the car when you leave for your cycle ride.

Using public transport

For those who want to leave their car at home, or who do not have access to a car, it is perfectly possible to use public transport. The nearest railway station to each of the featured cycle routes is provided in the text. In addition, information has also been provided on bus services, if appropriate, and the nearest cycle hire centre. Increasingly a number of bus companies are experimenting with on-bus cycle carrying facilities, and developing services on which bikes can be carried. These are still in their pioneering stage, but are well worth looking out for as they become more widespread.

The move towards the privatisation of Britain's railways has complicated the rules and regulations concerning the transport of bikes. In the North of England, the following rules currently apply and are provided as guidance only. It is always advisable to ring up and check with the railway operator, before turning up at the station, as on certain

routes bike spaces are limited and have to be booked in advance.

InterCity: On InterCity trains cycle places have to be booked in advance, for which there is a charge.

Regional Railways North West: Bikes are carried in the luggage space at the guard's discretion. Cyclists are advised to avoid peak travel periods — morning and evening rush hours. Spaces are extremely limited on Trans-Pennine Express services (Liverpool–Manchester–Leeds–Newcastle) and cyclists are strongly advised to book in advance.

Regional Railways North East: A maximum of two bikes are carried on all Regional Railways North East services, and cyclists are advised to check in advance on availability, but most are not bookable. It is generally wise to avoid peak times.

Greater Manchester — GMPTE: Bikes are carried free of charge, but cyclists should avoid peak travel periods.

Metrolink: No bikes can be carried on Metrolink services in Greater Manchester

West Yorkshire — METRO: Bikes are carried on local trains free of charge, but cyclists should avoid peak travel periods.

Merseyside — Merseyrail: Cycles are carried free of charge wherever space permits, but are not permitted on any Northern or Wirral Line electric trains during peak periods (Mondays to Fridays 6.30am–9.30am and between 4pm and 6pm).

Tyne & Wear Metro: No bikes can be carried on Tyne & Wear Metro services.

Above: It is essential that the right equipment is used when transporting bicycles by car. *Author*

THE LIVERPOOL LOOP LINE

This popular cycle path around the outlying suburbs of Liverpool provides a fine green traffic-free corridor around the western edge of the city, along semi-naturalised wooded embankments and through sandstone cuttings linking local communities, a nature park and two country parks, and several pleasant open areas. Because the route is frequently on raised embankment, there are extensive views as far as the Pennine foothills.

PLACES OF INTEREST ALONG THE ROUTE

Liverpool Loop Line
Opened in 1879 by the Cheshire Lines Committee, the Liverpool Loop Line was planned to provide a direct route to the Lancashire coast from Cheshire and Warrington, bypassing central Liverpool, as well as providing a rail link to such outlying villages as Gateacre, Knotty Ash and West Derby. Road competition caused the line to close in 1970, and the trackbed has been converted to a cycle and walkway by Sustrans and now forms part of the Liverpool section of the Trans-Pennine Trail.

Halewood Country Park
Halewood Triangle was once a busy railway junction. The land between the triangle of lines could not be developed, and now the Loop Line has gone, the area has been developed into an attractive area of woodland and meadowland, with picnic sites and a choice of footpaths and bridleways. Knowsley Borough Council has recently opened a Ranger and Visitor Centre to serve the park.

Knotty Ash
This village, now a pleasant suburb of Liverpool, has achieved wide fame thanks to Liverpool comedian Ken Dodd. Treacle mines may be hard to find, but this is a specially interesting section of railway through deep, fern and lichen-covered sandstone cutting. Steps past the old station platforms give access to a small park. The village has a handsome church whose churchyard is reputed to contain the graves of more Lord Mayors of Liverpool than any other in the city.

Croxteth Country Park
A magnificent 18th century country house set in 900 acres of parkland complete with a rare breeds farm, a miniature railway and miles of delightful walks. The park is easily reached from the old West Derby station on the Loop Line — however, the Park is open only to pedestrians.

Loop Line Nature Park
The area of the Loop Line around Walton, in the centre of heavy industry, is being replanted and allowed to regenerate as a semi-natural area for wildlife and wildflowers, to form a green corridor through this part of the city.

Left: The sylvan aspect of the Liverpool Loop line. *Author*

Starting Points: Halewood station, Halewood Triangle Country Park; Broad Green station; Walton Loop Line Nature Park car park and Rice Lane station.

Parking: In the car park on Okell Drive (off Church Road) by the Halewood Triangle Country Park Visitor Centre; in car park off Blackthorne Road, off the A580 near Walton Park. Limited off-road parking on Old Thomas Lane, Broad Green.

Public Transport: Merseyrail City Line (Warrington/Manchester branch) to Halewood; Merseyrail City Line to Broad Green; Merseyrail Northern Line (Kirkby branch) to Rice Lane. Cycles carried free of charge on Merseyrail but avoid peak times weekdays, especially on Northern and Wirral Lines.

Links to other cycle paths: It is expected that this route will be linked to the Cheshire Lines Southport Cycle Path (Route 2) in the near future. In the meantime the two routes can easily be linked using Merseyrail trains, changing at Kirkdale.

Distance: 15 kilometres, 9 miles

Map: Landranger 108

Surfaces & Gradients: Mostly tarmac; some sections near Halewood crushed gravel. Smooth — suitable for touring bikes. Sections of the route gently undulating — easy gradients.

Roads & Crossing Points: Hollies Road (busy) and Rainbow Drive — minor suburban road, on section from Halewood station, and busy crossing (traffic lights) at Rice Lane.

Refreshments: Light snacks and toilets at Halewood Country Park Visitor Centre; fish and chip shop at Broad Green; Safeway supermarket at Knotty Ash; coffee shop/café and three pubs at West Derby (Mill Lane), shops and pubs at Rice Lane.

ROUTE INSTRUCTIONS:
From Halewood Triangle
1. From the exit from Halewood station into Hollies Road, turn right and cross beyond the safety barrier to the playing field at Plantation Primary School, returning left to the railway embankment to join the path by the embankment, going left through the gateway and ascending the embankment.

2. At Rainbow Drive cross to continue directly ahead to pass the car park and Visitor Centre. (Visitors arriving by car join the trail at this point). Follow the signs to Gateacre.
3. For Broad Green station (7km) take the opening on the gateway after the three parallel bridges (main road, M62 motorway, railway) crossing directly to

Left: Information board at Halewood Triangle Country Park. *Author*

Old Thomas Street and Jubilee Avenue — entrance to station by narrow gate in the corner.

4. At Safeway's supermarket (Knotty Ash) the trail bears left around the outside of the supermarket fence. Keep ahead along to Walton and the Loop Line Nature park.

5. For Croxteth Country Park leave the trail at West Derby station (with the station house on the bridge) with exit path left which leads on to Mill Lane (heavy traffic). Turn right. Bear left at the junction and go directly ahead (350m) to the centre of West Derby village and the western pedestrian entrance to Croxteth Park by the church.

6. As you reach a recreation ground at Walton, with a low bridge ahead, take the tarmac path left which goes around the edge of the sunken football pitches, bearing right around the ground towards a red brick tramshed-style building and the exit along Whitfield Road into Rice Lane. Merseyrail Rice Lane station is almost directly opposite by the traffic lights.

From Rice Lane station

7. Cross Rice Lane at the traffic lights, turn left then first right along Whitfield Road and on to the trail.

From Broad Green station

8. Exit from the northern (Wigan) platform and go down Old Thomas Street to its junction with Thomas Lane. Gateway opposite leads to the cycle path.

Below: The metal bridge parapets help to emphasise th
Liverpool Loop Line

ROUTE 1
LIVERPOOL LOOP LINE

Rice Lane
⑥
Walton
P

Croxteth
Country Park
West
⑤ Derby
④ Knotty
Broad ⑦ ③ Ash
Green
P — M62

Gateacre
Halewood
Country
Park P②

①
Halewood

N

CHESHIRE LINES PATH TO AINSDALE

From the outskirts of Liverpool to the Sefton coast, this cycle route along the former Cheshire Lines Railway trackbed from Maghull to Southport crosses rich agricultural countryside and can easily be combined with a visit to the popular resort of Southport.

PLACES OF INTEREST ALONG THE ROUTE

Maghull

Though now a suburb of Liverpool, Maghull, on the Leeds–Liverpool canal, is an old town which keeps something of its own character. The little chapel of St Andrew dates back to the 7th century, whilst the parish church is 19th century. In the parish register an interesting entry refers to the packet fare on the canal for the carriage of a sick woman from Maghull to Wigan for 1s 10d – about 9p.

Downholland Moss

Moss is an old Lancashire word meaning marsh, and like much of this part of the West Lancashire plain this was former marshland which was drained in the 19th century to produce richly fertile farmland. With its mild, moist climate this area is famous for its excellent potatoes, green vegetables, flowers and market gardening. Much of the complex system of drainage channels feeding into Downholland Brook and the little River Alt will be seen from the cycleway.

Ainsdale

The dunes of Ainsdale Sands and the Formby Hills form part of an extremely important National Nature Reserve, celebrated for its botanic riches and wildlife. The pine woods close to the Liverpool–Southport railway line are one of the last sanctuaries of England's native red squirrel.

Southport

It's about seven kilometres (four miles) from Ainsdale by shore road (busy) into the centre of Southport; still an elegant and fashionable seaside resort and shopping centre, with a wide choice of facilities. On the right of the coastal road is the famous Birkdale Golf Course.

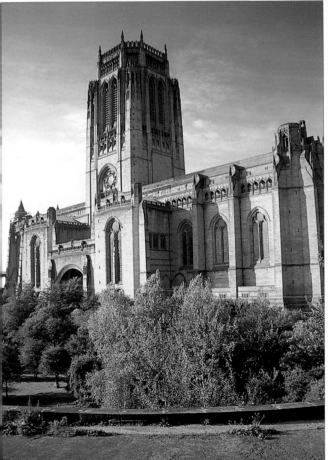

Left: The dramatic lines of Liverpool's Anglican Cathedral dominate the skyline. *AA Photo Library*

Starting Points: Maghull station or Ainsdale

Parking: Limited car parking at Maghull; greater choice at Ainsdale.

Public Transport: Maghull: Merseyrail trains Northern Line Liverpool Central/Moorfields to Ormskirk. Ainsdale: Merseyrail Northern Line Liverpool Central/Moorfields to Southport. Frequent services on both lines, Sundays included. Cycles are carried, but capacity is limited and peak times are best avoided.

Distance: 18 kilometres, 11 miles

Map: Landranger 108

Surfaces & Gradients: Compressed gravel, fairly smooth and dry, for most of the route — at the start a little stony, including sections on the Leeds–Liverpool canal towpath. A short section near Ainsdale (about 700m) is a very rough track made of old bricks and earth. The final section is on back lanes and a tarmac bike path. Acceptable for touring bikes except for the brick and earth section where care is required. Mountain bikes an advantage. No significant gradients.

Roads & Crossing Points: Sections of minor road in Maghull and near Ainsdale. Busy crossing of the A565 at Ainsdale — keep children under supervision.

Refreshments: Shops and pubs in Maghull; shops, cafés, pubs, toilets in Ainsdale.

ROUTE INSTRUCTIONS:

1. From Maghull railway station turn right along Station Road then take the second left turning by the Post Office. Follow this cul-de-sac to the end, over the footbridge to join the Leeds & Liverpool canal. Turn left, to continue on the towpath.

2. Turn off left at the sixth bridge over the canal, a level crossing marked by an

'8 T' sign and a small overhead pipeline. Follow the lane down; it soon narrows and enters open countryside.

3. After approximately one kilometre (half a mile), at a very sharp 90° bend, turn left off the lane. The cycle path starts here marked with a blue sign 'Cheshire Lines path'. The path bends round to lead to an old trackbed and turns right by some old concrete pipes to follow the old rail route.

4. The route crosses the open country of the West Lancashire plain. Where the path meets a minor road continue straight ahead under Moss Lane bridge, following the trackbed

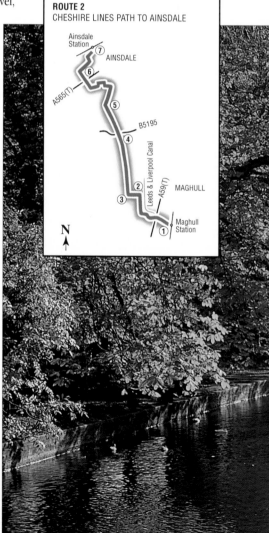

ROUTE 2
CHESHIRE LINES PATH TO AINSDALE

Ainsdale Station
⑦
AINSDALE
⑥
A565(T)
⑤
B5195
④
②
③
Leeds & Liverpool Canal
A59(T)
MAGHULL
N
①
Maghull Station

Right: Southport's Botanical Gardens.
AA Photo Library

until it meets North Moss Lane. Turn right on to the lane which soon becomes rough for the next 700m.

5. At the end of the track, turn left on to the tarmac lane which winds round into the edge of Instal. At the main road crossing, go straight across the A565 main Liverpool Road to continue along the bike path at the side of the coastal road, towards the railway level crossing.

6. At the end of the cycle path take Kendal Way opposite. Continue to the end then turn left to go along Easdale Drive to the end. Turn left to take the short bike lane which follows the railway up to Ainsdale station.

7. For Southport continue along Shore Road from the far side of the station, then left along the coastal road for approximately 7 km — 4 miles.

Below: A typical section of railway converted into cycle route. *Author*

SANKEY VALLEY PARK AND THE ST HELENS CANAL

Alongside one of Britain's oldest canals, to the shores of the Mersey — this is a cycle ride as rich in natural history as it is in industrial heritage interest, with landscapes of real grandeur along the Mersey estuary. This route is currently being extended for a further five miles into St Helens. With its variety of attractions, this is an especially good cycle route for children.

PLACES OF INTEREST ALONG THE ROUTE

The Sankey Valley Country Park
The Sankey Valley, an area of what is now woodland and parkland around the old St Helens Canal, and the little Sankey Brook, now forms a delightful countryside area with an extensive network of cycleways (soon to be extended into St Helens), a wildlife reserve, a maze and climbing and play areas for children. There is a Rangers Base and Information Point at Bewsey Old Hall (toilets in the park behind the Hall).
 The St Helens Canal Opened in 1757 to link the coalpits around St Helens with the River Mersey, this is Britain's oldest industrial canal, predating the more famous Bridgewater canal by three years. The canal was extended to Runcorn Gap, at Spike Island, in 1833, in order to take larger flat-bottomed sailing barges known as

Mersey Flats. Though now closed to traffic (apart from the 'yacht havens' by the locks at Fiddlers Ferry and Spike Island), this reed-edged waterway is a popular place for anglers and for birdlife.

Fiddlers Ferry
From at least the 12th century onwards, there was an important ferry across the River Mersey at this point, linking Cheshire with what in those days was south Lancashire. A large statue of Christ, now in Norton Priory, is said to have been placed here to protect travellers. The old Ferry Tavern, built to serve the physical needs of those same travellers, is now a popular haunt of boat people, walkers and cyclists — real ale, food and an outdoor beer garden. There are magnificent views along the Mersey and across to the low hills of Cheshire from this point.

Fiddlers Ferry Power Station
The eight massive cooling towers of Fiddlers Ferry power station make a notable landmark along the Mersey and have a gaunt beauty. This is one of Britain's largest power stations, with its own railway line and internal rail network.

Spike Island
A century ago this narrow strip of land between the canal and the River Mersey was busy with industry, especially soap and alkali manufacturing for a variety of industries. The West Dock, used to transport raw materials and finished goods, is now a wildfowl and angling centre, with a wildflower garden near by. Mersey Flat barges were built here, and

remains of two are to be seen offshore, as is a large rudder by the path. There is a small visitor centre and toilets near the marina.

Catalyst

Catalyst is the national museum of the chemical industry and gives a remarkable insight into the growth of one of Britain's major industries, which made this part of north Cheshire world famous. Hands-on interactive exhibits on aspects of science, displays on the growth of the industry, and from the top floor, reached by Observatory lift, are superb views across Runcorn Bridge, the Mersey and the modern industrial landscape of Widnes and Runcorn skilfully interpreted by audio-visual techniques. The museum is open 10am–5pm daily — except Mondays (apart from Bank Holidays).

Starting Points: Sankey Valley Park (near Bewsey Old Hall), Dallam, Spike Island.

Parking: Car parks to the east of the Bewsey Farm pub (follow the signs to the right before the pub, along track to car park on right among trees) and at Cromwell Avenue 400m north of junction with the A65 and at Tenby Drive (reached off Callands Road/St David's Drive); car park at Catalyst serves the museum and Spike Island. Some informal parking by the canal towpath at Sankey Bridges.

Public Transport: Frequent Regional Railways/Merseyrail services from Manchester/Chester/Liverpool to Warrington Bank Quay and Central.

Links to other cycle routes: A through route from Sankey Bridge (Trans-Pennine rail) to the 9km Warrington–Heatley Cycle Trail has been opened.

Distance: 12 kilometres — $7^1/_2$ miles. Additional 2km (over 1 mile) from railway stations and 2km into northern sections of the park.

Map: Landranger 108. Attractive map of Sankey Valley Park is available from the Rangers Base.

Surfaces & gradients: Tarmac and crushed gravel. Some rough sections on the canal towpath, otherwise generally good. Gradients virtually flat, slight descent from Sankey Valley Park.

Roads & Crossing Points: Care required at busy crossing of Liverpool Road at Sankey Bridges — otherwise everything off-road.

Left: The Sankey Canal. *Author*

Below: The Sankey Canal. *Author*

Refreshments: Bewsey Farm Inn near Old Hall; (toilets in the park close by Old Hall); the Ferry Tavern at Fiddlers Ferry; cafeteria at Catalyst Museum.

ROUTE INSTRUCTIONS:

1. From the car park near the Bewsey Farm pub or from the lower car park, head for the canalside and turn right along the tarmac track, passing southwards under the railway line with the wetland reserve on the left (cross footbridge to viewing platform), then past the Galleon and Rope Circus.

2. At main A57 Sankey Way expressway turn right to reach and cross the footbridge over the trunk road to pass Butterfly Gardens. Keep ahead to Liverpool Road.

3. Cross the Liverpool Road at Sankey Bridges with care, and level crossing (freight line to power station) ahead. Continue along the towpath bearing right at junction of paths. Where towpath narrows, follow the adjacent quiet cul-de-sac road. Keep ahead to Fiddlers Ferry by the Mersey.

4. Continue past the Ferry Tavern and the power station along straight stretch between wire fence, canal and railway.

5. Path enters Spike Island. Follow the tarmac path left around the shoreline to cross the lock gates to Catalyst.

Sankey Valley Park

6. To explore the northern part of the Valley Park, turn left on the canal path to the footbridge, cross and turn left along the canal

bank up to Bewsey Lock, crossing again to path which leads northwards by Twig Wood. Follow track past junction (track left leads past Gulliver's World to Ladywood) continuing northwards towards Dallam and Callands Estate, past play area and small ponds. Car parks on the left, but main path continues under the A574 and Winwick Quay towards St Helens.

From the railway stations

7. From Warrington Central, head for Bewsey Bridge turning right outside the station to the traffic lights, left along Tanners Lane then right at the lights along Bewsey Road ahead at next set of lights along Lodge Road to small island at the far side of which a footbridge crosses Sankey Brook. From Bank Quay station head across town centre to Central station then as above. A new section of Trail is being developed direct from Bark Quay to Sankey Bridge.

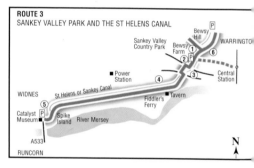

Below: A lifelike Heron appears to wait patiently for its next meal. *Author*

THE LUNE CYCLEWAYS

North and south of the ancient city of Lancaster, alongside the River Lune, run two attractive cycle tracks, each serving the city centre. The first operates down to the old port of Glasson Dock; the second upstream to the village of Caton beyond the Crook o' Lune. Both provide delightful cycling and a variety of riverbank and scenery.

PLACES OF INTEREST ALONG THE ROUTE

Lancaster

Lancaster is a city rich in history and heritage. Its great medieval castle, strategically situated on a hill overlooking the estuary, still dominates the town. Close by is the Priory Church of St Mary dating from the 14th and 15th centuries. The largely pedestrianised town centre contains several interesting buildings including the elegant Judges Lodging, now a museum, and down by the old quayside in the Old Custom House and warehouse, is the fine Maritime Museum with displays and exhibits telling much of the story of Lancaster's history as a major port and trading centre.

Glasson Dock

Glasson developed as a port in the 18th century when silting of the river Lune and the ever increasing size of ocean-going ships made access to Lancaster difficult. However, its distance from Lancaster was always a disadvantage and in 1826 a branch of the Lancaster Canal was constructed to link the port with the town, which in turn was augmented by the railway in 1887. Competition from such larger ports as Liverpool, Preston and Heysham was too much and the port declined, but the old canal basin and dockland area is now an attractive conservation area with a small marina, usually a hive of activity.

The Lancaster–Glasson Dock Railway

The railway was opened in 1887 to link Glasson Dock with the Lancaster–Preston Railway, with a station at Conder Green (now a picnic site) but services were an early victim of road competition. Passenger services ceased in 1930, freight in 1947. Lancashire County Council acquired the track in the 1970s and converted it into a cycleway.

The Lune Estuary

The estuary, now a Site of Special Scientific Interest, is a haven for a wide variety of wildlife, most notably birds including redshank, mallard, wigeon and shelduck, and a variety of plant life including rare plants

Above: The cycle path close to Glasson Dock. *D. Speakman*

which have colonised the limestone ballast of the old railway line. There are fine views from the cycleway over the estuary and to the Pennines in the east, and on a clear day, northwards to the Lake District.

The Lancaster–Wennington Railway

Until 1965, this was the main railway line between Lancaster and West Yorkshire, providing a direct link from the Skipton–Carnforth line at Wennington. The former Lancaster Green Ayre station at Skerton Bridge carried electric trains to Morecambe. The site has now been converted into a small park, with only a small warehouse crane from Hornby as a relic of the railway's history.

The Lune Aqueduct

This huge stone aqueduct carrying the Lancaster Canal across the River Lune was designed by the great canal engineer John Rennie. It is 600ft (about 190m) long, 51ft (16m) high and is designed in classical style, and was opened in 1799.

Crook o' Lune

A popular beauty spot, immortalised in a romantic painting of the river by Turner, Crook o' Lune makes a natural terminal point for the cycleway — with a picnic place. The 500m along the busy A683 main road into the pleasant village of Caton (refreshments) is also part of the Lancashire Cycleway. Between the Crook o' Lune and Forge Bank Weir is an important water extraction point — over 62 million gallons of water per day are taken by North West Water from this point for consumers in the region.

Starting Points: The best point to join both routes to Glasson Dock and Crook o' Lune is to take Long Marsh Lane, which runs down the hill at the railway side of Lancaster Castle. It can be reached from the railway station by taking the small path from the station and taking the lane up the hill. From the bus station take the cycle path leading from the rear of the Sainsbury's supermarket which follows the river — go left downstream to meet Long Marsh Lane.

Parking: Lancaster city centre, near bus station; Glasson Dock car park by exit of bike path; Conder Green picnic site; Denny Beck (off A683); Crook o' Lune picnic site (signed off A683).

Public Transport: Frequent rail services (InterCity and Regional Railways) to Lancaster station (500m from start of cycleways). Cycles carried on most services.

Cycle Hire: Duke of Lancaster Camal Hire. Tel: 01524 849484; Mike's Bikes, Alice Street, Morecambe. Tel: 01524 425 132.

Distance: Lancaster–Glasson Dock 9 kilometres — 6 miles; Lancaster–Crook o' Lune 8 kilometres — 5 miles.

Map: Landranger 97. An excellent leaflet of the two cycle paths, with detailed historical information and natural history notes, is produced by Lancashire County Council (available from local Tourist offices).

Surfaces & Gradients: To Glasson Dock, the trail is largely earth-covered which can be boggy in wet weather. However,

Left: The austere entrance to Lancaster Castle — now a prison. *Peter Waller*

Lancaster City Council have a programme of upgrading the route to tarmac. Tarmac, gravel and earth is found on the Crook o' Lune branch, but this is also being upgraded. Both routes are level and are suitable for touring bikes.

Roads & Crossing Points: In Lancaster centre (see route instructions). 500m along the busy A683 main road are required if accessing Caton village.

Refreshments: In Glasson Dock there are three pubs, a snack bar and café. Toilets are by the bus stop. Picnic site at Conder Green (old station). At Crook o' Lune is a picnic site and toilets; shop and pub in Caton. Wide choice of facilities in Lancaster city centre.

ROUTE INSTRUCTIONS:
To Glasson Dock
1. Take Long Marsh Lane which runs under the railway to its end. Then turn right and next left on to a road which follows the river. Just past Lune Industrial Estate the track begins, running straight ahead as the road finishes at a warehouse. The track is signed 'Aldcliffe Hill Lane 1', and lower down a less obvious sign 'Lancaster to Glasson Dock cycleway footpath 4½ miles (7km)'.

2. At the junction of paths continue straight ahead. The route continues for about 1km before turning left and continuing through a gate. (A parallel upper level path can avoid this section if it is flooded.)

3. The path follows the Lune Estuary, crossing a car park before bending left for the final stretch into Glasson Dock. The track peters out

after a last gate leaving the rider the choice of taking the short stretch along the road into Glasson Dock or going along a stretch of grassy trackbed.

To Crook o' Lune
4. From Long Marsh Lane, which runs down the hill at the railway side of Lancaster Castle, take the path which runs right from the road just before it runs under the railway. Otherwise the route can be accessed from either side of Sainsbury's supermarket by the riverside from the city centre.

5. The route runs along the riverside and through a park to follow the River Lune upstream. The route goes to the Crook o' Lune — a sharp bend in the river.

6. At Crook o' Lune cross over the river. Ahead are two wooden gates; take the first, then turn off right to take a track which joins the A683 road (caution) into Caton. The railway track is a footpath only beyond this point.

The Morecambe Link
7. By crossing Carlisle Bridge, the large railway bridge over the river in the centre of Lancaster, access can be gained to the cycleway which leads directly to Morecambe. Bikes have to be carried up the steps, however.

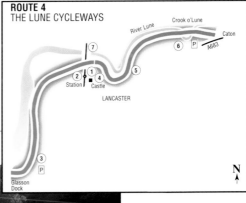

ROUTE 4
THE LUNE CYCLEWAYS

Left: Bridge over the River Lune.
D. Speakman

SALFORD'S LOOPLINES

Where commuter trains once carried workers and shoppers to Manchester and Liverpool, the Salford Looplines run behind housing estates and underneath main roads, through tunnels of trees. There are a couple of delightful parks at the start and midway, and the old line skirts Worsley Woods, a popular woodland, with opportunity to visit the celebrated Worsley Canal Basin on the Bridgewater Canal.

PLACES OF INTEREST ALONG THE ROUTE

Monton Green
Though Monton village has long been absorbed into the spreading conurbations of Eccles and Salford, Monton Green keeps something of its rural charm, thanks to the surviving areas of village green, now open green space, and a fine Victorian church

whose tall spire makes a prominent local landmark. The Duke's Drive, where the trail begins, is an attractive park and recreational ground lying between the old railway and the Bridgewater Canal, makes a pleasant start and finishing point to a cycle ride.

The Salford Looplines
The old London and North Western Railway between Manchester and Liverpool served the busy mill and mining towns of Leigh and Tyldesley and village of Worsley, for freight and passengers, with an extended loop which left the main line west of Eccles. A further branch extended to Farnworth and Bolton via Little Hulton. Both branches were an early victim of the Beeching axe and the loop was soon converted into a walk and cycleway — one of the earliest in the North West. An attractive feature is the directional signs in the form of railway signals, and the platforms of Worsley station which have been restored to make a small heritage feature and picnic area.

Worsley Woods
The woods at Worsley once formed part of the Duke of Bridgewater's extensive estates, and comprise a large area of mature semi-natural woodland — oak, alder, sycamore, birch, beech — which is one of the most attractive and popular woods west of Manchester, despite the effect of mining underground and industrial and suburban development close by. More serious has been the impact of the M61 and M62 motorways with their massive concrete viaducts and non-stop noise, but despite this the woodlands retain considerable charm, a haven for wildlife both within the woods and along the railway path.

Worsley Canal Basin
In the mid-18th century the Duke of Bridgewater was already exploiting the rich deposits from the Lancashire coalfield which lay under his estates. But transport of coal was a problem, being both slow and expensive by horse and cart. In 1759

Left: Worsley Basin — the red discolouration of the water is the result of iron polluting the water. *Author*

Right: A stone commemorates Little Hulton station. *Author*

he appointed the great Derbyshire engineer, James Brindley, to build a waterway — which became the Bridgewater Canal — to carry coal from his mines at Worsley to the mills and foundries of Manchester. The water in the canal basin is stained red from seeping from old mine workings. A Heritage Trail at the basin indicates main features of interest in this conservation area.

Parr Fold Park, Walkden:
The little Victorian park alongside the railway

Starting Points: Monton Green or Walkden. Access also possible from the A6 at Little Hulton.

Parking: Cyclists arriving by car should park in the large car park at Duke's Drive park just off Parrin Lane, to the west of its junction with Monton Green (about 120m west of Monton Church) — follow road signs to Worsley.

Public Transport: The most convenient access to the cycle path by train is from Walkden station on the Manchester Victoria–Wigan Wallgate line. From the station exit cross directly over the main A595 Walkden Road to the residential street opposite, Park Road, which runs parallel to the railway. Where this road reaches a junction by the bridge, look for a gap stile in the fence opposite (negotiable with a cycle) which leads down steps to the railway path. Patricoft Station (Liverpool–Manchester line) is about 1km away.

Distance: Monton Green–Little Hulton (M61) 7 kilometres — 4½ miles, plus 2km — just over a mile — on the 'branch' to Ellenbrook.

Map: Landranger 109

Surfaces & Gradients: Gravel and dirt, some cinder and grass. Generally good — acceptable for touring bikes. Slight gradients in the Little Hulton direction.

path is a gem, with beautifully kept rose gardens and flower beds, shrubbery, extended lawns, a bandstand, a small pond and a modern children's play area.

Little Hulton
A suburb of large housing estates with little to interest the visitor. However, the railway path is currently being extended to Farnworth and Bolton across the M61 which will create a more significant northern terminus.

Roads & Crossing Points: Minor roads to be crossed at Engine Fold (path only) and Little Hulton.

Refreshments: Pubs, shops and cafés at Monton Green and at Worsley Canal Basin, (especially along the main canal area) and along Manchester Road at Little Hulton.

ROUTE INSTRUCTIONS:
Monton Green to Little Hulton
1. From the entrance to Duke's Drive, take the tarmac path up the embankment on the left, through the gateway and on to the cycleway.

2. At the junction of tracks and picnic tables keep straight ahead for Little Hulton.

3. The entrance into Parr Fold Park lies up steps on the left, just before Park Road Bridge, Walkden (NB cycling is not permitted within the park).

4. Path ascends slope from cutting to cross street at access path. Continue down slope to rejoin route.

5. Steps at the Manchester Road bridge, Little Hulton, by the site of the former Little Hulton station, lead to busy main road with shops and pubs.

6. At next crossing point, still in Little Hulton, go over minor road to continue along the cycle trail between housing estates and school to a junction. A tarmac path leads towards the M61 and route extension to Farnworth. Otherwise return by the route you took.

Extension to Ellenbrook (2km)
7. To follow this pretty section, take the branch left (if coming from Monton Green) by the Greenleaf Lane overbridge. This leads to a tunnel (lit) underneath the East Lancs. Road and then along an increasingly narrow path through thick woodland, the path

Below: The Tydesley Loop. *Author*

eventually following the top left hand shoulder of the deep cutting. Rather overgrown at its western end, not much more than a footpath width.

Extension to Worsley Dam (1km)
8. 300 metres past the Worsley Road overbridge (beyond Worsley station), steps on the left by a wooden gateway lead into a bridleway. This crosses another railway path (leading to Worsley Road). Follow the bridleway past the garden of a house to where, in the woods, the track meets the track around Old Warke Dam. Turn left along the dam fence, the track leading into Mill Brow and down to Worsley Dam.

ROUTE 5
SALFORD'S LOOPLINES

THE ASHTON CANAL

The Ashton Canal has one of the few canal towpaths in the North West along which British Waterways have recently given permission to use for cycling. It forms an 11 kilometre, 7 mile traffic-free corridor from Ashton in the Pennine foothills directly into Manchester city centre. Whilst much of the canal is industrial, there are some attractive green areas, including gardens, recreation grounds and areas where vegetation and wildlife flourish by the canalside. Local electric train services (with guard's van for cycles) which operate between Manchester Piccadilly and Guide Bridge can be used for an outward or return trip — including the need to ascend to Ashton past 18 locks — but remember there are no trains on Sundays.

PLACES OF INTEREST ALONG THE ROUTE

Ashton Town Centre:

This bustling town, the administrative centre of Tameside, in Greater Manchester, has a large, attractive pedestrianised town centre and market place. The Parish Church of St Michael and All Angels is mentioned in the Domesday Book, whilst the present medieval building has some magnificent 15th century stained glass. In the Town Hall is the Museum of the Manchesters, which tells the story of the Manchester Regiment in a vivid manner. Exhibits include a reconstructed World War 1 trench, a World War 2 air-raid shelter and a feature about 'Women at War'.

Portland Basin Industrial Heritage Centre:

Portland Basin lies at the meeting point of three canals — the Ashton, the Peak Forest and the Huddersfield. The Portland Basin Industrial Heritage Centre, in a fine 1834 warehouse, has exhibitions which illustrate many aspects of local history. Goods are being loaded on to a traditional narrowboat in the loading bay, whilst further inside the warehouse exhibits and photographs recall the local cotton and printing industries, mining, engineering and even a nonconformist chapel. Don't miss the fine waterwheel by the quayside. Open daily 10am–5pm (except Mondays) all year — admission free.

Ashton Canal

The Ashton Canal was opened in 1797 and soon linked four important Northern canals: the Bridgewater, the Rochdale, the Huddersfield and the Peak Forest. It has 18 locks and by 1838 was carrying an estimated

Above: The Ashton Canal. *Author*

514,214 tonnes of freight annually — mainly coal and limestone. Parallel competing railway lines and later roads eventually took away much of this freight, and it was finally closed and abandoned in 1958. However, the growth of leisure traffic on the canals brought about its revival, and it was reopened in 1974 and now forms a key part of the popular 'Cheshire Ring'.

Fairfield Moravian Settlement

At the edge of Droylsden, between the A635 and the canal, is a village developed by the Moravian Church in 1785, a nonconformist religious sect which originated in what is now the Czech Republic. The village with its elegant Georgian houses was designed by Henry le Trobe, who also worked on the Capitol Building, Washington, and is now a conservation area.

Manchester City Centre:

It's only a short distance from Ducie Street Canal Basin to Piccadilly Gardens and the heart of Manchester with its huge choice of shops, museums and big city attractions. It's worth following the canal towpath along the opposite side of Ducie Street along the towpath of the Rochdale Canal, leading underneath the city to Castlefields, with its reconstructed Roman Fort and the excellent Manchester Museum of Science and Industry — but remember cycling is not permitted on this towpath.

Parking: Large free car parking area behind Portland Basin in Ashton — follow the brown signs from the centre of Ashton. Parking also available at Guide Bridge Station for rail users.

Public Transport: There are stations at Ashton (Manchester Victoria–Huddersfield–Wakefield line), Guide Bridge and Manchester Piccadilly (Manchester Piccadilly–Hadfield line). Hourly service between Ashton and Victoria; half-hourly service between Piccadilly and Guide Bridge. No trains on either line on Sundays.

Distance: 11 kilometres — 7 miles

Map: Landranger 109

Surfaces & Gradients: Gravel towpaths throughout — suitable for touring bikes. Steep gradients alongside each of the 11 locks.

Roads & Crossing Points: None on the towpath itself, but roads with busy traffic have to be negotiated in both Ashton and Manchester centres.

Refreshments: Choice of pubs and cafés in Ashton and Central Manchester. Look out for the Strawberry Duck pub in Audenshaw, a noted real ale house. It is on the right by the footbridge and the locks at Crabtree Lane, Openshaw.

Starting Points: The Portland Basin, Ashton; Ducie Street Basin, Manchester; Guide Bridge (see public transport access).

Above: The chancel of St Michael and All Angels, the parish church of Ashton.
Peter Waller

ROUTE INSTRUCTIONS:

1. From Portland Heritage Centre entrance, cross the footbridge over the Huddersfield Canal and the single arched stone bridge over the Peak Forest Canal, and follow the towpath westwards.

2. The towpath remains on the south bank of the canal as far as Forge Lane where, at the locks, the path crosses the canal at a spiral bridge, under the road bridge, and continues into central Manchester on the north bank.

3. Keep to the right of the lock-keeper's cottage as you enter Ducie Street Basin to return to the towpath.

4. Where the towpath ends, follow the tarmac path into Ducie Street. Turn left. About 220m on the left is the rear car park and entrance to Piccadilly station. Turn right at London Road traffic lights for Piccadilly Gardens.

From Ashton station

5. Ashton station is one kilometre (just over half a mile) from Portland Basin — best route from the station is to turn left from the station to Ashton Market, right down Old Street (pedestrianised) along Warrington Street, at the end of which an underpass under the A635 leads to Lower Wharf Street. Turn right, but bear right along a narrow passageway alongside the Asda store. Go through the underpass, keeping ahead along

Below: Manchester is home to one of the few second-generation tramways as yet built in Britain. It links Bury in the north with Altrincham in the south, with the street running through Manchester city centre. *Peter Waller*

Hill Street, then turn left (brown signs) to Portland Basin.

From Guide Bridge station

6. From Guide Bridge station turn left outside the station entrance, then first left into the station car park. Head for the far side of the car park where, in the right hand corner, a narrow enclosed footpath leads behind the signalbox to a long footbridge (steps) over the railway and sidings. The path turns right above and alongside the canal towpath for 250m to where, beyond a footbridge, steps lead down to towpath, 1km southwest of Portland Basin.

From Manchester Piccadilly station

7. From Manchester Piccadilly station take the side entrance on the right hand side of the ticket barrier (as you come out of the barrier), leading into the car park. Cross to the car park entrance which leads into Ducie Street. Turn right and Ducie Street Canal Basin is 220m on the right.

ROUTE 6
THE ASHTON CANAL   ASHTON-UNDER-LYNE

DROYLSDEN

Ashton Canal

Portland Basin (1)
(5) P

Ancoats
(3)   Openshaw
(4)
(2)
Guide Bridge (6)
(7) Piccadilly Station
MANCHESTER

N

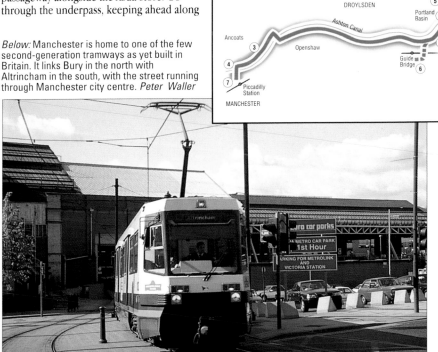

THE TAME VALLEY TRAIL AND THE DELPH DONKEY

The little River Tame, a tributary of the Mersey, comes down from the high Pennine moors, its fast flowing waters attracting early water-powered mills that brought industrial development, its steep-sided valley a natural communication route for road, canal and railway. These two linked cycle routes use former railway lines which now form corridors of delightful semi-wild countryside through a valley rich in industrial history and architectural interest, always with a backcloth of magnificent moorland scenery — yet so very close to the centre of Manchester.

PLACES OF INTEREST ALONG THE ROUTE

Uppermill
This former cotton mill village — one of several which make up the township of Saddleworth — enjoys new prosperity as a popular tourist centre, with speciality shops along its high street and in a converted mill. There's an attractive central park, and a former canalside woollen mill now houses the excellent Saddleworth Museum of local history. Close by is a statue commemorating Ammon Wrigley, Saddleworth's poet and local historian who died in 1946.

Greenfield
Greenfield in the Chew Valley, a side valley of the Tame, perhaps hasn't the immediate charm of Uppermill, but enjoys fine moorland surroundings. At Friezland, between Greenfield and Mosley, there is a horse access and exercising area alongside the trail.

Mossley
Like Greenfield, Mossley is very much a working community with mills and factories and has a busy town centre — though with some fine mill buildlings and areas of woodland between the trail and the Huddersfield Canal and River Tame in the valley bottom.

The Tame Valley Cycleway
The Micklehurst Loop, as it was known, was opened by the London and North Western Railway on the Manchester–Huddersfield –Leeds main line in 1883 between Stalybridge and Diggle. The six-mile line was built because the other side of the valley was too narrow to accommodate the two additional tracks required to carry the booming passenger and freight traffic of the time. The loop was closed in 1966 and its tunnels at Butterhouse, Royal George and Micklehurst were quickly filled in. Five kilometres (3 miles) of the route, between the long-vanished former Butterhouse and Micklehurst tunnels, have been converted into a route for walking, cycling and horseriding which offers a fine traffic-free corridor along the valley side.

The Delph Donkey

The Delph Donkey took its name from the little tank engine which regularly puffed its two coaches up this 1½-mile branch line which ran from a junction off the main line near Greenfield to the moorland village of Delph. Closed in 1963, about half the route has been converted into an excellent walk, and cycle path, with particularly good views across the Upper Tame Valley. The moorland village of

Delph is a further 2km from the terminus of the cycle path, but along busy roads.

Brownhill Vistor Centre

Converted canalside cottages by the Huddersfield Canal enjoy a dramatic setting under the huge stone arches of the Saddleworth viaduct. The Visitor Centre has displays of local and natural history, and a range of leaflets and guidebooks.

Distance: Five kilometres — 3 miles — along the Tame Valley Trail; plus 2 kilometres — 1 mile — approximately along the Delph Donkey from Brownhill.

Starting Points:
Brownhill Visitor Centre is the natural starting point to visit both the Tame Valley Trail and the Delph Donkey. The trail can also be joined from Uppermill — along Smithy Lane and Station Street — follow road right before the overbridge towards the swimming pool; at Greenfield; at Friezland Riding Arena (alongside the trail); and at Mossley.
From Mossley follow Station Road (reached off Micklehurst Road) to the start of the trail.

Parking: There is a small car park at Brownhill Visitor Centre on the A670 and an overflow car park 200m to the north at the Wool Road Transhipment Warehouse car park. There is also

a public car park on Smithy Lane in Uppermill and at Friezland. Limited car parking in Mossley and Greenfield (by sports centre) and near the Royal George.

Public Transport: Trains operate every hour between Manchester Victoria, Huddersfield and Wakefield (Mondays to Saturdays only) serving Greenfield and Mossley stations — each 1km (about ½ mile) from the Tame Valley Trail.

Links to other cycle routes: Route likely to be extended down the Tame Valley via Stalybridge and to the Ashton Canal (Route 6).

Map: Landranger 109

Surfaces & Gradients: Crushed sandstone and fine gravel throughout. Some short, steep sections to access both the Tame Valley Trail and the Delph Donkey from Brownhill. Gentle gradient up the Delph Donkey. Steep ascent on the main road into Delph.

Left: The Brownhills Visitor Centre. *Author*

Above: The Tame Valley Trail wends its way through the Pennine foothills. *Author*

Roads & Crossing Points: Great care needed to cross the A670 from Brownhills Visitor Centre or Wool Road car parks. Minor estate roads at Lower Arthur in Uppermill. Busy main road (A669) to be crossed at Greenfield and near The Roaches, and into the centre of Mossley and into Delph village. Keep children under supervision at all these points.

Refreshments: Excellent choice of cafés and pubs at Uppermill. Pubs in Greenfield and Mossley. Cafés and pubs in Delph. Limited light refreshments at the Brownhill Visitor Centre. Attractive picnic site on the far side of the canal from the centre — close to the start of the Delph Donkey Trail.

ROUTE INSTRUCTIONS:
The Tame Valley Trail
1. From Brownhill Visitor Centre, the Tame Valley Trail is reached about 500m along Brownhill Road, climbing the steep lane which leaves the A670 opposite the car park (walking recommended — the occasional car uses this narrow lane). Over the brow of the hill a pedestrian gate leads to a new track which runs past the vanished entrance to Butterhouse Tunnel. Follow the track as it bears right behind Uppermill.

2. To reach Uppermill, take the access road which leads from the swimming pool and sports centre along Station Road and Smithy Lane.

3. Keep directly ahead across the main road at Greenfield.

4. At the Royal George triangle, cross the main

Below: Rail, canal and cycleway in close proximity. *Author*

road to the track across a triangle between roads, uphill, keeping slightly left to join the continuation of the trail to Micklehurst.

5. Track descends left to an attractive mill and canalside area below Quickwood.

The Delph Donkey
6. To reach the Delph Donkey from Brownhill Visitor Centre, take the path to the left of the visitor centre to the canalside, cross the stone bridge below the locks and follow the lane past the picnic area climbing steeply uphill, under a railway bridge. The entrance to the Delph Donkey Trail is a few metres beyond the bridge on the right.

7. The trail ends after a little over a kilometre (about three quarters of a mile), but a narrow cul-de-sac path on the trackbed, somewhat overgrown, can be followed beyond this point, which ends at a highway depot — no public access. Though the route is signed from the exit point down to the main road and up to Delph village, this is along a busy main road including a very busy crossroads over the A62 and is not recommended for inexperienced cyclists.

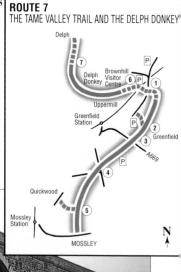

ROUTE 7
THE TAME VALLEY TRAIL AND THE DELPH DONKEY

Delph

7

Delph Donkey

Brownhill Visitor Centre

6

1

Uppermill

Greenfield Station

2

3 Greenfield

A669

4

Quickwood

5

Mossley Station

MOSSLEY

N

LEEDS—LIVERPOOL CANAL
ALONG THE AIRE VALLEY

Airedale is the Yorkshire dale which reaches into the very heart of the city of Leeds. Despite two centuries of industrial and urban development, it provides an extended green corridor into the city centre which remains remarkably unspoiled. There's no better way of discovering this hidden beauty than from the towpath of the Leeds–Liverpool Canal.

PLACES OF INTEREST ALONG THE ROUTE

Leeds-Liverpool Canal

The oldest surviving trans-Pennine waterway, the Leeds–Liverpool Canal was opened between Bingley and Shipley by 1777, and has many features from that period: locks, bridges, sluices and wharfside cottages, dating from the late 18th century. Where heavily laden barges once carried coal, chemicals, limestone and wool between Lancashire and Yorkshire, leisure craft and anglers now enjoy the peace and quiet, through an area as rich

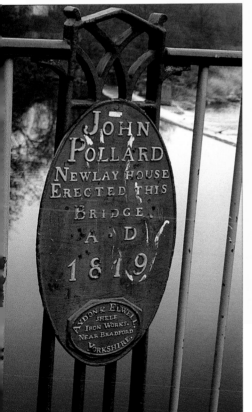

in early industrial history as it is in natural beauty. The cycle path is likely to be improved to the village of Saltaire in the near future.

Shipley

This busy mill town has largely been absorbed in the outskirts of Bradford, but keeps its own identity with a market place, a Regency church, and unique five-platform triangular junction railway station dating back to Midland Railway days.

Buck Wood

This long deviation past attractive Buck Wood and around the hill known as the Nosegay obviates the need for a tunnel — as used by the railway — reflecting the fact that the Leeds–Liverpool Canal was built before later tunnel techniques had been fully developed. The sewage works at Esholt (well screened) take its name from a village where in medieval times there was a nunnery, and which is now the setting for the television soap opera *Emmerdale*.

Apperley Bridge

Apperley Bridge refers to an ancient bridge across the River Aire. A fine old coaching inn — the George and Dragon — is to be found nearby. Dobson's Lock is one of the most picturesque on the canal. Canal cottages at this point contain the area offices of the Leeds–Liverpool Canal. The next stretch of the canal below Calverley Woods is one of the loveliest along the entire Leeds–Liverpool Canal.

Rodley

Another small canalside mill settlement, Rodley was famous for its crane works, Smiths and Booth cranes being found all over the world. The whole of the canalside from here to the centre of Leeds now forms part of the Leeds Waterfront Heritage Trail.

Newlay Bridge and Bramley Fall Woods

The 18th century Abbey Inn at Newlay offers

Left: A cast sign at Newlay, near Leeds, records the history of this bridge over the Leeds-Liverpool canal. *Author*

welcome refreshments. Nearby is one of the oldest iron bridges in England, built across the Aire by John Pollard of Newlay House and dating from 1819. Bramley Fall with its series of locks was the site of extensive quarries from where gritstone was taken for use in many famous buildings — including Kirkstall Abbey itself.

Kirkstall Abbey
It's worth deviating from the canal (see route instructions) to explore the ruins of this remarkable 12th century Cistercian abbey, set in beautiful parkland, with a small museum close by.

Armley Mills
There is easy access from the canal to the huge riverside Armley Mills, a vast early 19th century water-powered mill complex. It now houses the Leeds Industrial Museum, one of the best museums of its kind in Britain, packed with displays of the industries that made Leeds famous — textiles, tailoring, engineering, together with a water-powered fulling mill, steam engines and even an early cinema.

Leeds Canal Basin and Granary Wharf
There's no more spectacular entry into Leeds than along the canalside and into the historic canal basin where the Leeds–Liverpool Canal feeds into the Aire and Calder Navigation. This leads directly into the remarkable Granary Wharf shopping and market area inside the dark arches below Leeds station, where the River Aire roars underneath.

Starting Points: Shipley station and Granary Wharf. Access is also possible at several other points along the canal, including Apperley Bridge, Rodley, Newlay and Kirkstall Bridge.

Parking: Large car park at Shipley (rail users only) and in Leeds Granary Wharf — access from Neville Street (by railway station) or along Water Lane.

Public Transport: Fast, frequent rail services between Leeds and Shipley on electric MetroTrain services Leeds–Keighley–Skipton (Airedale Line) and Leeds–Shipley–Bradford Forster Square. Trains have cycle-carrying capacity in guard's van.

Cycle Hire: Watson Cairns & Co, Lower Briggate, Leeds, LS1 6NG. Tel: 0113 245 8081.

Distance: 21 kilometres — 13 miles

Map: Landranger 104

Surfaces & Gradients: Good — well surfaced gravel. Gradients level apart from

Above: Leeds Basin — eastern extremity of the Leeds-Liverpool Canal has seen much investment over recent years. *Author*

short sharp descents (in the Leeds direction) alongside the locks.

Roads & Crossing Points: None except for crossing the main road at the entrance to Shipley station. Heavy traffic in Leeds city centre along Neville Street to Leeds station (200m) — walking may be advisable.

Refreshments: Pubs at Apperley Bridge (George & Dragon) Rodley (The Railway, Rodley Barge), and Newlay (Abbey Inn). Small picnic area at Newlay. Choice of facilities in central Leeds, in and around Granary Wharf.

ROUTE INSTRUCTIONS:
1. From Shipley station main car park (reached off the main Leeds road from Shipley traffic lights) cross to the Bull Inn on Briggate, to the left of which a footpath leads to a metal bridge over the canal. Turn right along the canal towpath. The towpath remains on this side of the canal, alongside several locks down to Leeds Canal Basin.

2. For the George and Dragon Inn leave the towpath at Apperley Road, at Millman Swing Bridge just after Dobson's Lock and follow (quiet) lane to Apperley Bridge.

3. For the Abbey Inn and Newlay Bridge, leave the towpath at the little picnic area by Newlay Bridge into Pollard Lane and turn right to the inn close by the railway. Newlay Bridge lies another 100m beyond the railway bridge.

4. To reach Kirkstall Abbey, leave the towpath at Leeds Bradford Road Bridge and continue along Bridge Road to the traffic lights, turning left along Abbey Road at the lights — extremely busy with traffic. To avoid the traffic, a footpath (no cycling) leads from Bridge Road beyond the

Right: A typical stretch of the Leeds-Liverpool Canal tow path.
Author

department store and Kirkstall Light Railway into the abbey grounds.

5. At Leeds Canal Basin keep left past the car park into Granary Wharf and under the Dark Arches. Turn left at the entrance to Granary Wharf along Neville Street to City Square and City station (steps on the left by the pedestrian lights provide a short cut into the station).

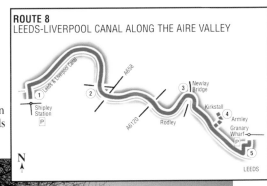

ROUTE 8
LEEDS-LIVERPOOL CANAL ALONG THE AIRE VALLEY

THE HARLAND WAY — WETHERBY TO SPOFFORTH

Where once the crack 'Queen of Scots' Pullman ran between London, Leeds, Harrogate and Edinburgh, a cycleway meanders from the market town of Wetherby through lush countryside to the village of Spofforth with its medieval castle. Part of the proposed through cycle route from York to Harrogate, this section is named in memory of Peter Harland, President of Wetherby & District Lions Club, one of the moving spirits of the project who died during its planning stage.

PLACES OF INTEREST ALONG THE ROUTE

Wetherby
Wetherby, an ancient market town overlooking the River Wharfe, has a fine stone bridge downstream from the ancient weir which once powered the town's corn mill. The town, now mercifully bypassed by the A1(M), was an important staging post on the Great North Road to Scotland. Several old stage-coach and posting inns remain, including the Swan &

Talbot and The Angel, once known as 'Halfway House' because it was midway between London and Edinburgh. There's also a choice of cafés and shops, whilst the attractive local cream-coloured limestone gives a warm feeling to the many historic buildings and narrow streets in the town including the Town Hall, Church Street and The Shambles.

The Wetherby–Harrogate Railway Line
The York and North Midland Railway — later the North Eastern Railway — between Church Fenton and Harrogate was opened as far as Spofforth on 10 August 1847. A spur direct to Leeds via Cross Gates opened in 1876 and a new station was built in 1901 south of the triangular junction (now the car park) on Linton Road to allow express trains from Leeds to use the line without reversing. Despite its potential for commuter traffic into Leeds, the line was closed to passengers on 4 January 1964, an early and much lamented victim of the Beeching Axe, and converted for cycle use between Wetherby and Spofforth in 1993.

Spofforth
A large village which keeps its character despite its new commuter housing. There's a main street of mellow cottages, a church dating from late Norman times, a Georgian rectory and village green.

Above: A group of youngsters enjoy the freedom and security offered by the Harland Way. *Author*

Spofforth Castle

Really a large fortified house rather than a castle, this splendid ruin dates from the 14th century when Henry Percy, ancestor of Shakespeare's Hotspur, was given permission by the King to fortify his house. Built from fine red sandstone, remains of a tower, the kitchen and Great Hall with 15th century windows can be seen. Owned by the village but in the care of English Heritage, the castle is open at all times.

Kirk Deighton

Reached by a bridleway spur off the Harland Way, as it name implies Kirk Deighton is dominated by its handsome Norman church with a 14th century tower and spire — a notable local landmark. A pleasant street of period cottages leads uphill to the church.

Starting Points:
Easiest access is at the southern point of the triangle at the former Wetherby station car park on Linton Road — reached just along Westgate, the A661 Harrogate road, from the centre of Wetherby, bearing left at the first junction to Linton. The alternative route is reached along North Street and Deighton Road. From Spofforth direction, the way is accessed directly off the A661 in Spofforth village along an estate road by the old station site.

Parking: Large free car park at the start of the way on Linton Road (ample additional parking in Wetherby town centre). Restricted parking in Spofforth village.

Public transport: Frequent bus from Leeds — less frequent from Harrogate and York. No cycle-carrying facilities.

Cycle Hire: Harrogate Spa Cycles, 1 Wedderburn Road, Harrogate HG2 7HQ. Tel: 01423 887000.

Distance: 5 kilometres — 3$\frac{1}{2}$miles — plus 1.5km — 1 mile — to Spofforth Castle and 3km — 2 miles — to Kirk Deighton.

Map: Landranger 104

Surfaces & Gradients:
Fine compressed gravel throughout. Gradients slight, but modest ascent along the bridleway into Kirk Deighton village.

Roads & Crossing Points: None on the Harland Way, but to reach Spofforth village centre and Spofforth Castle it is necessary to cross the A660. Busy main roads have to be negotiated into the centre of Wetherby. Short stretch of lane into Kirk Deighton village.

Refreshments: Large choice of pubs and cafés in Wetherby. The Railway Inn at Spofforth has a direct access from the Harland Way, a child-friendly beer garden, food and real ale.

Left: An attractively laid out board giving information about the route.
Author

Route instructions:

1. From Wetherby station car park, it is worth completing the eastern section of the triangle — an attractive, tree-lined path in deep cutting. Otherwise take direct path along old trackbed into the outskirts of Spofforth.

2. Informal path branches off the Harland Way as you reach Spofforth direct to the beer garden of the Railway Inn.

3. For Spofforth Castle, turn right along the (busy) main A661 for 150m, then where the main road bends keep straight ahead along a quiet lane. Continue past the village hall and recreation ground to a narrow path, left, which leads to the castle (signposted and open at all times).

4. For Kirk Deighton village, take the narrow bridlepath (earth-surfaced) which leaves the Harland Way to the right (coming from Wetherby) just beyond modern housing on the outskirts of Wetherby, soon reaching a farm track which ascends a gentle hill to join the lane into Kirk Deighton. The church is at the top of the village.

ROUTE 9
THE HARLAND WAY – WETHERBY TO SPOFFORTH

Right: Spofforth Castle. *Author*

THE SELBY TO YORK CYCLE PATH

This cycle path links the cycle-friendly city of York with the old town of Selby, lower down the shallow Vale of York. One of the first cycle paths in North Yorkshire, it was opened in 1987 by former world champion racing cyclist Beryl Burton. Much of the route uses the former East Coast main line railway and is on embankment which gives fine views across the surrounding, mainly flat, arable countryside, punctuated by clumps of attractive woodland.

PLACES OF INTEREST ALONG THE ROUTE

The York–Selby Railway

The former Great Northern main railway line between London and York was threatened by the massive new Selby coalfield in the 1970s, when constant risk of mining subsidence would have prevented InterCity trains from operating at high speed. A new stretch of main line was therefore financed by the National Coal Board and opened in 1983. The old route was converted in stages by Sustrans into a walking and cycling route. A notable feature is the number of modern sculptures at Mileposts along the route, many of them reflecting a strong link with deep coalmining.

Bishopthorpe

Now a modern commuter village, Bishopthorpe takes it name from the ornate Bishopthorpe Palace on the River Ouse, official seat of the Archbishop of York.

Naburn Swing Bridge

The railway path goes across this fine swing bridge over the River Ouse, built to permit large vessels to go up river as far as the city of York. There is now a busy marina and camp site close by. At Howden Lane Bridge nearby there is a viewpoint looking across to York Minster.

The Maze

An unusual feature, in a cutting just south of the minor road and car park between Escrick and Stillingfleet, this maze makes an interesting diversion and a challenge for children old or young.

Left: The dramatic lines of York Minster, one of the greatest of all English Gothic churches.
Peter Waller

Riccall

A pleasant village, with two inns. The village is most notable for its church with a richly decorated Norman doorway on the south side and many other interesting features. There is the tower of a windmill to the southwest of the village.

Selby

Reputedly the birthplace of King Henry I, this medieval port on the River Ouse has a magnificent abbey church, founded in 1069 by the monk Benedict of Auxerre who is said to have had a vision of three swans, signifying the Holy Trinity, alighting on the riverside close to where the church and town now stands. The swans are incorporated in the town's coat of arms. There are many fascinating old buildings, including Yorkshire's oldest railway station (not the present one but close by) now used as a warehouse.

Starting Points: York, Selby or Riccall.

Parking: Public car parks in York (eg the 'park and ride' on Tadcaster Road) and Selby. Street parking in Riccall. There is a car park on the cycle path near the maze on the Stillingfleet–Escrick road.

Public Transport: Excellent local and express rail services from Leeds and Manchester to both Selby and York — and (more limited) local train services between Selby and York. Cycles carried free on local trains without booking if space permits.

Cycle Hire: York — Cycle Scene, 2 Radcliffe Street YO3 6EN. Tel: 01904 653286 York Cycle Works (April-September only), 14–16 Lawrence Street, York. Tel: 01904 626664

Distance: 24 kilometres — 15 miles

Map: Landranger 105. York City Council have an excellent map of cycle routes within the city — available at any tourist office.

Surfaces and gradients: Crushed gravel — firm, clean — good for touring or mountain bikes. Mostly flat — hardly any gradient.

Roads & Crossing Points: Minor roads, some traffic-free in York. Through Riccall, the route follows a quiet lane round the back of the village. Some terraced back streets into the centre of Selby.

Refreshments: Excellent choice of facilities in both York and Selby. Two inns and a shop in Riccall.

ROUTE INSTRUCTIONS:
From York
1. From York station turn left outside the entrance down Station Avenue, going straight across at the traffic lights, bearing right under the city walls and across the lights into Rougier Street. Turn left at the opening by the bridge to the riverside by Tanners Moat, the start of the bike route, marked with a small blue bike lane sign.

2. Follow North Street round until the traffic lights across Micklegate. Go straight ahead and take the bike route which forks off left soon after. This tarmac bike path follows the

Right: The Norman great west door at Selby. *Peter Waller*

River Ouse out of the city, before eventually bending sharply right up an embankment.

3. The path crosses Bishopthorpe Road before crossing a playing field and the edge of The Knavesmire, York Racecourse.

4. At the next junction turn sharp left to go under the bridge. The path follows the side of the A64 York bypass dual carriageway (the cycle path along Sim Walk from the Tadcaster Road 'park and ride' joins here) before descending to another junction. Turn left under the road tunnel to join the railway trackbed.

5. The route passes alongside a housing estate in Bishopthorpe, turning right to follow an estate road for a short distance before rejoining the railway trackbed. The path now follows the route of the former East Coast main line, taking a very straight course.

6. Soon after the car park on the Escrick road you reach the maze in a cutting — a good lunch stop.

7. At Riccall the old railway line is occupied by the new A19 trunk road, so the bike route turns into the village along a back lane. Go through Riccall until the road meets the A19 again and take the bike path which runs alongside the main road.

8. After about one kilometre (half a mile), the bike path turns off again to run down a back road. Follow this until the roundabout, where the path turns to the right, marked by blue bike path signs.

9. The route into Selby centre goes down to the river bank and runs by the Rank Hovis river frontage, before dropping down the embankment to run along quiet back streets to the old toll bridge in Selby.

10. From the bridge turn left down the road to the railway station. The station is on the right just before the railway bridge.

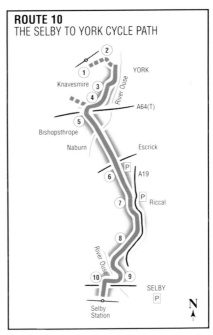

ROUTE 10
THE SELBY TO YORK CYCLE PATH

Below: Converted railway lines make ideal cycle routes. *Author*

THE SOUTH HOLDERNESS RAIL TRAIL

Holderness, the most easterly part of Yorkshire, has a character all of its own — an area of quiet, gentle countryside dominated by attractive villages, rich in history, many with magnificent churces, including those at Hedon and Patrington, easily accessible off this route which begins barely a kilometre from the centre of the city of Hull.

PLACES OF INTEREST ALONG THE ROUTE

The Hull and Holderness Railway
The Hull and Holderness Railway was built to serve the new coastal resort of Withernsea and opened in 1853. Suffering financial problems at first, it was taken over by the North Eastern Railway in 1862 and was soon bringing thousands of visitors to the seaside, not only from Hull but from as far away as Nottingham and Newcastle, as well as serving local communities. It was still carrying 132, passengers per year and 800 tonnes of produce a week when it was closed as part of the Beeching policy of eliminating rural branch lines in 1965. It was bought by Humberside County Council in the 1970s as a recreational route. Much of the line is now a nature reserve, and cyclists are asked to respect the vegetation and wildlife.

Hedon
Astonishing as it seems, Hedon, now inland, was one of the most important ports on the Humber in medieval times, being developed in the 12th century to export wool and cloth. It soon prospered, and though the harbour eventually silted up and its trade transferred to Hull, it still has many fine old buildings including a superb church and a fine town hall with an impressive coat of arms.

Burstwick
Burstwick once had a castle, the most important in Holderness, in which the wife of Robert the Bruce was imprisoned in 1306. It was abandoned in Elizabethan times when the owner, Sir Robert Constable, Lord of Holderness, moved to Burton Constable.

Keyingham
Keyingham, now five kilometres — three miles — from the river, was once, like Hedon on the Humber, a small port. In 1642 a French ship carrying arms came up Keyingham Creek in support of King Charles I, who was already being harassed by the Parliamentarians.

Above: A view looking east along the South Holderness Rail Trail. *D. Speakman*

The King visited the ship and people from Holderness declared their loyalty to the King, unlike those in Hull who were to close their gates to him, thus starting the English Civil War.

Winestead

This small village was the birthplace of Andrew Marvell (1621–78) one of the greatest poets of the 17th century. He was born in the Old Rectory and lived in the village until he was six.

Patrington

This village is famous for its church with its soaring spire. Known as the Queen of Holderness, it is a landmark over the flat countryside for many miles. With its cathedral-like proportions and rich medieval carving, this is reputed to be the most beautiful parish church in England.

Starting points: Hull city centre, Hedon or Patrington.

Parking: Hull city centre, Hedon or in Patrington.

Public Transport: Hull is served by Regional Railways services from many parts of England — cycles carried on most trains. Bus services (East Yorkshire) only from Patrington to Hull.

Links with other cycle routes: There is an extremely pleasant route along minor roads following the coast to Hornsea about 24km — 14 miles. This can be easily combined with the Hornsea Railway Path (Route 12) to make a longer or even a two-day trip.

Distance: 21 kilometres — 13 miles

ROUTE 11
THE SOUTH HOLDERNESS RAIL TRAIL

Below: Hedon Church. The scale of the building gives some indication of the wealth of the region during the Middle Ages. *Peter Waller*

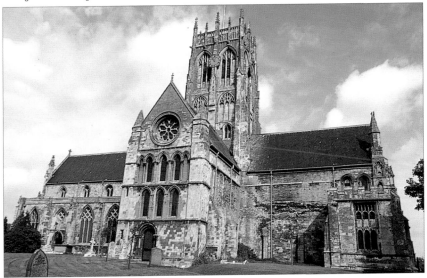

Map: Landranger 107. Humberside County Council publish a detailed map of the railway path.

Surfaces & Gradients: Cinder, earth, rough grass. Fairly rough going at the eastern end — more suitable for mountain bikes. No gradients.

Roads & Crossing Points: Minor roads from the centre of Hull, and along two points on the trail where the line is blocked. Patrington can be reached by approximately two kilometres (just over one mile) of main road.

Refreshments: Hull city centre, Hedon, Patrington — choice of shops, pubs and cafés. (The resort of Withernsea, with a good choice of refreshments and accomodation, lies 8km (5 miles) from the end of the route and can be reached by minor lanes — see below.)

ROUTE INSTRUCTIONS:

1. From Hull railway station turn right, take the first turn left, Albany Street, and follow the street along the bus/bike lane until the end. Turn right on to Alfred Gelder Street and continue straight ahead past the traffic lights, over the bridge (short bike lane provided) and straight across again at the next road junction. After about 100m turn right down East Street (or Wilson), a short street, then left on to a back road. Pass the Blacksmiths Arms, and continue straight ahead over the next junction to the end of the street to meet Abbey Street by a children's playground.

2. Turn left on to Abbey Street then turn right shortly after, on to a short bike lane which crosses the main road and joins Ellis Street. Continue straight ahead under the railway bridge to round the estate (Victor Street) and down to Belmont Street, straight ahead at the next junction. Continue straight ahead to a path marked by a sign 'Middleham Close'. Take the gravel path which soon widens and follows the route of an old railway. The track leads through the suburbs to the outskirts of Hull.

3. At the first diversion from the old railway at Keyingham take the track which leads off

on the immediate right. The track soon rejoins the rail trackbed once the house has been passed.

4. After Ottringham, the second short diversion, the route takes a narrow lane south, turning left at the first junction to rejoin the rail trackbed which narrows, becoming grassy and rougher as it continues.

5. The track ends abruptly south of Winestead by a garage. Turn right to go to Patrington which is about a mile down the main road.

6. For Withernsea take the minor lanes leading northwards from the A1033 via Winestead village and Willow House.

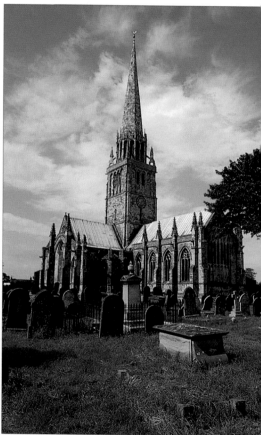

Above: The 'Queen of Holderness' — the superb parish church of Patrington. *Peter Waller*

THE HORNSEA RAIL TRAIL

The old railway line which runs from Hull to the busy resort of Hornsea across the central part of Holderness, crosses countryside of quiet beauty, rich in natural history interest, providing an ideal way to visit this popular East Coast resort.

PLACES OF INTEREST ALONG THE ROUTE

The Hull–Hornsea railway:

Joseph Wade of Hornsea, a Hull timber merchant who lived in Hornsea prompted this railway in order to develop Hornsea into a fashionable resort. It opened in 1864, despite costing 75% more than planned. Soon becoming part of the North Eastern Railway, which doubled the track and provided new stations, the line prospered for more than a century serving the needs of local agriculture as well as seaside trippers. The last passenger trains ran in 1964, and freight trains ceased a few months later in 1965. The line was acquired by East Riding County Council in 1971 for development into a walking and cycling route. It is now rich in natural history and users are asked to respect wildlife and not disturb vegetation.

The Foredyke Stream

The first section of the trail does not use the railway but the course of a stream which in medieval times was used by the monks of Meaux Abbey as a canal to take their wool in barges via Hull to fairs at Boston or Lincoln and even as far as Flanders or Italy.

Swine

There was a Roman fort just to the north of Swine village where, last century, a hoard of copper coins was

found. In 1150 a priory for Cistercian nuns was established here, and for a period it also housed monks. The Priory Church still serves the village as its Parish Church.

Skirlaugh

Skirlaugh derives its name from the Anglo-Saxon Skirle — the name of a local headman — and leah (meaning an area of woodland). The station was 1½ miles from the village it served.

Goxhill

A deserted medieval village with traces of a field system can be seen near the crossroads to the west. The present village has an unusual church, well worth a visit. The station was, however, called Wassand to avoid confusion with another station called Goxhill in Lincolnshire, but only had two market day trains per week and closed in 1904.

Hornsea

Described in railway posters as 'Lakeland by the Sea' because of its extensive mere, the largest freshwater lake in Yorkshire, rich in birdlife. Hornsea is famous for its pottery which is now a major visitor and leisure centre. Though no longer as busy as in its railway heyday, it is still an attractive sand and sea resort, and much of the old town, with stone and pebble cottages, has survived. In the main street is the Holderness Museum of Village Life. There is an excellent choice of accommodation.

Right: Market Weighton station — once a crossroads for a number of railway lines linking York, Hull, Driffield and Selby. *Author*

Starting Points: Hull, Hornsea or from the Skirlaugh picnic site and small car park.

Parking: Public car parks in Hull and Hornsea. Small car park on the A165 south of Skirlaugh where there is a picnic site directly on the trail. Car park by the end of the cycle path by the police station.

Public Transport: Rail services to Hull; bus services (East Yorkshire) only from Hornsea.

Distance: 23 kilometres — 13 miles

Map: Landranger 107

Surfaces & Gradients: Tarmac and compressed gravel (generally very good) but some sections of earth and cinder. Suitable for touring or mountain bikes. No gradients.

Roads & Crossing Points: Minor roads and cycle paths in the centre of Hull and in Hornsea.

Refreshments: In Hull and Hornsea — wide choice of facilities. Railway Inn near the old station at Ellerby.

ROUTE INSTRUCTIONS:
From Hull
1. From Hull railway station turn right, take the first turn left, Albany Street, and follow the street along the bus/bike lane until the end. Turn right on to Alfred Gelder Street and continue straight ahead past the traffic lights, over the bridge (short bike lane provided), and go straight across again at the next road junction along Clarence Street to the start of

Above: The cycle way opens up a completely different vista of the English landscape. *D. Speakman*

the trail at Spyvee Street on the right, turning along the now filled-in Foredyke Stream to the rear of Reckitt and Colman's factory, heading to and past the huge Bransholme Estate.

2. After 2 km (1¹/₂miles) you leave the path to branch right along the Hull-Hornsea railway line (waymarked). Follow the line which leads directly to Hornsea.

At Hornsea
3. Leave the line at the

Right The church of Holy Trinity, Hull. *Peter Waller*

southern end of Marlborough Avenue adjacent to Hornsea Pottery and close to the site of Hornsea Bridge station, and pass some new houses. A yellow waymark leads you on to the old trackbed of the rail trail again to the site of Hornsea Town station, close to the police station — built on the site of the old railway turntable.

4. If joining the trail from Hornsea, head for

the police station, close to the promenade and car parks overlooking the sea. The rail trail begins by the old station buildings and runs through the town to a roundabout on the edge of town. Take the minor road opposite, Marlborough Avenue, and turn right at the next junction past some new houses. A yellow waymark leads you on to the old trackbed of the railway again.

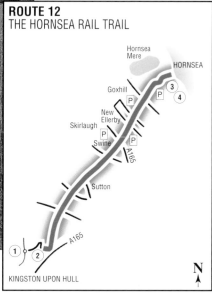

ROUTE 12
THE HORNSEA RAIL TRAIL

Hornsea Mere

HORNSEA

Goxhill
P ③
P ④

New Ellerby
Skirlaugh
P
Swine P
A165

Sutton

A165

① ②

KINGSTON UPON HULL

N

THE HUDSON WAY — BEVERLEY TO MARKET WEIGHTON

This cycle route through the gentle, undulating chalk hills of the southern Yorkshire Wolds links the historic town of Beverley with the little town of Market Weighton, and offers downland scenery with open fields and scattered woods more typical of southern than northern England. It's also an area rich in interest for the botanist, with important nature reserves alongside the track — enjoy but do not pick the wildflowers.

PLACES OF INTEREST ALONG THE ROUTE

Beverley
One of the most ancient and lovely towns in Yorkshire, with its cream stone and red pantiles, Beverley was the county town of the old East Riding of Yorkshire. It is particularly famous for its superb Minster, St Mary's church, its historic town walls and bars, its Guildhall and many outstanding attractive buildings in and around its largely pedestrianised town centre.

The Beverley to Market Weighton Railway Line — The Hudson Way
George Hudson, the York railway entrepreneur and financier, the so-called 'Railway King', planned the railway from York to Hull which was opened as far as Market Weighton in 1847, even constructing his own private station from nearby Londesborough Hall. Opposition by local landowners delayed the extension of the line for many years, until, after Hudson's disgrace, it was finally built by the North Eastern Railway in 1865. The line was the main freight and passenger route between York and Hull until becoming a controversial closure under the Beeching axe in 1965. It was acquired by East Riding County Council in 1971 for road improvements, but in 1983 Humberside County Council converted it into a cycleway and footpath.

Kiplingcotes Station
The hamlet of Kiplingcotes is notable for having one of England's oldest racecourses. The station is at the highest part of the route and now houses 'Grannies' Attic' a popular tea room and antique shop. There is a small car park and picnic area close by.

Kiplingcotes Chalk Pit Nature Reserve
Much of the line in this area has been designated a linear nature reserve, whilst the small quarry and chalk pit is carefully managed by Yorkshire Wildlife Trust. Access is on foot only and visitors must keep to the paths, and should respect wildlife. Look out for orchids, trefoil, thyme and campion, and a variety of butterflies in the summer.

Goodmanham
The village is reached by turning north at the

Below: The disused signalbox at Kiplingcotes has been restored and now stands sentinel over a different type of traveller — one who makes the trip from Market Weighton to Beverley under his or her own steam rather than behind the steam-powered locomotive. *Author*

point where the track meets a narrow lane to the village. The church of All Hallows in the village is believed to be on the site of a pagan temple which, in AD627, after the conversion of King Edwin and his kingdom of Deira to Christianity, was destroyed by Edwin's High Priest Coifi, and one of the region's first Christian churches built on the spot.

Market Weighton

Also Anglo-Saxon in origin, Market Weighton was granted a Royal Charter for a weekly market in 1252, and its geographic importance on trade routes between the Wolds and the Vale of York helped the town to grow in importance, as did its former role as a railway junction. Its greatest claim to fame was perhaps as the birthplace of England's tallest man, William Bradley (1787–1820) who reached the height of 7ft 9in and a weight of 27st. The son of a local butcher, he lived at Bradley House in the Linegate, now France's Cycle Shop, where a cast of his foot is to be seen in the wall, and he is buried in the church.

Starting Points:
Market Weighton — The Hudson Way starts from the old station site reached along Hall Road off Londesborough Road or north of Station Road which runs behind the church.

Beverley — New car park just off the new A1035 Beverley bypass north of the town; 2km (1¼ miles) from Beverley railway station.

Parking: Choice of car parks in both Market Weighton and Beverley; on Hudson Way car park off A1035 bypass; in Beverley; Kiplingcotes station; small car park off lane parallel to Hudson Way in Goodmanhamdale west of Kiplingcotes Chalk Pit Reserve.

Public Transport: Beverley station (2km from the eastern terminal of the way) is on the Hull–Bridlington–Scarborough Wolds Coast Line. Cycles carried on trains free of charge at guard's discretion. East Yorkshire Buses (every 2–3 hours) link York, Market Weighton and Beverley.

Links to other cycle routes: Market Weighton–Bubwith: a 19km (12 mile) railway path route from the Wolds westwards across the Vale of York. Starts 1km west of Market Weighton.

Distance: 11 miles — 17 kms.

Maps: Landranger 106, 107.

Humberside County Council issue a series of excellent route cards to the Hudson Way.

Above: Beverley Minster. *AA Photo Library*

Surfaces: Compressed chalk/gravel, ash or grass. Acceptable for touring bikes, but mountain bikes preferred.

Roads & Crossing Points: Minor lanes crossing at Goodmanham, and farm access tracks. However, busy and dangerous crossing — steps and ramps — along the B1248 north of Cherry Burton. Traffic travels at high speed — visibility poor, care required. Keep children under strict supervision at this point.

Refreshments: Excellent choice of inns and cafés in both Beverley and Market Weighton. Café at Kiplingcotes station; pubs in Goodmanham and Etton.

ROUTE INSTRUCTIONS:

1. From Beverley station follow Railway Street into the town centre, turning right along Eastgate and Butcher Row (pedestrianised) to Market Place, heading past St Mary's to North Bar Without, then turning right along Hengate to the traffic lights. Turn left along Manor Road, continuing into Woodhall Way (busy suburban road — care required) towards Molescroft. Where area of open grassland appears as the road forks, take the quiet road on the right which ends at a cycle and footway leading to the new bypass. Follow the signed path to the right, over the new

foot and cycle bridge over the bypass, to the start of the Hudson Way at the far side (car park close by).

2. At the B1248 past old Cherry Burton station take the steps and ramp down to the main road, crossing with extreme care (fast traffic) to the ramp and steps back up the embankment. (Safer access to both Cherry Burton and Etton village is available at the next overbridge).

3. In Market Weighton take the path which forks left behind the community centre and behind the church leading into the main street. (Access from Market Weighton market place is along St Helen's Square behind the parish church and into Station Road, which leads to an area of waste land, the old station site, where, on the right, the cycle path starts.)

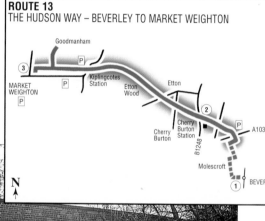

ROUTE 13
THE HUDSON WAY – BEVERLEY TO MARKET WEIGHTON

Above: On all the disused railway lines converted to cycleways there will be evidence of former use — here is a road over bridge. *Author*

DALBY, LANGDALE AND SNEATON FORESTS

The North Riding Forest Park in the North York Moors National Park is made up of a series of forests covering 27,000 hectares of trees stretching from South Durham into North Yorkshire. The forest in total produces 100,000 tonnes of timber per annum, but at the same time the area has been developed by Forest Enterprise for recreational use, with an excellent network of waymarked cycle routes.

This route follows the waymarked Forest Drive and a series of forest tracks to travel the length of the North Riding Forest Park between Dalby Forest and Sneaton Forest, crossing the spectacularly beautiful heather-clad moors above Goathland. For those who wish to shorten the route there are a number of waymarked alternatives, some of which use forest tracks.

PLACES OF INTEREST ALONG THE ROUTE

Dalby Forest
An attractive area of commercial forest, mainly of conifer plantations, but including Staindale Lake, an attractive small lake fringed by trees which is a popular place for picnics. The Dalby Visitor Centre is open 10.30am–4.30pm Easter–May, September–October and 10am–5pm May-September and includes an exhibition about the forest and the different trees within it.

Langdale Forest
A 45,000 hectare coniferous forest, planted between 1967–1977. The route crosses the forest climbing steadily up to the edge of Goathland Moor.

Goathland Moor
The route crosses Goathland Moor up to the summit of Stony Leas 299m above sea level. On the right is Lilla Cross and a dramatic viewpoint across the moors to the golf balls at Fylingdales Early Warning Station. The cross dates from the 7th century and was named after Lilla, a minister to King Edwin of Northumbria, who was supposedly murdered at this spot and buried in the ancient barrow on which the cross now stands.

Sneaton Forest
Sneaton Forest is also mainly coniferous trees, but as the route descends to May Beck it passes an attractive area of waterfalls. The woodland around the valley of Little Beck has recently been designated a Forest Nature Reserve and is a haven for birds and wildflowers.

Below: The North Yorkshire Forest. *Author*

Starting Point: Low Dalby Visitor Centre, just north of Thorton-le-Dale. Motorists will have to pay a toll to reach Low Dalby car park and visitor centre.

Parking: Low Dalby Visitor Centre car park. Parking is also available at Bickley Forest Gardens, Langdale Forest and at May Beck and Falling Foss in Sneaton Forest. There are also various smaller car parks at points along the forest drive. These include: Seive Dale, Staindale Lodge, Staindale Lake and Adderstone Rigg.

Public Transport: The nearest railway station at the southern end of the route is Scarborough and at the northern end Ruswarp. It is also possible to travel to Low Dalby by bus, using the MoorsBus service from Malton, York and Leeds. Cycles are, however, carried on the North York Moors Railway to Levisham (8km from Low Dalby) and Goathland (daily services in summer months, weekends only in spring and autumn) which links with the Esk Valley line from Middlesbrough or Whitby at Grosmont — Tel: 01751 472508 for details).

Links to other cycle paths: There are three promoted routes within Langdale Forest: a 4 mile (7km) route along forest roads, a 15km (8 mile) and a longer 24km (15 mile route) aimed at more experienced cyclists. There are also a number of challenge routes designed for mountain bikers. Contact the Forest District Office on 01751 72771 for further details.

Cycle hire: Cycle hire is available from Dalby Visitor Centre and at Bickley Forest Gardens throughout the summer and at weekends March–September. Also from Wardill Bros Thornton-le-Dale. Tel: 01751 474335.

Distance: 27 kilometres — 17 miles. This route can easily be shortened either by taking a circular route within Dalby Forest (12 kilometres or 7.5 miles) or by starting and finishing the route at intermediate car parks along the way.

Maps: Ordnance Survey Outdoor Leisure 27, North York Moors-Eastern area. A map is also available from Low Dalby Visitor Centre showing this route and others within the North Riding Forest Park.

Surfaces & Gradients: Forest roads, rough in places. Some steep gradients — mountain bikes recommended.

Roads & Crossing Points: This route uses part of the Forest Drive, for about half of its distance, which in the height of summer can sometimes be busy with other vehicular traffic, though speed restrictions are in force.

Above: The North Yorkshire Forest. *Author*

Refreshments: Low Dalby Visitor Centre.

ROUTE INSTRUCTIONS:
1. From Low Dalby Visitor Centre, turn right to follow the Forest Drive past Staindale Lake and Adderstone Rigg. For those who wish to shorten the route and return to Low Dalby Visitor Centre where the Forest Drive turns 90° left, turn right along a forest road, which bends sharply left and then right before descending down Housedale to Low Dalby.

2. To continue along the forest drive until a road junction, turn left and follow the road to where it crosses a stream, turn right and then left to follow a forest road through Langdale Forest to emerge at an area of open moorland, Goathland Moor.

3. Go straight ahead into Sneaton Forest, continuing through the forest to where the route joins the B1416. Take the first left back to Little Beck.

ROUTE 14
DALBY, LANGDALE AND SNEATON FORESTS

Ruswarp

Littlebeck

Whitby

P

Sneaton Forest

Lillacross

Langdale Forest

Scarborough

Toll

Dalby Forest

Forest Drive

Low Dalby Visitor Centre

Optional loop to shorten route

i P

Toll

Thornton-le-Dale

N

Above: Cycle hire at Dalby in the North Yorkshire Forest. *Author*

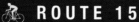
GUISBOROUGH FOREST

Forming the largest single block of woodland in Cleveland, Guisborough Forest stretches from the town of Guisborough southwards up a steep escarpment to the open moorlands of the North York Moors National Park. The Forestry Commission has recently developed a cycle route through Guisborough Forest on the flanks of Roseberry Topping, aimed at mountain bikers. For those who are looking for something less strenuous, the car park at Pinchinthorpe is sited midway on the 3.5km (two mile) Guisborough Branch Walkway, an attractive level path open to both pedestrians and cyclists.

PLACES OF INTEREST ALONG THE ROUTE

Guisborough Walkway
Until 1960 the line between Middlesbrough and Whitby had a branch line serving Guisborough station on a short spur from Morton Carr, near Nunthorpe, via Pinchinthorpe (where there was a station by the level crossing) and Hutton Gate. This meant that all through trains on leaving Guisborough had to reverse back on to the main line. This section of the line is leased by Cleveland County Council from British Rail under licence to use as a walkway and a cycleway.

Roseberry Topping
At 320m — 1,051ft high, with its pointed summit, Roseberry Topping, an outlier of the Cleveland Hills, is a major landmark and viewpoint in Cleveland. Its craggy western, stepped outline was caused by a landslip resulting from ironstone mining on the flank of the hill.

Guisborough Forest
An attractive area of mainly coniferous woodland, including Hutton Lowcross and Hanging Stone Woods, full of interesting wildlife. Access is possible for mountain-bikers along a network of bridleways and forest tracks easily accessed off the walkway.

Hutton Village
A small former mining village on the northern edge of the North York Moors National Park. This was an area of extensive ironstone mining in Elizabethan times; much of the old working is now concealed by forestry. The incline railway to Cod Hill mine above Hutton has long vanished.

Guisborough
Guisborough (3km or 2 miles) from Pinchinthorpe car park was once the ancient capital of Cleveland. It is an attractive market town, dating back to Saxon times and with a market cross and a long linear street fringed with cobbles. A market is held on Mondays and Saturdays. Guisborough still has its 12th century Augustinian Priory now in ruins and in the care of English Heritage (open 1 April–31 October, daily; 1 November- 31 March, Wed-Sun 10am-4pm).

Below: Guisborough Forest. *Author*

Starting Point: Pinchinthorpe car park off the A173 just after the junction with the A171 between Middlesbrough and Guisborough.

Parking: Pinchinthorpe car park on the A173 south of Guisborough.

Public Transport: The nearest railway station is Nunthorpe on the Middlesbrough–Whitby line, 2km (1 mile) from the start of the route.

Distance: 8.5 kilometres — 5½ miles — plus 3km — 2 miles — along the railway path.

Maps: Landranger 93 Middlesbrough, and 94 Whitby. A leaflet showing the route is also available from Forest Enterprise tel: 01751 72771.

Surfaces & Gradients: Rough and stony terrain. Steep hills at various points. Mountain bikes strongly recommended. However, the railway path is perfectly suitable for touring bikes.

Roads & Crossings Points: Short section of road (1.6km on the route).

Refreshments: None on route. There are a number of pubs and cafés in Guisborough.

ROUTE INSTRUCTIONS:
1. Leave Pinchinthorpe car park and go on to the A173 southwards. Continue for 150m then take the grassy bridleway, left, heading towards the forest.

2. Ignore the turning on the left and continue straight ahead following the blue waymarks along the forest track.

3. Follow the waymarks through the forest to emerge at a minor road. Turn left and continue through Hutton Village. Just beyond the village, take a bridleway on the left and follow it back to Pinchinthorpe car park.

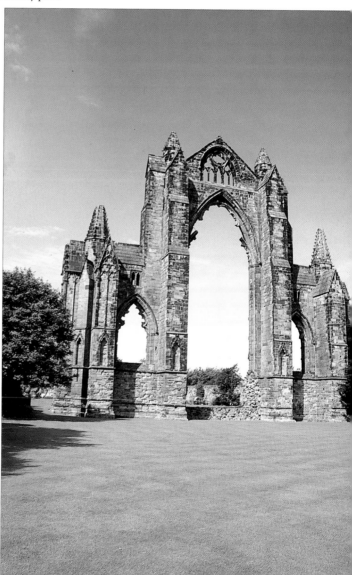

Below: The stark ruins of the east front at Guisborough Priory. *Peter Waller*

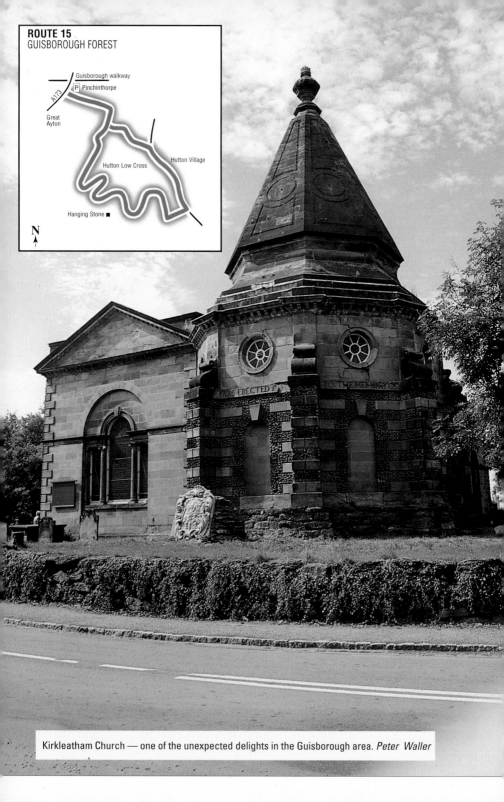

Guisborough walkway

P Pinchinthorpe

A173

Great
Ayton

Hutton Village

Hutton Low Cross

Hanging Stone ■

N

Kirkleatham Church — one of the unexpected delights in the Guisborough area. *Peter Waller*

THE SCARBOROUGH–WHITBY TRAILWAY

The Scarborough–Whitby Trailway in the North York Moors National Park follows the line of the old Scarborough to Whitby railway along a spectacular route around the North Yorkshire Heritage Coast. It offers some dramatic views over such famous landmarks as Robin Hood's Bay, Boggle Hole and Whitby Abbey. This cycle route is probably one of the most scenic in the North of England, serving an area mostly inaccessible by road, across undulating pasture and wooded dales, skirting the edge of some of Britain's finest and grandest cliffs.

The Scarborough–Whitby line was opened in 1885, having taken 13 years to build and represents a dramatic piece of engineering which included the 13-arched, 915ft-long viaduct over the River Esk and the climb between Robin's Hood's Bay to Ravenscar, once one of the steepest gradients on English railways at 1 in 39. Not only did the line cost substantially more than was envisaged, with many investors losing money, but it was never profitable and finally closed in 1965.

PLACES OF INTEREST ALONG THE ROUTE

Scarborough

An elegant seaside resort, with fine beaches and attractive Victorian promenades, Scarborough was a fashionable watering place where the Victorians came to enjoy sea-bathing and fresh air. Today, Scarborough is still a popular seaside destination with visitors enjoying its elegant parks and cliff-top walks. The town is dominated by its 12th century Castle, now in the care of English Heritage. Scarborough castle is open 1 April–31 October 10am–6pm; 1 November–31 March 10am–4pm. Admission charge.

Ravenscar

From Ravenscar there are some dramatic views over Robin Hood's Bay. This section of the coast is managed and owned by the National Trust, which owns over 10 miles of the North Yorkshire and Cleveland Heritage Coast. An introduction to the coast is provided in a series of exhibitions at the Coastal Centre; open daily from Easter to the end of September, which stands adjacent to the trailway. At Ravenscar the railway went through a 279yd tunnel which was built on the instructions of one of the directors of the line who owned Raven Hall and didn't wish the line to obscure his view of the coast. In the 1890s, there were plans to develop Ravenscar as a seaside resort. Roads, a water supply and drains were laid and over 1,500 plots offered for sale, but in this rather windswept location the idea never caught on.

Peak Alum Works

Close to the trailway, linked by footpath, lies the Peak Alum Works which was founded in 1650 and eventually closed in 1862. Alum was used for fixing cloth dye and tanning leather. Ships moored at a purpose-built jetty to bring in iron, lead and barrels of urine – an essential ingredient in the alum-making process. The

Below: The Whitby-Scarborough route near Ravenscar. *Author*

alum works have now been restored by the National Trust.

Robin Hood's Bay

Known locally as Bay or Bay Town, Robin Hood's Bay is a delightful collection of tightly packed houses and narrow streets connected by narrow cobbled passageways and short flights of steps. Standing huddled against the sea, the brightly coloured cottages with their pantile roofs and tiny wooden porches were said to have been so closely built together so that the womenfolk would have company, when the men were away at sea. Once a thriving fishing centre, in the 17th and 18th centuries, Robin Hood's Bay was also a haven for smugglers. It was said that a bolt of silk could be passed from the houses near the sea to

the cliff top, without it seeing daylight, via interconnecting doors and cellars.

Whitby

An attractive fishing town, based around a harbour from which lead narrow cobbled streets. Whitby is famous for its jet, a black stone found only in and around the town and which became popular in Victorian times when it was elaborately carved into cameos and other pieces of jewellery. Standing above the town and reached by 199 steps, is Whitby Abbey, an ancient holy place and once the burial place of kings. The abbey was host to the famous Synod of Whitby in the 7th century, presided over by Abbess Hilda where the Roman and Celtic churches agreed the date of Easter. The remains of the abbey date mainly from the Benedictine Church of the 13th and 14th centuries. It is open daily 10–6pm (4pm October– March). Admission charge.

ROUTE 16
THE SCARBOROUGH-WHITBY TRAILWAY

WHITBY
River Esk
Viaduct
B1447
Robin Hood's Bay
Tunnel
Ravenscar
North Sea
A171
Cloughton
Scalby
Scalby Cut
N
A170   SCARBOROUGH

Starting Point: Scarborough, Safeway's car park. Just off West Parade on Falsgrave Road. The trail could also be started/finished at Scalby, Cloughton, Ravenscar, and Robin Hood's Bay

Parking: Various public car parks in Scarborough; parking at Ravenscar and Robin Hood's Bay.

Public Transport: The nearest railway station is Scarborough. There are also railway stations at Whitby and Ruswarp at the end of the route.

Below: Robin Hood's Bay. *Author*

Cycle hire: At Robin Hood's Bay: Bay Bike Hire, Glenray, Station Road, Robin Hood's Bay. Open all year, but notice preferred. Also at Whitby. Tel: 01947 880488/820326. North Road Cycles, Whitby. Tel: 01947 820326.

Distance: 29 kilometres — 18 miles. The trail can be shortened by beginning the route at various mid points.

Maps: Landrangers 94 and 101. A leaflet is also produced by Scarborough District Council showing the route and providing a brief history of the line. Tel: 01723 373333.

Surfaces & Gradients: Gravel, stony in some sections. Generally a level route with only a few slight gradients.

Roads & Crossing Points: Several minor road crossings and two short sections of quiet road at Scalby and Ravenscar.

Refreshments: Café in Ravenscar; large selection of pubs and cafés in Robin Hood's Bay and Whitby.

ROUTE INSTRUCTIONS:
1. The trail starts at the far end of Safeway's car park where a tarmac path follows the line of a former cutting through northern Scarborough, passing a cemetery and continuing along the edge of a housing estate towards Scalby.

2. The trail continues to Scalby where the route crosses the Scalby Cut at a brick viaduct. From the viaduct continue up Chichester Close to the road. Cross the road and then turn up Field Close Road on the opposite side of the road and then right along Lanchester Way to rejoin the trail.

3. The trail continues to the outskirts of Cloughton where it deviates from the former trackbed through the old goods yard and then continues to Staindale and Ravenscar.

4. At Ravenscar the original tunnel has been closed and the trail continues along a minor road through the village. Where the road swings sharply left, continue down a rutted track which is signposted to rejoin the old railway just north of the tunnel entrance. The trail continues to Robin Hood's Bay, where part of the trackbed is used as a linear car park.

5. The trail ends at Esk Viaduct $2\frac{1}{4}$km ($1\frac{1}{2}$ miles) from Whitby, where there is a path from the embankment down to the road below. Cyclists wishing to continue to Whitby should turn right along the road to where it meets the A171 at crossroads. Continue straight ahead following the River Esk into the centre of Whitby. For those cyclists preferring to end their journey at Ruswarp (1km — $\frac{3}{4}$ mile — railway station) turn left along the road to where it meets the B1416 and a Bridge over the river Esk. Ruswarp station is on the right hand side.

Below: The Whitby-Scarborough route near Ravenscar. *Author*

THE HART–HASWELL WALKWAY

Like many of the Durham cycle paths, the Hart–Haswell Walkway and Cycleway follows the line of an old railway. It passes through some very attractive countryside with views of the coast and to the Cleveland Hills. The first section of the route between Castle Eden and Hart provides a high quality level surface, without any major road crossings. The second half of the route is more suitable for mountain bikes, when the terrain becomes stony and grassy in places; the route also crosses the Wingate bypass beyond Castle Eden.

PLACES OF INTEREST ALONG THE ROUTE

The Hart–Haswell railway line

Originally the line's promoters intended to build a line between Moorsley near Houghton-le-Spring to the new docks at Hartlepool, and George Stephenson was employed to survey the line. However, during construction the cost of the line escalated and the company decided to revise the original scheme and open the line from Hartlepool only as far as Haswell with a branch line to Thornley.

The line was heavily used until 1905 when the Sunderland–Hartlepool line was built and new pits were opened along the coast. Despite the withdrawal of passenger services in the 1960s, the line continued to be used for freight, and only closed in 1980 after the closure of Thornley colliery.

Crimdon Beach

A footpath from Hart station leads to Crimdon beach — a large expanse of sand dunes which includes the Hart Warren dunes, a Site of Special Scientific Interest by virtue of its rich plant and insect life which includes the rare Durham Argus butterfly as well as the common lizard and slow worm.

Castle Eden

A scattered community which has maintained much of its rural charm. Unlike many of the neighbouring communities, Castle Eden's development was based not on the exploitation of coal but on the patronage of a local family, the Burdon family, who settled here in the 18th century and completely rebuilt the medieval church and castle. Castle Eden is also the home of the Castle Eden brewery, which is now owned by the Whitbread group. The brewery was once attached to Castle Eden Inn, but moved to their present premises in 1826 where Castle Eden Ale is still brewed.

Above: The Hart-Haswell Walkway. *Author*

Shotton Colliery

Shotton was once famous for having the biggest pit heap in the UK, which was disparagingly described by J. B. Priestley as a 'depressing smoking volcano'. The colliery was first opened in 1840 and by 1913 employed 1,833 men producing over 400,000 tonnes of coal. The colliery finally closed in 1972, making nearly 800 men redundant.

Tuthill Quarry

This was once the site of a former World War 2 munitions factory. When the rail lines were removed, the area was flooded and this has now been developed as a wetland area with a boardwalk to provide access to the pond, now home to the crested newt.

Haswell:

This pleasant linear settlement dates back to medieval times, but it was in the 19th century that it grew into a small town. The first pit was sunk in 1831 and it was in Haswell that the cage pulley system was first pioneered. In 1844 tragedy hit the Haswell pit when an explosion killed 95 men. When an official inquiry concluded that there was 'no blame attributable to anyone' the owners had no moral or financial liability to provide for the miners' widows and children which left many in financial hardship, dependent on a relief fund which was set up to help them. The Haswell colliery pit head still stands as tribute to the history of this mining community.

Starting Point: Hart station, just off the A1086 between Hartlepool and Blackhall colliery. Take the first turning on the left before the first roundabout on the approach to Hartlepool.

Parking: Hart Station; Hesleden; Castle Eden, opposite the Castle Eden Inn; Shotton Colliery old station and Haswell village.

Public Transport: The nearest railway station at the present time is Hartlepool (3½miles, 6km away), but there are plans to reopen Hart station in the near future.

Distance: 14.5 kilometres — 9 miles. It is possible to shorten the route by finishing at Castle Eden (6.5km, 4 miles).

Maps: Landrangers 88 and 93. A leaflet is also produced by Easington District Council. For details — Tel: 0191 527 0501.

Surfaces & Gradients: Wide, fine gravel path for first part of the route to Castle Eden. Route then narrows and becomes grassy in places and a little overgrown, suitable only for mountain bikes. No gradients — a level path.

Above: Crimdon Beach. *Author*

Roads and Crossing Points: Three road crossings, one of which is the busy A181.

Refreshments: Pubs in High Hesleden, Hesleden, Castle Eden, Shotton Colliery and Haswell.

ROUTE INSTRUCTIONS:

1. From Hart station follow the cycle path under the iron footbridge which continues through the edge of Crimdon Dene to a road.

2. Continue along the cycle path skirting the edge of Hesleden to reach Castle Eden where a road bridge crosses the route and a path on the left hand side leads to the inn and car park.

3. To continue, cycle straight ahead under the A19 to where the route ends at an embankment and set of steps at the Wingate bypass (A181). Ascend the steps and cross the road with extreme care and continue along the railway track which runs straight ahead.

4. Follow the cycle path through woods to Shotton Colliery to a road; continue straight ahead past the old station. Keep straight ahead past a pond, to a cutting and the end of the Hart–Haswell Walkway.

5. To continue to Haswell village, turn left along the farm track to a road and then right into Haswell.

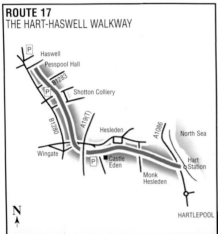

ROUTE 17
THE HART-HASWELL WALKWAY

Haswell
Pesspool Hall
B1283
Shotton Colliery
B1280
A19(T)
Hesleden
A1086
North Sea
Wingate
Castle Eden
Hart Station
Monk Hesleden
HARTLEPOOL
N

Below: The signposting along the Hart-Haswell Walkway. *Author*

THE AUCKLAND WALK

The Auckland Walk follows the line of the former railway which ran between Byers Green and Bishop Auckland, which was closed in 1939. Today the seven kilometre — four mile — section between Spennymoor and Bishop Auckland is an attractive tree-lined route for cyclists and pedestrians, providing fine open views over the Wear Valley towards the North Pennine hills.

PLACES OF INTEREST ALONG THE ROUTE

The Byers Green Railway

The railway line was built in two stages. In 1841 the section between Byers Green and Spennymoor was opened as part of the Clarence Railway Company's Byers Green railway which served Port Clarence on Teesside. This was used to carry coal from around Byers Green and Willington. In 1885 the NER opened a new section of the line between Byers Green and Bishop Auckland to passengers, and an extension was built to link the line to the present day East Coast main line at Cornforth.

Spennymoor

The trail begins on the outskirts of Spennymoor, a Victorian town which developed as a focal point for the mining communities which came to provide the labour force for the many mines in the surrounding area. Despite some unsympathetic modern developments, the town centre has recently been improved in ways which recapture its 19th century origins, complete with a Victorian-style bandstand.

Whitworth Hall

This is the former family home of 'Bonnie Bobbie Shafto', hero of the famous nursery rhyme. Whitworth Hall is reached by turning right where the cycle path meets Whitworth Road and is one mile (1.5 km) down the road. It is an attractive house which has been extensively restored, with some superb gardens which include a walled garden with greenhouses and a vineyard, Dene Gardens, two lakes and a deer park. Whitworth Hall also has its own brewery, winery and bottling plant. It is open Easter–September at weekends and Bank Holidays. Also open Mon, Tue and Wed from Spring Bank Holiday; Gardens 11am-6pm, Hall 1pm-5pm. Admission charge.

Below: The Auckland Walk. *Author*

Westerton Folly

Situated on a hill top in the middle of the village of Westerton, to the left-hand side of the Auckland Walk, is a round stone tower. This is Westerton Folly which was built in 1770 as an observatory tower by the astronomer and mathematician Thomas Green, famous for his work on the Milky Way.

Binchester

Binchester is now no more than an attractive group of cottages, but in Roman times it was a military station on Dere Street, the Roman road which linked Hadrian's Wall with York. The site of the fort, known as Vinovia, which means pleasant place, is a mile southwest of the present village. It includes the house of the fort commander which contains one of the best examples of a Roman military bath suite in Britain. Open Easter– October daily 11am–5pm. Admission charge.

Auckland Park

The Auckland Walk passes alongside the 800-acre Auckland Park which is the deer park belonging to the Bishop of Durham. When the line was first constructed, the then Bishop of Durham, Bishop Lightfoot, insisted that if the line had to cross the park, it should be hidden from view. So to placate the Bishop an extra wide railway bridge was constructed and planted with trees and the railway hidden in a deep cutting. Within the park there is an unusual Gothic-style deer shelter built in 1767 which consists of a square-walled enclosure surrounded by a higher arcaded outer wall, enabling the deer to shelter in the passage between the inner and outer walls. The entrance to the Bishop's Park is in Bishop Auckland and it is open to the public daily. Admission is free.

Starting Points:
Spennymoor, Princess Street. From the roundabout at the top of Spennymoor High Street turn up Clyde Terrace, signed Whitworth Hall, and then turn right at the Crown pub, into Princess Street. The route can also be started at Whitworth Road car park.

Parking: Spennymoor town centre, either at the leisure centre or limited parking at

Below: The Auckland Walk. *Author*

Right: The Bishop's Palace, Bishop Auckland. *Author*

Princess Street. Parking is also available at Whitworth Road car park.

Public Transport: The nearest railway station is Bishop Auckland, enabling the route to be cycled in reverse.

Links to other cycle paths:
Brandon–Bishop Auckland Walk begins north of Bishop Auckland. There are also proposals to open a new cycle

path from Bishop Auckland to Barnard Castle in the near future.

Distance: 6½ kilometres — 4 miles

Maps: Landranger 93. Durham County Council also produce a route card as part of the railway walks series. Tel: 0191 383 3354 for further details.

Surfaces & Gradients: Stony and rough in places, but mostly level with a few gentle gradients. Mountain bikes recommended.

Roads & Crossing Points: The route crosses two minor roads. Main roads have to be followed into Bishop Auckland town centre from the end of the trail.

Refreshments: Pubs and cafés in Bishop Auckland. Picnic site at Byers Green station.

ROUTE INSTRUCTIONS:
1. From Princess Street, turn immediately left and then right to pass a Methodist chapel and Victorian school. The cycle path starts on the far side of the school, by Princess Court. Continue past some allotments to emerge at a road opposite Whitworth Road car park.

2. From Whitworth Road car park follow the old railway track to intersect a road. Continue across the road, passing the old Byers Green railway station. The route continues past Auckland Park on the right and old Coundon station on the left, before emerging at a small car park just off the main A689.

3. There is no traffic-free route from here into Bishop Auckland and cyclists wishing to continue into town will need to use the busy main road, turning right at the next roundabout to reach the town centre.

ROUTE 18
THE AUCKLAND WALKWAY

BRANDON AND BISHOP AUCKLAND WALK

This route follows the line of the former Brandon–Bishop Auckland railway which was built to carry coal and coke for Wearside and Tyneside industry. It is an attractive route following the River Wear north from Bishop Auckland along the old Newton Cap railway viaduct which spans the river. This route provides wonderful views over the Wear Valley and is a haven for birds, with woodcock, common sandpiper, jay and nuthatch regularly seen along the route.

PLACES OF INTEREST ALONG THE ROUTE

Bishop Auckland
As its name suggests, the town derives its name from the Bishops of Durham who have used the town as their principal residence since Norman times. At its centre is a fine 19th century town hall and clock tower, overlooking an attractive market place. The Bishops' association with the town began in the 12th century when Bishop Puiset built a manor house as a more spacious alternative to his home, Durham Castle. In the 13th century under Bishop Beck, the manor house was converted into a castle and as the principal country residence of the Bishops was continually enlarged and beautified. Although much of the Palace was destroyed in the 1650s, after the restoration of the monarchy it was restored to some of its former glory by Bishop Cosin. The Palace's chapel, St Peter's, was originally a sumptuous banqueting hall, but was converted under Cosin to a chapel, and it is reputably one of the largest private chapels in Europe. Both the chapel and the state rooms, including the Bishop's throne room, are open to the public May–September, Bank Holiday Mon, Sun, Wed & Thur 2–5pm and Tue 10am–12.30pm, and Saturdays in Aug 2–5pm. Admission charge. The 800-acre Bishop's Park is open to the public throughout the year and admission is free.

Hunwick
The area around Hunwick was an important producer of bricks and within a four-mile stretch along the Wear Valley there were six brickworks. There is still a large brickworks perched on the brow of the hill at Todhills.

Above: Brancepath Castle. *Author*

Willington

A pleasant linear town stretched along the A690, with several old coaching inns. Willington was an important centre for coke production, when it became the headquarters of Messrs Straker and Love who leased the collieries in this area and made a fortune from a process which used poor quality coal to make good quality coke.

Brancepeth

Where the route crosses a road by Brancepeth station, turn right to visit Brancepeth, a 19th century estate village which was rebuilt as part of the developments created to improve the

approach to Brancepeth Castle. This originally medieval castle was bought in 1796 by a Sunderland banker for £70,000. His son, Matthew Russell, rebuilt the castle at a cost of over £100,000 in Norman style with towers modelled on chess pieces and an imposing gateway complete with portcullis. The castle is now a private residence, but it is possible to visit the church which is situated in wooded grounds. The church is one of the finest in County Durham; it is a large important looking building with a 12th century tower and fine 17th century woodwork including an impressive rood screen, pews, pulpit and ceiling.

Starting Point: Newton Cap Viaduct car park, just off the A689 road to Crook, north of Bishop Auckland town centre.

Parking: Parking at north end of Newton Cap Viaduct. If cycling the route in reverse, parking is also available at Broompark car park near Durham. From the A167, take the A690 towards Crook and take first right (B6302). Broompark picnic site is signposted on the left hand side.

Public Transport: Bishop Auckland railway

station is at the south of the town. Durham station is 3.25km (2 miles) from the end of the route.

Cycle hire: Nearest outlet is in Durham: Dave Heron Cycles, 6 Neville Street. Tel: 0191 384 0287 – selection of mountain bikes to suit all sizes; 24 hours' notice required.

Links to other cycle paths: From Bishop Auckland it is possible to join the Auckland Walk which starts one mile south of the town. There are also plans in the near future to

Below: Bishop Auckland — the principal residence of the Bishop of Durham. *Author*

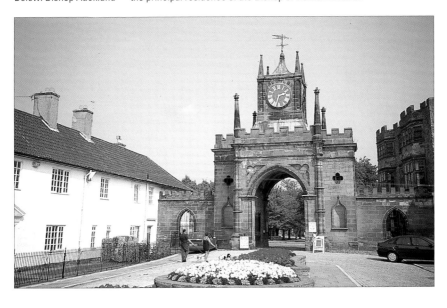

develop a cycle path between Bishop Auckland and Barnard Castle. There are links from Broompark picnic site to the Deerness Valley Walk and the Lanchester Valley Walk.

Distance: 14 kilometres — 9¹/₂ miles

Maps: Landranger 88, 92 and 93. Durham County Council also produce a route card as part of the Durham Railway Walks series. Tel: 0191 383 3354 for details.

Surfaces & Gradients: Gravel track for most of the route, stony in places. Level with a few gentle gradients.

Roads & Crossings Points: Several minor road crossings; care needed at Willington where the route crosses the A690.

Refreshments: Pub alongside cycle path near Hunwick village. Pubs at Willington and Brancepeth.

ROUTE INSTRUCTIONS:
1. From the car park at Newton Cap Viaduct, follow the cycle path through trees following the line of the River Wear to the edge of Willington.

2. At Willington the route continues over the road and through a set of concrete bollards to follow a tarmac path for a short distance to a road. Continue along a narrow path which runs to the left of a block of flats to emerge by Willington Library, at a main road, the A690. Cross this road with care and look for a set of gates on the right which marks the continuation of the trail.

3. Continue along the trail, past Brancepeth station and through Brandon. The path descends a hill steeply, to cross the River Deerness via a footbridge and continues up the hill to Broompark car park.

ROUTE 19
BRANDON AND BISHOP AUCKLAND WALK

Above: The Brandon and Bishop Auckland Walk. *Author*

THE DEERNESS VALLEY WALK

The Deerness Valley Walk is a cycle and walkway which goes through a part of County Durham whose landscape has been entirely shaped by the coalmining industry in the 19th century, with the creation of new towns and villages surrounding the pit heads. Today little is left from the mining era — the collieries and drift mines have all disappeared leaving a landscape which looks deceptively rural.

PLACES OF INTEREST ALONG THE ROUTE

The Deerness Valley line
This railway, which opened in 1853, was once one of the main arteries serving this section of the Durham coalfield with branches to New Brancepeth, Ushaw Moor, Stanley, Hedleyhope and Consett. The line finally closed in 1965 and has been transformed into an attractive tree-lined cycling route from the outskirts of Durham to the edge of the Durham Dales.

Ushaw Moor
The picnic area at Ushaw was once the site of Ushaw Moor Colliery and the pit head gear still survives. On the right is Ushaw College, a Roman Catholic seminary with an impressive Victorian chapel. The college once had a swimming pool which was filled with water raised hydraulically by the power of the river.

Esh Winning
A typical mining village whose importance is demonstrated by the size of its Miners' Hall. Indeed, Winning means a successful shaft or coal face. Largest of the former colliery villages, there are pubs, shops and a café by the village green.

Waterhouses
Another former pit village with an attractive church built of locally-fired distinctive off-white bricks. From Waterhouses the route continues up the Stanley Incline where a stationary steam engine at the top of the hill hauled trucks up and gravity took them down.

Crook
There are plans to extend the Deerness Valley Walk into Crook, but at the moment those wishing to visit Crook have to continue by busy road (see directions overleaf). Crook derives its name from its location on an obvious bend in the River Wear. A market town which is now the administrative centre of Weardale, it has a large square at its centre which in summer is bedecked with flowers.

Above: Durham Cathedral. *AA Photo Library*

Starting Point: Broompark picnic site. From the A167, take the A690 towards Crook and take first right (B6302). Broompark picnic site is signposted on the left hand side.

Parking: Broompark picnic site. Also available at Ushaw colliery and at Esh Winning.

Public Transport: Durham station is 3.5km (2 miles) from Broompark picnic site.

Cycle hire: Nearest outlet is in Durham: Dave Heron Cycles, 6 Neville Street. Tel: 0191 384 0287 — selection of mountain bikes to suit all sizes; 24 hours' notice required.

Links to other cycle paths: Links from Broompark picnic site to Lanchester Valley Walk and Brandon–Bishop Auckland Walk.

Distance: 13 kilometres — 8 miles

Maps: Landrangers 88 and 92. A route card showing the route of the Deerness Valley Walk together with other railway walks is available from the Environment, Department Durham County Council. Tel: 0191 383 3354.

Surfaces & Gradients: Fine gravel, stony in places. Level path with moderate gradients, but steep climb at the end of the route.

Roads and Crossing Points: Four minor road crossings on the trail. Busy roads from the centre of Durham and from the end of the trail into Crook.

Refreshments: Pubs and café in Esh Winning and Crook. Pub at Hamilton Row.

ROUTE INSTRUCTIONS:
1. Begin at Broompark picnic area and at the junction of cycle paths turn right to follow signs to the Deerness Valley Walk, turning right to follow the path along the River Deerness. The trail crosses a road and continues straight ahead over a narrow footbridge crossing the River Deerness.

2. The trail crosses another footbridge; a path on the right leads to a picnic site. Keep to the main route under a large bridge. The trail continues through Esh Winning and Waterhouses and emerges at a road junction at Hamilton Row.

3. Continue straight ahead with the trail climbing steeply to emerge at a road. Continue straight ahead to another road, the B6299, on the outskirts of Crook where the route terminates.

4. For those wanting to continue into Crook, take the first road on the right and then turn right again into the centre of Crook (2.5 km, 1½ miles; steep descent).

Below: Converted railway tracks provide a safe environment for cyclists of all ages. *Author*

Right: Cyclists will encounter a great variety of road surfaces — from mud through sand and gravel to tar macadam. *Author*

ROUTE 20
THE DEERNESS VALLEY WALK

Esh
Winning

Ushaw
Moor
Colliery

Ushaw
Moor

B6302

A167

Waterhouses

Hamilton
Row

River Deerness

P

Broompark
Picnic site

A690

B6299

CROOK

N

ROUTE INSTRUCTIONS:

1. From Broompark car park cross an area of open grassland, signed railway paths, and at the junction of paths turn left to follow signs to the Lanchester Valley Walk.

2. Continue along the trail to a road and the edge of Langley Park village. Continue over the road and take a ramped path on the left hand side which leads back on to the old trackbed.

3. The path continues through Malton picnic area past Lanchester station. The route continues over Accommodation Bridge to Hurbeck Farm, where the route has recently been extended into Consett.

4. From Hurbeck Farm turn left along a farm track, past some cottages. Then follow a way-marked stony path alongside the road and turn right down a track. The track bends right to emerge at a road. Continue across the road and follow the trail to cross a road and go under a rail bridge to a second bridge marked by a large iron smelt wagon. Follow the cycle path on to the bridge. Straight ahead is Hownes Gill car park.

5. This is Lydgett's Junction where the four cycle paths meet: the Lanchester Valley Walk, Consett–Sunderland Railway Path, Derwent Walk and the Waskerley Way. For Consett turn right and follow the Consett–Sunderland path into Consett. To reach the town centre, where the path forks alongside the A692, ignore the right hand fork signed 'C2C' and continue straight ahead past a row of terraced houses, Gill Street, to a cyclists' and pedestrian bridge crossing the main road. Go over the bridge and continue straight ahead into the town centre.

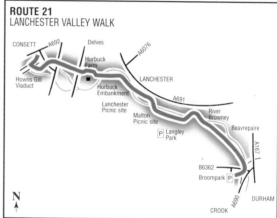

ROUTE 21
LANCHESTER VALLEY WALK

Below: The Lanchester Valley Walk follows a disused railway line. *Author*

CONSETT AND SUNDERLAND RAILWAY PATH

This railway path is constructed on one of Britain's oldest railways, the Stanhope and Tyne Railway, which was first opened between Stanhope and South Shields in 1834. The western half of the line now forms the Waskerley Way and like that section of the line, the line east was also made up of a number of inclines between Annfield and Chester-le-Street, which were worked by horses and stationary engines. Through running was only achieved in 1893, with a nine-kilometre (six-mile) detour. The line was mostly employed carrying iron ore, coal and other minerals, through a landscape of typical Durham mining communities.

The track was lifted in 1985 and Sustrans acquired the section between Consett and East Washington to create a traffic-free route. Throughout the 35km (22 miles), the railpath is decorated with various environmental sculptures using materials which reflect the industrial heritage of the area. These include the two famous earthwork sculptures by Andy Goldsworth: 'The Lambton Worm' and 'The Maze'. There is also

David Kemp's menacing 'Head for the Hills' built out of scrap transformers and Sally Matthew's quizzical 'Beamish Shorthorns', a herd of grazing cows made of scrap iron.

PLACES OF INTEREST ALONG THE ROUTE

Consett

Consett was once home to the massive Consett Steel Works, the largest steel complex in Europe. This Victorian town is now fighting back from the recession-hit 1980s, with the building of new superstores and the refurbishment of its town centre. Consett acts as the hub of four major cycling routes within County Durham and has a network of cycle paths serving its town centre.

Stanley

Stanley is a windswept market town which was once a mining community. In its churchyard stands a memorial to 168 men and boys who were killed in an underground explosion in 1909.

Beamish, The North of England Open Air Museum

Buildings from throughout the North East have been brought to Beamish and carefully re-erected brick by brick. The museum features a high street with its Co-op and dentist, a station, pit village and working farm, linked by vintage tram and bus. Beamish sets out to re-create life

Below: The Consett-Sunderland Railway Path at Stanley. *Author*

ROUTE 22
CONSETT AND SUNDERLAND RAILWAY PATH

in the North East in the early 1900s, and the buildings and their contents are brought to life through staff dressed in the period of the day. Open April–October 10am-6pm, and in winter till 5pm except Mondays. Admission charge.

Chester-le-Street

A pleasant market town on the River Wear, Chester-le-Street holds an open air market on Tuesdays and Fridays. The town dates back to Roman times when it was the site of a fort and civilian settlement on the Roman road between Brough and Pons Aelius on the River Tyne. Close to the town centre is the church of St Mary and St Cuthbert which dates from 1250 and has a spire more than 50m tall. The remains of St Cuthbert were placed here for a short time on their way to Durham Cathedral. An exhibition at Anker House Museum tells the history of church and town. Open April–September, 10am–4pm daily except Sundays.

Washington

This is a relatively new town, built in the late 1960s in a series of districts or numbered estates, around a group of older villages. About a mile from the route is Washington Old Hall, a small sandstone manor house, owned by the National Trust, in which the ancestors of George Washington lived. Closer to the route is the Washington Arts Centre, venue for a variety of exhibitions and which has a licensed bar. The Washington Wildfowl and Wetlands Centre on the banks of the River Wear is a 100-acre site and home to over 1,200 birds. It is open between 9.30am–5pm daily in summer.

Penshaw Monument

The Penshaw Monument dominates much of the Consett–Sunderland Path, which beyond Washington finally skirts around the bottom of Penshaw hill on which its stands. It was built in the form of the Greek Temple at Theseus in 1844, to the memory of the Earl of Durham, John George Lambton, who had died four years earlier.

Sunderland

Dominated by the magnificent 1928 Wearmouth Bridge, Sunderland is one of Britain's newest cities, having been elevated to city status in 1992. Once the home of shipbuilding, coalmining and glass making, Sunderland's shipyards were formerly second only to the Clyde in output. Today the city is looking to new hi-tech industries to revive its fortunes and much of the Wear has been landscaped to provide an attractive riverside area. The church of St Peter, founded in AD674, is one of the country's most important early Christian sites and is attractively situated overlooking the harbour.

Below: A signpost on the Consett-Sunderland Railway Path records part of The Celestial Railroad. *Author*

Starting Point: Hownes Gill picnic site, signposted off the A692 between Consett and Castleside. It is also possible to start the route from Consett town centre. This route may be shortened by using a number of alternative starting points along the way.

Parking: Hownes Gill car park. Also available at Consett, Annfield Plain, Stanley, Beamish, Chester-le-Street and James Steel Park, Washington.

Public Transport: There are railway stations at Chester-le-Street and Sunderland.

Cycle Hire: Darke Cycles, 113 High Street West, Sunderland SO1 1TR. Tel: 0191 510 8155

Links to other cycle paths: At Hownes Gill Viaduct, links to Waskerley Way, Lanchester Valley Walk and the Derwent Walk.

Distance: 35 kilometres — 22 miles.

Maps: Landranger 88. A map of the route is also available from Sustrans on 0117 926 8893.

Surfaces & Gradients: Fine gravel and tarmac for the majority of the route. Level for the majority of the route with moderate gradients. Two steeper sections at Washington where the route crosses the River Wear.

Roads & Crossing Points: There are a number of minor road crossings. Small section of road near Washington at crossing of River Wear, and in Pallion, Sunderland.

Refreshments: Pubs and cafés at Consett, Stanley, Chester-le-Street. Pubs in Annfield Plain, Beamish village and at the Washington Arts Centre.

ROUTE INSTRUCTIONS:
1. From Consett go down Sherburn Terrace, by the Braes Hotel, and then turn right down Wear Street to a bridge over the A692 which provides a safe crossing over the road for pedestrians and cyclists. Turn right on the other side of the bridge to follow a shared cyclist and pedestrian pavement to join the Consett–Sunderland rail path.

2. From Hownes Gill picnic site follow the trail through the outskirts of Consett and Leadgate to cross the A693 into Annfield Plain. Continue through the town, crossing the main road via the crossing and continuing towards Stanley, passing several sculptures along the route.

3. From Stanley continue past Beamish, Pelton and under the A1 to reach the outskirts of Washington.

4. Following the 'C2C' signs on the far side of Washington to turn right down a footpath which runs alongside a railway. After a short distance turn left under a bridge to enter the James Steel Park. Turn immediately right and follow a path through the park to reach the River Wear. Cross the river by the footbridge.

5. From the footbridge, turn left and follow the road up a steep hill and then turn left on to the old railway just before the T-junction is reached. Continue along this path to join the road at Pallion.

6. Continue along the road for a short distance and then turn right to follow the cycle path into Sunderland city centre. The trail ends in a park, opposite Sunderland Bus Station.

Below: The North of England Open Air Museum at Beamish has recreated many typical scenes of urban and industrial life from the Durham area, including preserved vehicles and reconstructed buildings. *Author*

WASKERLEY WAY

The Waskerley Way, between Consett and
Waskerley, near Stanhope, provides a dramatic
route into the heart of the Durham Dales and
offers outstanding views across the surrounding
moors and reservoirs, making the long climb
from Consett more than worth while. This
route should be avoided in bad weather, as the
majority of the trail can be bleak and
windswept, easily obscured by heavy mist.

PLACES OF INTEREST ALONG THE ROUTE

The Stanhope and Tyne Railway

This cycle path has been created on the former
Stanhope and Tyne railway which opened in
1834 to carry limestone from Stanhope in
Weardale to the steel works at Consett and coal
from Medomsley to the Tyne at South Shields.
At the time of its construction, it was an
exceedingly ambitious railway. At the Stanhope
end the railway crossed many miles of non-
traffic-producing moorland and it involved
several changes of motive power. It comprised
10 miles worked by horse, 11 miles worked by
stationary engine, three self-acting inclines and

nine miles worked by locomotives. In addition,
it had to cross the 150ft deep Hownes Gill
ravine. Gradually the line was improved,
through a series of diversions and the
construction of the Hownes Gill Viaduct to
allow through running. The line finally closed
in 1968.

Hownes Gill Viaduct

This impressive viaduct crossing Hownes Gill
was built by Sir Thomas Bouch of Tay Bridge
fame in 1857. At 150ft high, the viaduct was
constructed from over 2.5 million bricks.
When the line first opened in 1834, the
waggons had to be lowered one at a time
down into the valley and a winding engine in
the bottom of the ravine was then used to haul
the waggon up the other side, restricting the
traffic to 12 waggons each way per hour. Later
a funicular railway was built on each side of
the ravine which was capable of hauling three
trucks at a time.

Rowley Station Picnic Area

The original Rowley station and platform were
dismantled stone by stone and have been
rebuilt at the Beamish Museum. Just beyond
the station, horses were once used to pull
waggons to the foot of Nanny Mayor's Incline
(Mrs Mayor kept a lineside alehouse) where
the weight of the down-coming laden waggons

Above: The churchyard of the Parish Church of St Thomas, Stanhope. *AA Photo Library*

was used to haul trucks up the incline. The incline was made redundant in 1859 when the line was diverted via Burnhill Junction.

Waskerley

Waskerley was once a busy railway centre with goods station, sidings and a shed for six engines and a waggon repair shop. The village, which stands 1,150ft above sea level, had a church, chapel, shops and a school. But the closure of the lead mines and the opening of easier to work railways led to the village's slow decline. When the railway finally closed in 1969, Waskerley became a ghost village.

West of Waskerley the line was originally worked by gravity and horses. A 40-horse power stationary steam engine was then used from Meeting Slacks to haul trains up from the village. Later a diversion allowed locomotives to travel to Weatherhill 1,445ft above sea level, where originally the Weatherhill engine (now in the National Railway Museum in York) had hauled the waggons by rope from Crawley Bank Head, where another incline hauled the waggons the first half mile (1km) from the limekilns up the northern slopes of the Wear Valley above Stanhope.

Stanhope

Stanhope is the largest village in Weardale and is home to the Durham Dales Centre which provides an introduction to the area through exhibitions and the sale of local crafts. An attractive collection of lead mining cottages, Stanhope was once an important market town and still has its fine market cross which stands outside St Thomas's churchyard. In the same churchyard is a remarkable fossilised tree which was found between Stanhope and Edmundy Byers. It has been identified as a giant plant similar to the small mare's-tails which still grow today in damper areas and would have been in existence 250 million years ago when the moorlands of Upper Teesdale were swamps full of giant trees. The church itself dates back to Norman times and inside is a Roman altar dedicated to Silvanus, the god of woodland.

Below: The Waskerley Way. *Author*

Starting Point: Hownes Gill Viaduct car park and picnic site, signposted off the A692 between Consett and Castleside.

Parking: Hownes Gill picnic site. There is also parking at Rowley station, Waskerley picnic site and Meeting Slacks.

Public Transport: There is no railway station within easy reach of either end of the route, though it is likely that Stanhope on the Weardale Railway will re-open in the near future for regular summer services. However, there are frequent buses from Newcastle and Durham to Consett where bikes can be hired.

Left: North Durham is littered with the debris of an industrial past. *Author*

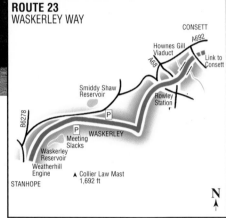

ROUTE 23
WASKERLEY WAY

CONSETT

Hownes Gill Viaduct

A692

Link to Consett

A692

Smiddy Shaw Reservoir

Rowley Station

B6278

P

P WASKERLEY

Meeting Slacks

Waskerley Reservoir

Weatherhill Engine

▲ Collier Law Mast 1,692 ft

STANHOPE

N ↑

Cycle hire: From Consett Bicycle Company, 62/64 Medomsley Rd, Consett. Tel: 01207 581205. Mountain bikes and folding bikes; 24 hours' notice required; Derek McVicker Sports, 23 Front Street, Consett DH8 5AB. Tel: 01209 505121

Links to other cycle paths: The Waskerley Way links with three cycle routes at the Hownes Gill Viaduct picnic site: Consett–Sunderland, Derwent Walk and Lanchester Valley Walk. The Waskerley Way is part of the 140-mile C2C route and from Waskerley the C2C route continues to Rookheads and Allenheads, finishing at Whitehaven. Further details of the C2C route can be obtained from Sustrans. Tel: 01207 281259.

Distance: 15 kilometres — 9¹/₂ miles

Maps: Landrangers 87 and 88. A route card is also produced by the Environment Department, Durham County Council as part of its Railway Walks series. Tel: 0191 383 3354 for further details.

Surfaces & Gradients: Stony and grassy in places, suitable only for mountain bikes. Long, gentle uphill gradient towards Waskerley along most of this route.

Roads & Crossings Points: One minor road crossing, but sections of fairly busy minor road (B6278) into Stanhope.

Refreshments: Picnic sites at Rowley station, Whitehall and Waskerley. Choice of pubs and cafés in Consett and Stanhope.

ROUTE INSTRUCTIONS:

1. If joining the route at Consett, go down the road towards Delves and then use the footbridge to cross the A692. Turn right along Gill Street, a row of terraced houses, and join the Consett–Sunderland rail path at its far end. Continue in the same direction to Lydgett's Junction and the start of the Waskerley Way.

2. From Lydgett's Junction, at Hownes Gill picnic site, join the cycle route and cross the viaduct. Follow the trail to a road and continue past Rowley station and Whitehall picnic site.

3. Just past Whitehall picnic site at Burnhill Junction, turn sharply right and continue along the trail past the car parks at Waskerley and Meeting Slacks.

4. The trail ends at Weatherhill summit. The off-road footpath into Stanhope is accessible to walkers only. For those cyclists wishing to continue down to Stanhope, follow the B6278, Crawleyside Bank Road, taking great care as the road is extremely steep — keep children under supervision.

HAMSTERLEY FOREST

Hamsterley Forest is a popular destination for mountain-bikers. This cycle ride follows forest tracks for the first half of the route, with stunning views of the surrounding countryside including Pikeston Fell. The second part of the route is through Bedburn Valley Nature Reserve and offers attractive open pastureland fringed with mature trees. For the more adventurous there are several waymarked cycle trails through the forest to cater for most abilities.

PLACES OF INTEREST ALONG THE ROUTE

Hamsterley Forest

Set in the midst of Upper Weardale, where the West Durham Moors meet the North Pennines, Hamsterley Forest is one of the most attractive of the Forestry Commission's Forest Parks. The forest covers an area of 2,000 hectares and mostly consists of European larch, Norway spruce, Scots pine and Western hemlock. In between there are open hay meadows and old broadleaf woodlands of ash, birch and oak which ensures the forest offers a wide variety of habitats. Both the red squirrel and roe deer are native to the forest, and there are a huge variety of birds which in winter include the redwing, fieldfare, crossbill and siskin and in summer the curlew, tree and meadow pipit and woodcock.

Hamsterley Forest Visitor Centre

Situated in the main car park, the centre provides an exhibition on the history of the forest. Open from Easter–September 10am–4pm weekdays and 11am–5pm weekends.

Bedburn Valley Nature Reserve

Bedburn Beck is a tributary of the River Wear and forms a narrow dale through the centre of the forest. The land around the valley bottom has not been planted with trees but retained as sheltered pasture. This is now a nature reserve and contains a wide variety of trees and wildflowers. Of particular interest are the large trees in the area around The Grove (an elegant 18th century house) and Redford Meadows which are designated a Site of Special Scientific Interest.

Below: Hamsterley Forest, County Durham.
AA Photo Library

ROUTE 24
HAMSTERLEY FOREST

Starting Point: Hamsterley Forest Visitor Centre, one mile from Hamsterley village. A toll is payable on the road from Bedburn to the visitor centre.

Parking: Car parking at the visitor centre. There is also parking at The Grove.

Public Transport: The nearest railway station is Bishop Auckland 14.5km (9 miles) away.

Links to other cycle paths: There are two other waywarked trails within Hamsterley Forest of 11km and 25km (7 and 16 miles), both of which are suitable only for mountain bikes, and more are planned. Further details from Forest Enterprise. Tel: 01669 620569.

Cycle hire: Hamsterley Forest Bike Hire, Hamsterley Forest. Open for a long summer season. Tel: 01388 528129 for details.

Distance: 7 kilometres — 4 miles

Maps: Landranger 92. A map is also available at a small charge from Forest Enterprise at the visitor centre, or from the offices in Rothbury (number as above).

Surfaces & Gradients: Gravel tracks for the first part of the route, then tarmac. The first part of the route is quite hilly with one fairly steep bank at the start of the route and two sharp descents; the section along the Forest Drive is level.

Roads and Crossings Points: The route follows the Forest Drive, forest tracks and a county road, with some light local traffic.

Refreshments: Refreshment kiosk available at the visitor centre; pub in Hamsterley village, 1.5km (1 mile) away.

ROUTE INSTRUCTIONS:

1. The route is waymarked from the visitor information centre. Turn left to follow the Forest Drive and then take the first left to follow a forest track over Bedburn Beck. The track climbs steeply and at the top of the hill turns right.

2. Follow the forest track to a gate where it meets a road. Turn right along the road and follow the road to where it descends to a bridge crossing the beck opposite The Grove.

3. Turn right along the Bedburn Valley following the Forest Drive back to the visitor centre and car park. Turn right over the river to follow a road for a short distance, before turning left along a waymarked forest track which leads to a bridge to rejoin the Forest Drive. Turn right to the visitor centre.

Opposite and left:
Hamsterley Forest,
County Durham.
AA Photo Library

DERWENT WALK

The Derwent Walk Country Park, a linear Park, is one of the largest in the North East. This extremely popular foot and cycle path follows the route of the old Derwent Valley Railway. Starting at Swalwell, west of Gateshead, it follows the River Derwent, a tributary of the Tyne, passing through attractive birch woods, and continues past hay meadows and scattered woodlands before ending on the outskirts of Consett at Blackhill.

PLACES OF INTEREST ALONG THE ROUTE

The Derwent Valley Line

At its peak, this North Eastern Railway Company branch line between Newcastle, Gateshead and Consett transported over 500,000 people per year and served six stations along its route. It was also an important freight line with regular goods traffic including timber, bricks and coal into Newcastle and iron ore to Consett. The railway was opened in 1867 and took three years to build. Zigzagging its way up the Derwent Valley, the line crosses the river four times over four impressive viaducts.

Hollinside Manor

On the left hand side of the Rowlands Gill Viaduct it is possible to see the ruins of Hollinside Manor, a 13th century manor house hidden in the trees. It was the home of the Harding family for centuries, but fell into ruin when it became part of the Gibside estate in 1730. The manor is accessible on foot only.

Gibside

The trail offers panoramic views of the Gibside Estate. The 140ft high Column of Liberty can be seen on the left hand side of the trail and was erected in 1757. Now a National Trust property, the estate was landscaped in the 18th century and although the 17th century hall is now in ruins, there are attractive walks through the parkland to a mausoleum chapel and the banqueting

hall. This fine mausoleum was designed by James Paine for the Bowes family, ancestors of the Queen Mother, who made their wealth from coal. It is open daily April–October 11am-5pm except Mondays. Admission charge. The entrance to the estate can be reached by ignoring the turning on to Rowlands Gill Viaduct and continuing along the B6314 for a short distance.

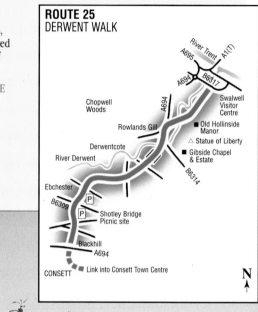

ROUTE 25
DERWENT WALK

Ebchester

Ebchester's Norman church is partly built of second-hand stone taken from the ramparts of Vindomora, the Roman fort on which Ebchester is based. The fort was built to protect Dere Street as it crossed the river. Ebchester's name is derived from St Ebba to whom the 12th century church is dedicated and it is possible to see various Roman stones which were used in its construction, including a pagan carving which has been incorporated into the tower.

Derwentcote

The Derwent Valley Steel Works were once the centre of the British steel industry. Derwentcote, a small 18th century cementation furnace, is the earliest and most authentic to have survived. It has been restored by English Heritage and together with a small exhibition is open to the public, 1 April–30 September, daily 10am–6pm. Small admission charge. It can be reached by turning right down the B6310 where it intersects with the Derwent Walk and then going left along the A694 for a short distance.

Shotley Bridge

For a short time in the 19th century Shotley Bridge became a popular spa town when people came to partake of its waters. However, by the time the railway line had been built, Bath and Buxton had become more firmly established as fashionable watering holes and its popularity rapidly declined.

Starting Point: Swalwell Visitor Centre, signposted off the A694 between Blaydon and Dunston.

Parking: Swalwell Visitor Centre; also at Rowlands Gill, Pontburn Wood, Ebchester station, Shotley Bridge station for those wanting to shorten the route.

Public Transport: Nearest railway station is at the Gateshead Metro Centre on the Tyne Valley Line where the South Tyne cycle path links directly to Swalwell. There are also buses to Swalwell Visitor Centre from Newcastle and Gateshead.

Links to other cycle paths: The South Tyne Cycleway at Swalwell. From Consett the Derwent Walk feeds into the Consett–Sunderland railway path, Waskerley Way and Lanchester Valley Walk.

Left: The Statue of Liberty, Gibside. *Author*

Below: The view from one of the Derwent Walk's viaducts draws an audience. *Author*

Cycle hire: Derwent Valley Bikes, Station Road, Rowlands Gill. Tel: 01207 545005. Also Consett Bicycle Company, 62/64 Medomsley Road, Consett. Tel: 01207 581205. Mountain bikes and folding bikes; 24 hours' notice required.

Distance: 18 kilometres — 11 miles

Maps: Landranger 88. A leaflet is also produced by Gateshead Leisure Services and Durham County Council Environment Department. Tel: 0191 383 3354 for details.

Surfaces & Gradients: Fine gravel path for most of the route; can be muddy after heavy rain. Gradual ascent from Swalwell to Consett, with a few steeper sections near road crossings.

Roads & Crossing Points: The trail intersects fairly busy roads at four places and there is also a short section of road for 400m at Rowlands Gill.

Refreshments: Pubs in Rowlands Gill, Ebchester and Shotley Bridge.

ROUTE INSTRUCTIONS:
1. From Swalwell Visitor Centre look for a gate by the visitor centre which leads to a path across an area of open grass, to a second gate and the start of the Derwent Walk.

2. Continue along the trail until the outskirts of Rowlands Gill where the trail joins the road for a short distance. Take the first road left (B6314) and rejoin the trail at the viaduct reached by taking the first right to a small car park.

3. The Derwent Walk ends at the outskirts of Consett at Blackhill. A link has been constructed here to the Waskerley Way, Consett–Sunderland path and Lanchester Valley Walk. Continue straight ahead over the A694 and follow the trail through the edge of an industrial estate and then across open ground to cross the A692 down to the Hownes Gill Viaduct picnic site. To visit Consett continue straight ahead over the A694 to where the cycle path meets a road. Continue straight ahead and then turn left following signs to Consett town centre.

Below: The disused platform to the left reminds cyclists that the Derwent Walk was once an important railway line linking Gateshead with Consett.

Beginning in the heart of Newcastle city centre and continuing through its industrial suburbs, the North Tyne Cycle Way includes the Tyne Riverside Country Park, an attractive area of tree-lined paths along the Tyne. Not only is the route rich in industrial heritage, which is interpreted through a series of panels along the first three kilometres of the route, it also has strong associations with the development of the railways, passing the birthplace of George Stephenson and of two other great railway pioneers, Timothy Hackworth and Nicholas Wood.

The Cycle Way is being extended and developed and will ultimately stretch from Tynemouth, where the Tyne meets the North Sea, to Prudhoe in Northumberland. It is currrently possible to cycle from Newcastle city centre to Prudhoe along a traffic-free cycleway for all but 500m of the 17.5km route. The route can easily be shortened by beginning the route either at Newburn, the gateway into the Tyne Riverside Country Park, or at Wylam.

PLACES OF INTEREST ALONG THE ROUTE

The Wylam Waggonway

The North Tyne Cycle Way uses newly-constructed landscaped walkways along the banks of the River Tyne and the old Scotswood, Newburn and Wylam Railway and the Wylam Waggonway. The Wylam Waggonway was built around 1748 to transport coal from Wylam Colliery to Lemington where the River Tyne was deep enough to enable keels or barges to transport the coal to the coast. The waggonway later became part of the North Wylam railway line constructed in 1876 and in constant use until it closed in 1968.

The River Tyne

The river has played an important role in the development of Tyneside, being an important route for the transport of coal and iron which led to the development of the celebrated shipbuilding industry. At Newcastle the river is dominated by a series of bridges, the most famous being the Tyne Bridge built in 1928 which has become the

symbol of the city. Close by is the two-tier road and rail High Level Bridge constructed by Robert Stephenson and T. E. Harrison between 1845–9 to link the Darlington–Gateshead railway to the Newcastle-Berwick

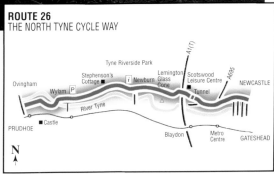

ROUTE 26
THE NORTH TYNE CYCLE WAY

Above: George Stephenson, in many ways the father of modern railways, was born alongside the route of the North Tyne Way. His cottage, now under the care of the National Trust, is open to the public. *Author*

Railway, and also the Swing Bridge. The Swing Bridge was constructed between 1868–76 and was originally worked by hydraulic pumps. It is estimated that over half a million ships have passed through the Swing Bridge since it was built, though the bridge is now rarely opened.

Lemington

On the left hand side of the cycle path is the 120ft high Lemington Glass Cone which is the only reminder of the Northumberland Glass Company, established in 1787. There were originally four large glass cones here which produced flat glass, but in 1906 the site was purchased by GEC who expanded the works to produced bulbs and tubing for all types of electrical lamps. The surviving glass cone was cleaned and repaired in 1993.

Newburn

Newburn has strong connections with George Stephenson who was twice married in its church. The route also passes the Boat House Inn at Newburn, where a plaque commemorates the fact that George Stephenson worked near here between 1798 and 1801 when he was in charge of Robert Hawthorn's new pumping engine at Water Row Pit, where George's father Robert was fireman.

George Stephenson's Cottage

The trail passes the cottage where George Stephenson was born in 1781. This small cottage was once the home of four families, one to each room. The Stephenson family room has been restored and is the only room open to the public. The cottage would have been an ideal place to stimulate the interest of a boy who was to become one of the world's greatest engineering pioneers. Stephenson would have grown up surrounded by machines and coalmine workings and would have watched the horse-drawn waggons trundling along the waggonway. The cottage is now in the care of the National Trust and is open to the public on Thursday, Saturday and Sunday afternoons 1–5pm, during the summer between April and October.

Wylam

The Wylam Railway Museum on Falcon Terrace (just north of the car park) illustrates Wylam's remarkable place in the development of the railways as the birthplace of three important railway pioneers: George Stephenson (1781–1848), Timothy Hackworth (1786–1850) and Nicholas Wood (1795–1865). Wylam was also where William Hedley built his experimental steam locomotives, 'Puffing Billy' and 'Wylam Dilly'.

Ovingham

Linked to Low Prudhoe by a rather precarious bridge, unsuitable for heavy traffic, is the attractive village of Ovingham dominated by its church, St Mary's, a mainly 13th century church with a tall late Anglo-Saxon west tower.

Prudhoe

Prudhoe Castle can be seen in the distance from the cycle path and is only a short distance (400m) from the end of the route. Originally a 12th century keep and gatehouse, Prudhoe Castle was extended in the 13th century by the Percys when it played an important role in the Border Wars, due to its location at the intersection between key north–south, east–west routes. It was in a semi-ruinous state by the late 16th century and was partly restored by the second Duke of Northumberland between 1808 and 1818. The castle is now managed by English Heritage and contains a fascinating exhibition about castles in Northumbria. Open 1 April–31 October 10am–6pm daily. Admission charge.

Above: The graceful neo-classical lines of All Saints Church, Newcastle-upon-Tyne. *AA Photo Library*

Right: Prudhoe Castle, once one of many castles held by the Percy family and now owned by English Heritage, is located near the end of the North Tyne Way. *Author*

Starting Point: The Swing Bridge, Quayside, Newcastle city centre

Parking: Car parking in Newcastle city centre; to shorten the route car parking is also available at Newburn Leisure Centre, Wylam and Prudhoe.

Public Transport: This route is well served by rail, running parallel to the Newcastle–Hexham Tyne Valley line. There are railway stations at Newcastle, Wylam and Prudhoe.

Links to other cycle paths: There is a link to the South Tyne Cycle Way at Scotswood Bridge.

Cycle hire: From Newcastle Cycle Centre, 265 Westgate Road. Tel: 0191 222 1695 for details.

Distance: 17.5 kilometres — 11 miles.   The route can be shortened by starting at Newburn Leisure Centre (8 kilometres —   5 miles).

Map: Landranger 88

Surfaces & Gradients: Mixture of tarmac and fine gravel. Level path throughout.

Roads & Crossing Points: Short section of road between Newcastle Business Park and start of old railway line at Scotswood. Minor road crossing at Newburn.

Refreshments: The Boat House, Newburn; pubs and café in Wylam and Prudhoe.

ROUTE INSTRUCTIONS:
1. Begin at the Quayside and go under the High Level Bridge to follow the newly-created walk and cycleway along the River Tyne past Newcastle Business Park. The walkway ends and joins a road up to a mini-roundabout. Continue for a short section along the road and rejoin the cycle path on the right hand side of the road following the line of the old railway.

2. The cycle path continues to a tunnel, which has recently been breached to create more light for pedestrians and cyclists. The tunnel emerges at a fenced tarmac path leading up a hill to an area of open grass. Continue along the tarmac path towards Scotswood Leisure Centre. Just before the leisure centre take a left fork over the footbridge crossing the western bypass. Over the bridge drop down to the left, turn right along the road and then take the first right to rejoin the old railway line.

3. Continue along the old railway to The Boathouse pub and continue straight ahead following the cycle path which runs parallel to the river. Turn left to follow the old Wylam Waggonway to the car park, at Wylam before swinging right to a road.

4. Continue along the cycle path, cross the river at Hagg Bank west of Wylam and turn right for Prudhoe where the cycle path ends at the Tyne Riverside car park.

RISING SUN COUNTRY PARK — NORTH TYNESIDE

As in Durham, many of the old railway lines and waggonways around Tyneside are being converted into cycle routes by the local authorities. North Tyneside has a particularly good network of routes, which is constantly being developed. This route begins within the Newcastle city boundary and follows the old Coxlodge Waggonway for much of its route into the Rising Sun Country Park which has been created on the site of a former colliery.

PLACES OF INTEREST ALONG THE ROUTE

Coxlodge Waggonway
This waggonway was used to carry coal from Jubilee and Regent pits at Gosforth to the River Tyne. Previously coal had been carried in carts by road to the quayside. The line was constructed between 1806–1809 by the owners of Kenton Colliery to Walker on the riverside, although west of South Gosforth the actual route of the railway changed several times to accommodate different pits during its period of operation. A native of Walker, John Blenkinsop, helped pioneer a rack and pinion locomotive on Hunslet Moor in Leeds, and in 1813 this system was adapted for the Kenton–Coxlodge waggonway.

Rising Sun Country Park
400 acres of woodland and grassland surround a marshy lake, which is now a nature reserve. This is the site of the former Rising Sun Colliery which was opened in 1908 when a shaft was sunk to the Bensham Seam. A second shaft was sunk in 1915. The colliery finally closed in 1969. It was the last colliery on the north bank of the Tyne. Since the colliery's closure, the area has been extensively landscaped to create a country park for local recreation. The Rising Sun Countryside Centre has a small exhibition area, a herb garden and a children's play sculpture. The centre is open Mon-Fri 9am–5pm and on Sun (May–Sept only) 1–5pm.

Above: Information board at the Rising Sun Countryside Centre. *Author*

Starting Point: South Gosforth; the cycleway starts on the A191, just off the roundabout with the A189.

Parking: Limited parking around South Gosforth; more parking at Rising Sun Country Park.

Public Transport: Bikes cannot be carried on the Tyne & Wear Metro. The nearest railway station is Newcastle, 3 kilometres (2 miles) away.

Links to other cycle paths: There are links to Wallsend and Killingworth on a mixture of quiet roads and off-road routes. See the map produced by North Tyneside Council (detailed below).

Cycle hire: From Newcastle Cycle Centre, 265 Westgate Road. Tel: 0191 222 1695 for details. Bike hire is also available from the Rising Sun Countryside Centre. Tel: 0191 266 7733 for details.

Distance: 8 kilometres — 5 miles

Maps: Landranger 88. A map and guide

showing cycle routes in North Tyneside is available from the Environment Strategy Team, North Tyneside Council. Tel: 0191 201 0033.

Surfaces & Gradients: Mixture of tarmac and gravel, suitable for mountain bikes. A level path throughout.

Roads & Crossing Points: Three road crossings, one over the very busy A188 and another over the equally busy A186 (keep children under strict supervision) and a short section of quiet lane near Rising Sun Farm.

Refreshments: Newton Park pub at Longbenton where the route intersects the A188; the shop at Rising Sun Countryside Centre sells light refreshments.

ROUTE INSTRUCTIONS:
1. The cycle path begins just off the A191, opposite a garage on the right hand side. Follow an attractive tree-lined tarmac path to where it emerges at a main road, the A188.

2. Cross the road with care and continue

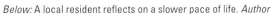

Below: A local resident reflects on a slower pace of life. *Author*

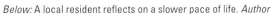
97

straight ahead along the track to another road. Continue straight ahead past Little Benton Farm to a railway line. At the railway turn left. Continue parallel to the railway to a junction of paths. Turn right to cross over the railway and continue along a lane to a road, the A186.

3. Cross the road with care and continue straight ahead to the edge of a plantation of trees, turn right and follow the path to where

Below: The path of the route stretches towards the horizon. *Author*

it joins a lane. Turn left along a quiet lane to Rising Sun Farm and then continue straight ahead to a junction of paths. Turn right and then left. At the next junction of paths turn left to the Rising Sun Countryside Centre.

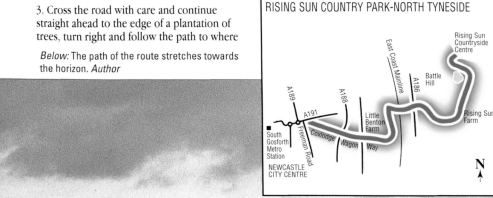

ROUTE 27
RISING SUN COUNTRY PARK-NORTH TYNESIDE

Rising Sun Countryside Centre

East Coast Mainline

A186

Battle Hill

A189

A191

A188

Little Benton Farm

Rising Sun Farm

South Gosforth Metro Station

Freeman Road

Coxlodge Wagon Way

NEWCASTLE CITY CENTRE

N

WHITEHAVEN TO ENNERDALE CYCLE PATH

This 18 kilometre (11 mile) cycle route, which forms part of the Sustrans Coast to Coast Cycle route, runs from industrial West Cumbria on the coast through the western edge of the Lake District offering spectacular views of the Lakeland fells as it climbs slowly from the old port of Whitehaven to the edge of Ennerdale — and most riders will want to complete the extra 7km (3 miles) down minor roads to Ennerdale if only to enjoy the glorious views of Ennerdale Water.

PLACES OF INTEREST ALONG THE ROUTE

Whitehaven

Whitehaven developed as one of Britain's most important ports in the 17th and 18th centuries, exporting coal and iron to Ireland and Europe, and importing Virginia tobacco. Inspired by the rebuilding of London after the Great Fire, the Lowther family provided the town with many elegant buildings, many of which have been preserved.

The Whitehaven to Rowrah Railway

This line was built and opened in 1852 by the Whitehaven, Cleator and Egremont Railway Company to exploit the rich deposits of coal and iron, but soon operated passenger services to the towns and villages in the ironfield. An additional mining and quarry branch, used by the cycle path, was opened soon afterwards from Rowrah to Kelton Fell. Services ceased in the 1950s, but as well as the trackbed being converted to a cycleway, decorated signposts, seats and sculptures have been provided as part of a Community Arts Programme.

Cleator Moor

The Whitehaven Iron and Steel Company, discovering the massive mile-wide seam of rich iron ore which ran across Cumbria, developed a large ironworks at Cleator Moor to exploit this wealth. The town developed rapidly to serve the ironworks. St Mary's Catholic church, between Cleator Moor and Cleator, is notable for its grotto on a similar scale to that at Lourdes.

Ennerdale

Ennerdale Bridge, a small village on the River Ehen, stands at the entrance to Ennerdale, the most western of the major Lakeland valleys, and the setting of Wordsworth's poem 'The Brothers'. It is also one of the quietest lakes, being, apart from at its western end, inaccessible by car. However, a bridleway around the northern shore makes it accessible to the more energetic with a mountain bike.

Above: An original railway bridge, evidence of which is visible either side of the cycleway, has been carefully modified to accommodate cyclists. *Author*

Starting points: Whitehaven, Corkickle station or Rowrah (car park).

Parking: Choice of car parks in Whitehaven. Small car park on the cycle path at Rowrah.

Public Transport: Cumbria Coast Line. Corkickle station in the south of Whitehaven is close to the start of the bike route. The station is a request stop for trains on the Carlisle/Whitehaven–Barrow route. Services are approximately every 2 hours. Whitehaven has a greater frequency of trains served by extra trains from Carlisle as well as trains from Lancaster/Barrow. For request stops a hand signal to the driver or a request to the guard on the train is necessary for the train to call at the station. Very limited services on Sundays.

Distance: 18 kilometres — 11 miles

Map: Landranger 89

Surfaces & Gradients: Nearly all tarmac. Last 1.5km (1 mile) to Kirkland is of compressed gravel. Minor back roads to Kirkland village and Ennerdale. A steady gradient from Whitehaven to Kirkland.

Roads & Crossing Points: Minor roads in Whitehaven and near Ennerdale.

Below: The Whitehaven-Ennerdale Cycle Way. *Cumbria County Council*

Refreshments: Wide range of facilities in Whitehaven. Shops and pubs in Cleator Moor and Rowrah. Pub in Ennerdale Bridge village.

ROUTE INSTRUCTIONS:
1. From Whitehaven station go out of the station forecourt to the main road. Turn right along the road. Continue straight ahead, following the brown Cumbria Cycle Way sign, as the traffic turns right. Continue to the end and right down the short Michael Street. Turn left at the bottom along the main road (note blue 'C2C' sign) for about 300m, passing the college. Turn right then immediately diagonally left, ('C2C' sign) then turn left again down Calder Avenue.

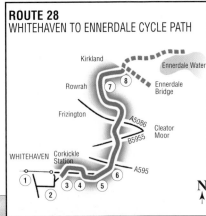

ROUTE 28
WHITEHAVEN TO ENNERDALE CYCLE PATH

2. From Corkickle station turn right out of the station up the street, and take the first right, Calder Avenue. This is the easiest way for public transport users to join the route.

3. From the centre of Whitehaven, follow the main A595 out of the town, turning left down Coach Road then first left to Corkickle station, and then right into Calder Avenue.

4. At Calder Avenue continue along this street, which runs through the estate, up a short hill before meeting another road, Esk Avenue, the official start of the cycle path. Turn right and go down to the school on the corner. Turn left on to a tarmac path here — marked on the surface 'C2C' with a bike symbol.

5. The bike path crosses playing fields at the bottom of the valley before bending right to go under the railway. Follow the decorated metal signs for the bike route.

6. The cycleway follows the railway line, before entering another estate. Continue straight ahead (noting the blue sign on the lamp post) along the street. Turn left at the concrete posts, signposted for the bike lane. The path goes under the railway again, past a sculpture.

7. The bike trail leaves the outskirts of Whitehaven, to climb very gradually through the fields and into the hills. The trail is marked along all its route with metal sculptures. The high Lakeland fells soon come into view ahead.

8. At Rowrah, the bike route turns off the main railway track. A car park is provided on the left, and the bike route continues on the right, through woodland, before making its way through a cutting to ascend through old quarry workings, now grassed over. After about 1.5km (1 mile) the route ends by a little cattle grid and a narrow wooden arch, to join a minor road. You may wish to follow the road to the right for a few metres for an excellent view of the Lakeland fells along Ennerdale.

9. Follow the minor road left for Kirkland village (no facilities). At the primary school turn right up the short hill to the village. Fine views of Ennerdale appear ahead. In Kirkland continue straight ahead ('C2C' route) at the crossroads if you wish to go on to Ennerdale and into the Lake District National Park, including the famous viewpoint at Bowness Knott, or right if you wish to go down to the village of Ennerdale Bridge

Below: The border hills are often snowbound; although cycling is an all-weather hobby, cyclists should always ensure that they have the correct equipment with them for the conditions. *Author*

THE KESWICK RAILWAY PATH

The little River Greta which flows from the shoulders of Blencathra and White Pike into the River Derwent north of Derwentwater forces its way through a deep, rocky gorge, which a little over 130 years ago was penetrated by a single track railway which for more than a century brought tourists in their thousands to the lakeside resort of Keswick. Sadly, the line closed in 1972, but thanks to the Lake District Special Planning Board, seven kilometres — four miles — of it have been redeemed to provide one of the most romantic and beautiful railway paths in England. National Park Interpretation Boards are strategically placed to explain aspects of the line's history, and several fine 'bowstring' bridges over the river give attractive views along the valley and to the surrounding hills — Latrigg, Blencathra and White Pike are especially dominant.

PLACES OF INTEREST ALONG THE ROUTE

Keswick

Copper mining once formed the basic industry of this lakeside town. However, the coming of turnpike roads in the 18th century and the railway in the 19th, together with the work of painters such as Turner; Romantic poets such as Wordsworth, Coleridge and Southey (who is buried in the town) and the writings of Ruskin, established Keswick as one of the most fashionable inland resorts of the British Isles and a leading centre for climbing and walking; a reputation which continues into the late 20th century.

Low Briery Bobbin Mill

Demand for wooden bobbins for the Lancashire and Yorkshire textile trade was strong in the 19th century, and ample supplies of suitable wood and fast flowing streams to provide waterpower made the Lake District ideal for bobbin manufacture. Demand decreased with the decline and modernisation of the textile industry, and the mill at this site — which once had its own rail siding — closed in 1961. There was also a woollen mill nearby.

Brundholme Wood

These natural sessile oak woodlands form a dominant feature of this trail, and the embankments and cuttings have been attractively colonised with oak, alder and birch. The entire route is a haven for wildlife, with native red squirrels frequently to be seen as well as such birds as chaffinch, blue tit and blackbird, and a wide variety of wildflowers.

Wescoe Tunnel

This short tunnel makes its way through an outlier of mudstone above the valley to create an interesting feature on the path.

Threlkeld village

Threlkeld's name is pure Norse, meaning the serf's spring, suggesting a Viking settlement. This little linear, typically Cumbrian village below Blencathra is notable for its two inns, both closely linked to local traditional foxhunts, but otherwise there are no tourist facilities.

Left: Autumn colours amidst the woodland of the Keswick Railway Path. *Author*

Threlkeld Quarry

With its workers' village close by, the former Microgranite Quarry at Threlkeld is closer to the old Threlkeld station than the village and now houses a quarry, geological and mining museum. There is a footpath but no cycle access at present (1995) eastwards from Threlkeld station towards Penrith.

Starting Points: From Keswick Leisure Pool by the old station; from Threlkeld station.

Parking: At the start of the railway path by the leisure centre — follow the main street over Greta Bridge towards the A66, then turn right along Crosthwaite Road past the Hospital, turning right again into Briar Rigg, continuing beyond Brundholme Road to Station Avenue and access to the car park by the leisure pool. Limited car parking also available along Station Road at Greta Park.

For Threlkeld station car park take the B5322 road off the main A66 at Threlkeld to the well signed car park. Steps from rear of car park lead to the lane. Cross the road to another gate and steps up the embankment and the official start of the Keswick Railway Path.

Limited access (short stay) for disabled users on level central section at Low Briery (brown signs off A591)

Public Transport: 555 bus serves Keswick from Lancaster and Windermere railway station; X5 bus serves Threlkeld and Keswick from Penrith — no cycle carriage facilities. Nearest rail station is Penrith.

Cycle Hire: Braithwaite General Stores, Braithwaite, near Keswick CA12 5SZ. Tel: 01787 78273.

Distance: 7 kilometres — 4 miles

Map: Landranger 90

Surfaces & Gradients: Compressed gravel, generally very good, but there are sections of rougher rail ballast at the eastern (Threlkeld) end. Wooden plank surfaces on bridges can be slippery in wet or frosty weather. With several sets of steps, and two short steeply-graded sections, this makes the path more suitable for mountain bikes.

Roads & Crossing Points: Three sets of steep steps underneath the A66 Greta Viaduct, east of Keswick, require cycles to be carried. There is also a steep incline at this point. Central

UTE 29
KESWICK RAILWAY PATH

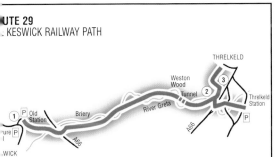

N

Below: Castlerigg Stone Circle.
AA Photo Library

sections level, but a further incline and steps at Threlkeld Bridge where a minor road (quiet) has to be crossed, and also the B5322 to Threlkeld station car park. Access to Threlkeld village requires a short section of grassy and gravel verge alongside the A66 and 500m of quiet lane (steady climb) into the village centre.

Refreshments: Choice of pubs and cafés (and public toilets) in Keswick. Two pubs in Threlkeld village; no facilities at Threlkeld station.

ROUTE INSTRUCTIONS:
1. From Keswick town centre follow Bank Street past the Post Office, bearing right along Victoria Street to junction with Station Road, left, at Greta Park, past the YHA to entrance to leisure pool. Cycle and pedestrian path leads to the right of leisure pool and into car park and old station area which is the start of the railway path.

2. At bridge when the second A66 concrete viaduct comes into view, the path through the bridlegate on the right leads off the main path along the side of the valley to join the road at a small gate. Turn left for 100m to where the waymarked path (white arrow) on the right goes through a gate and down steps to rejoin the old railway track for 500m over bridge over the River Greta to emerge at steps by the B5322. Cross road and either take the steps ahead into car park, or turn right along road then first left to car park. The Threlkeld Quarry Museum is 400m along the lane beside the station car park, turning right and uphill at the business park.

3. For Threlkeld village keep on the main track under the viaduct when it comes into view, to emerge alongside the main A66 road. Keep on the narrow verge to junction with the lane into Threlkeld village (500m).

Below: One of the typical bridges of the former railway line east from Keswick towards Penrith.

KIELDER WATER AND THE BORDER FOREST

The Border Forest is an outstanding area for off-road cycling and there are a large number of well-promoted routes within the forest. The Castle Hill route is designed to give a taste of this vast area of forest and reservoir. It offers superb views of the Border Hills, the Forest and Kielder Water.

Cyclists should be aware that they may encounter forest traffic on some of the routes through the forest and just occasionally routes are diverted or closed because of forest management operations. Alternative routes will be clearly signposted.

PLACES OF INTEREST ALONG THE ROUTE

Kielder Forest

Kielder Forest is Britain's largest man-made forest covering over 600 square kilometres in the far west of Northumberland and east Cumbria. Planting began in the 1920s and continues up to the present day to create one of the largest forest areas in Europe. Kielder Forest is a working forest with 1,400 tonnes of timber harvested every day. Increasingly, however, the forest is being designed with tourism and conservation in mind. Forest Enterprise is moving away from monolithic blocks of conifer trees to more mixed plantations with broad-leaved trees and a network of open spaces, more in keeping with the natural contours of the landscape, improving wildlife habitats and recreational opportunities. In addition to a rich birdlife which includes birds of prey, the forest is also home to red squirrels and roe deer.

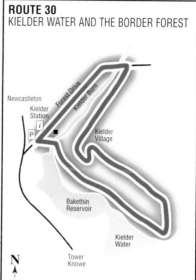

ROUTE 30
KIELDER WATER AND THE BORDER FOREST

Above: Kielder — Europe's biggest man-made lake. *Author*

Kielder Castle

Kielder Castle was built in 1775 as a hunting lodge by Earl Percy, Duke of Northumberland. The castle is now a visitor centre managed by Forest Enterprise containing an excellent exhibition on the workings of the forest and of the birdlife to be found within the forest. The exhibition is open Easter to October 10am–5pm and at weekends only at other times of the year, 11am–4pm. Admission is free.

Kielder Water

Kielder Water is northern Europe's largest man-made lake with a surface area of 2,684 acres and a shoreline of 27.5 miles, created by the flooding of the Upper North Tyne Valley to supply industrial Tyneside and Teesside. Kielder Water has a storage capacity of 44 billion gallons, which has meant that unlike other regions in unusually dry summers, the North East has been spared a water shortage. Kielder Water has also become a popular recreational centre offering sailing, wind surfing and other water sports as well as angling. Northumbria Water's Visitor Centre at Tower Knowe on the eastern end of the lake provides an introductory exhibition to the area. Open Apr-Oct 10am–5pm (6pm June & July). Admission charge.

Below: The dramatic nature of the border country. *Author*

Bakethin reservoir

Bakethin reservoir holds 233 gallons of water and feeds into Kielder Water, with a weir separating the two which has been designed to prevent mudflats appearing when the level of Kielder Water drops. Bakethin reservoir is now a conservation area. Three islands have been constructed in the centre of the reservoir, each of which has been designed to provide different habitats for a different range of animals and birds. In the summer it is possible to see goosander, teal and great crested grebe on the lake, while in winter, wildfowl include golden-eye, pochard and tufted duck.

The North Tyne Railway

The route passes Kielder Viaduct on the now dismantled Border Counties Railway which was constructed in 1862 to transport coal mined in the North Tyne Valley to new markets. It ran from Hexham via Bellingham to Riccarton Junction in Scotland and operated until closure in 1956. Kielder Viaduct was built in 1862 and is an impressive example of what is termed 'skew arch construction' whereby the arches are set at an angle to the line of the viaduct or bridge. This meant the railway could cross the river diagonally, whilst still allowing the river below to flow straight through the arches without battering against the piers.

Right: The austere lines of Hermitage Castle, which is located just north of the Scottish border, bring to life the nature of border warfare in the Middle Ages. *AA Photo Library*

Starting Point: Kielder Castle Visitor Centre.

Parking: Kielder Castle.

Links to other cycle paths: There are 10 cycle routes within the forest, with other routes being planned. The routes include the 16-mile circuit of Kielder Water, some of which uses the public highway. All the routes cater for a range of abilities, with some of the more demanding routes including prolonged gradients and rough terrain. There is also a special challenge area for mountain bikes, the Trail Quest Orienteering Course. For details of all the routes contact Forest Enterprise on 01434 220242.

Cycle hire: Cycle hire is available at Kielder Castle and Hawkhope (01434 253392 & 220392) and at Leaplish Waterside Park (01434 250312).

Distance: 12 kilometres — 7.5 miles.

Maps: Landranger 80. An excellent map showing all the different cycle routes within the Border Forest is also available from Forest Enterprise at Kielder Forest Information Centre.

Surfaces & Gradients: Some tarmac roads, but mainly stony forest roads. Some moderate climbs. Mountain bikes recommended.

Roads & Crossing Points: This route follows the Forest Drive for a short section which is used by vehicular traffic and a short section of the North Haul road which is used by occasional forest vehicles.

Refreshments: Café at Kielder Castle. There is also a pub in Kielder village.

ROUTE INSTRUCTIONS:

1. The Castle Hill route is waymarked by blue arrows. From Kielder Castle follow the tarmac Forest Drive uphill to where it crosses over Kielder Burn.

2. Take the next right to follow an undulating forest road which descends to where Bakethin reservoir meets Kielder Water.

3. Turn right along the North Haul road following the edge of the reservoir through Kielder village to Kielder Castle.

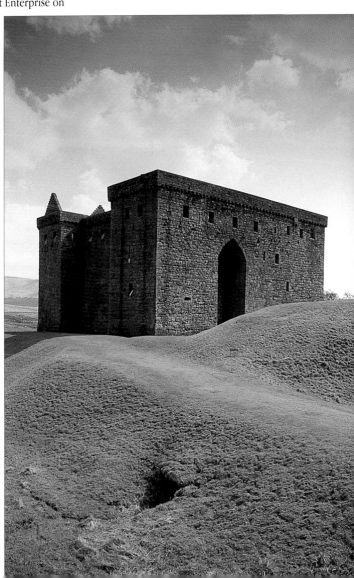

There are an increasing number of cycle paths being created within Northern England and many existing ones are being extended. In addition to the routes featured in the book, including the Trans-Pennine Trail, the following off-road routes are also available for cyclists:

Market Weighton–Bubwith, Humberside: a 19km (12 mile) railway path route from the East Yorkshire Wolds to the Vale of York.

South Tyne Cycle Way: A route from Swalwell to Jarrow using a combination of minor roads and cycle paths along the southern bank of the River Tyne.

Wirral Country Park, Merseyside: Cycling is not permitted on the old railway itself, which is for walkers only, but cyclists may use a parallel 11km (7 mile) bridleway along the shores of the Dee estuary, which is suitable for mountain bikes only.

Forestry Commission

There are also a number of other routes through Forestry Commission land. These include:

Cropton Forest — an off-road route from Levisham station on the North York Moors Railway exploring the forest
Langdale Forest — offers three cycle routes, plus various challenge routes for mountain-bikers
Boltby Forest — offers one route
Guisborough Forest — offers one route
Dalby Forest — offers one route
Sneaton Forest — offers one route
Hamsterley Forest — offers four cycle routes
Kielder Forest — offers ten cycle routes, plus challenge routes for mountain bikers
Grizedale Forest — several routes are available through this forest in the Lake District

For details of these and other areas where cycling is permitted contact:

Forest Enterprise, North York Moors Forest District, 42 Eastgate, Pickering, N. Yorks YO18 7DU. Tel: 01751 472771/473810
Forest Enterprise, Rothbury Forest District, 1 Walby Hill, Rothbury, Morpeth, Northumberland NE65 7NT.
Tel: 01669 620569/620062

Forest Enterprise, Kielder District, Eals Burn, Bellingham, Hexham, Northumberland NE48 2AJ. Tel: 01434 220242

Forest Enterprise, Lakes. Tel: 01229 860373

Canal Towpaths and Regional British Waterways

Cycling is allowed along the following canals within the region:

The Ashton Canal (see text)
The Leeds-Liverpool Canal —
Leeds–Saltaire (see text)
The Aire and Calder Navigation —
Leeds–Woodlesford
(see Trans-Pennine Trail)
The St Helens' Canal (see text)

Sections of other canals may be opened in the future as further improvements permit.

For more information contact your local British Waterways office: British Waterways, Pennine and Potteries, Top Lock, Church Lane, Marple, Cheshire SK6 6BN.
Tel: 0161 427 1079; Yorkshire Regional Office, 1 Dock Street, Leeds LS1. Tel: 0113 243 6741; Leeds–Liverpool (East), Dobsons' Lock, Apperley Bridge, Bradford BD10 0PY.
Tel: 01274 611303

Below: The sylvan delights of the Derwent Valley. *Author*

Various local authorities and other organisations in the North of England have produced leaflets detailing cycling routes and recommended cycle rides on some of the region's quieter country lanes. These include the following:

Durham: Durham County Council have produced an attractive pack of leaflets detailing five cycle routes within the county.

Countryside Cycling, Teesdale and Richmondshire: three on-road cycle routes designed for families, leaflet available at a small charge.

Cleveland: Cycle rides in Cleveland — three quiet road-based routes 16–25 miles in length around Guisborough and Staithes.

Cumbria: The Cumbria Cycle Way — a 250-mile round the county route on quiet roads and byways, plus circular routes. Large fold-out map of the route available priced £2 from Cumbria County Council.

Talkin Tarn: Mountain bike routes leaflet available for a small charge.

Humberside: A 25-card pack is available from the County Council which provides details of various cycle rides including several rail trails within Humberside.

Lancashire: The Lancashire Cycle Way. A 250-mile waymarked route devised by Lancashire County Council in the form of two loops, north and south. The route has been designed to reflect the different landscapes of Lancashire and includes the Fylde coast, Arnside, Lune Valley, Bowland Fells, Pennine Moors and West Lancashire plain.

Cycle route cards have also been produced for Lever Park and Rivington in the West Pennines.

Pedal Power: four cycle rides in and around Blackburn between 6 miles and 25 miles; all the routes are graded.

Greater Manchester: Bike rides in Greater Manchester: a series of bike rides throughout Greater Manchester including Dunham Town, Reddish Vale and Saddleworth. Small charge per leaflet. Published by the Cycling Project for the North West.

The open road ahead — the Lanchester Valley route. *Author*

Medlock Valley Bridle and Mountain Bike Route: an 18-mile route from Daisy Nook, mainly on bridleways and quiet lanes and byways, to Bishop Park Development. Published by the Greater Manchester Cycling Project.

North Tyneside: A map showing the various different cycle routes within the District, including quieter lanes and bridlepaths suitable for cycling, is available from North Tyneside Council.

West Yorkshire: A 150-mile route around West Yorkshire mainly on quiet lanes and bridleways with some short sections on minor roads. A leaflet is available from local tourist offices describing the route.

Mountain bike trails — Upper Calderdale: short and long routes mapped out by Calderdale Council.

North Yorkshire: Ryedale mountain bike routes: a set of four routes exploring the countryside around Malton; leaflet available from Ryedabike (01653 692835) at a small charge.

Yorkshire Dales Cycleway: 121 miles exploring the Yorkshire Dales National Park on quiet back roads. Leaflet produced by the Yorkshire Dales National Park Authority.

Cumbria County Council: Economy & Environment Dept, Highways Division, Citadel Chambers, Carlisle CA3 8SG. Tel: 01228 812388

Calderdale MDC: Leisure Services, Wellesley Park, Halifax HX2 0AY. Tel: 01422 359454

Cleveland County Council: Dept of Environment, PO Box 77, Gurney House, Gurney Street, Middlesbrough, Cleveland TS1 1JJ. Tel: 01642 248155

Durham County Council: Environment Dept, County Hall, Durham DH1 5UQ. Tel: 0191 383 3354

Humberside County Council: Prospect House, Prospect Street, Kingston upon Hull HU3 8PU. Tel: 01482 867131

Lake District National Park: Murley Moss, Oxenholme Road, Kendal, Cumbria LA9 7RL. Tel: 01539 724555

Lancashire County Council: County Hall, Preston PR1 8XJ. Tel: 01772 263536

Kirklees MDC: Countryside Dept, The Stables, Ravensknowle Park, Wakefield Road, Huddersfield HD5 8DJ. Tel: 01484 443704

North Tyneside Council: Environment Dept, Graham House, Whitley Road, Benton, Newcastle upon Tyne NE12 9TQ. Tel: 0191 201 0033

North York Moors National Park: The Old Vicarage, Helmsley, York YO6 5BP. Tel: 01439 770657

Northumberland County Council: County Hall, Morpeth, Northumberland NE61 2EF. Tel: 01671 514343

Northumberland National Park: Eastburn, South Park, Hexham, Northumberland   NE46 1BS. Tel: 01434 605555

York City Council: Dept of Development & Transportation, 9 Leonard's Place, York YO1 2ET. Tel: 01904 650349

Yorkshire Dales National Park: Hebden Road, Grassington, via Skipton, North Yorkshire BD23 5LB. Tel: 01756 752748

British Cycling Federation and British Mountain Bike Federation: The National Cycling Centre, 1 Stuart Street, Manchester M11 4DQ. Tel: 0161 2232244

The Cyclists Touring Club (CTC): Cottrell House, 69 Meadrow, Godalming, Surrey GU7 3HS. Tel: 01483 417217

The Cycle Campaign Network: c/o London Cycling Campaign, 3 Stamford Street, London SE1 9NT. Tel: 0171 928 7220

Cyclists' Public Affairs Group, CPAG: 3 Stamford Street, London SE1 9NT. Tel: 0171 252 3696

Environmental Transport Association (ETA): The Old Post House, Heath Road, Weybridge, Surrey KT13 8RS. Tel: 01932 828882

The Greater Manchester Cycling Project: Environmental Institute, Bolton Road, Swinton, Manchester M27 2UX. Tel: 0161 794 1926

Rough Stuff Fellowship: Secretary, Belle Vue, Mamhilad, Pontypool, Gwent NP4 8QZ. Tel: 01873 880384

Sustrans: 35 King Street, Bristol BS1 4DZ. Tel: 0117 926 8893

Trans-Pennine Trail: Pam Ashton, Trans-Pennine Trail Officer, Planning Services Dept, Barnsley MBC, Central Offices, Kendray Street, Barnsley S70 2TN. Tel: 01226 772574

Transport 2000: 10 Melton Street, London NW1 2EJ. Tel: 0171 388 8386

Below: Alexander Bridge, Sunderland, on the Consett-Sunderland route. *Author*

A smelting wagon on the Consett-Sunderland route provides both a useful prop to a bicycle and a reminder of the region's industrial heritage. *Author*